The Community Book Project:

CELEBRATING 365 DAYS OF GRATITUDE

Donna Kozik, lead editor
Theresa Scandale, assistant editor
Susan Veach and Gregory Paul Hoffmaster, cover designers
Susan Veach, formatter

Limits of Liability and Disclaimer of Warranty

The author/publisher shall not be liable for your misuse of this material. This book is strictly for informational and educational purposes.

Warning/Disclaimer

The purpose of this book is to educate and entertain. It is distributed with the understanding that the publisher is not engaged in the dispensation of legal, psychological or any other professional advice. The content of each entry is an expression and opinion of its author and does not necessarily reflect the beliefs, practices or viewpoints of the publisher, its parent company or its affiliates. The publisher's choice to include any material within is not intended to express or imply any warranties or guarantees of any kind. The authors and/or publisher do not guarantee that anyone following these techniques, suggestions, tips, ideas or strategies will become successful. The authors and/or publisher shall have neither liability or responsibility to anyone with respect to any loss or damage caused, or alleged to be caused, directly or indirectly by the information contained in this book.

Get Your Free Gratitude Journal!

Keep a daily record of life's positive moments (big and small) with this printable gratitude journal filled with a year's worth of positive affirmations, insightful prompts, inspiring quotes, and room for reflecting on all the things that make your life a blessing.

- Take 60 seconds to shine a light on what's good!
- Affirmations and inspirational quotes to lift you up.
- Delivered via a colorful PDF printable.

Pick up your free gratitude journal!
www.TheCommunityBookProject.com

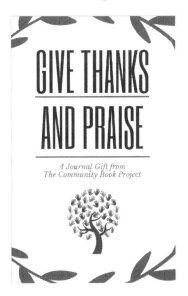

About Donna Kozik

USA TODAY & WALL STREET JOURNAL and Amazon best-selling author Donna Kozik shows people how to write a book fast and easy to use as a "big business card" for themselves and their businesses.

She does this with her signature online program, Write a Book in a Weekend, which she has conducted over 80 times in the past 12 years, showing thousands of people how to get a short and powerful book done in just two days.

Get a free book planner at www.FreeBookPlanner.com to get started on your book today.

Need editing, proofreading, cover design or other publishing help? Check out www.DoneForYouPublishing.com.

Want to be a part of the next Community Book Project?
Go to www.TheCommunityBookProject.com to find out what we have cooking next.

Acknowledgments

I give great thanks to so many people for their help in putting together this edition of The Community Book Project. My gratitude and appreciation go to the contributors, designers, proofreaders and more. Thank you Susan Veach, Gregory Hoffmaster and Theresa Scandale, and Tammy Atchley for help in putting the book together. Thank you to Teresa and Brad Castleman for constant support and cat pictures and Ruth Strebe for the fun found at a distance. Finally, heaps of love go to all the cheerleaders in the Business Authors Association who left encouraging words in our Facebook group.

I am grateful for you!

~ Donna Kozik, lead editor

For our readers...we appreciate you!

Note from the Editor

This book, almost a year in the making, is ready to make your year. (Or at least some days in it.) The idea was simple: bring together 365 entries that give a glimpse of gratitude from everyday people. Inside you'll find stories about grandchildren, weddings, kindness and, of course, those wonderful pets! We hope they make you smile--and lead you to reflect on the people and things you are grateful for.

~ Donna Kozik

P.S. Go to www.TheCommunityBookProject.com to see what we have cooking next!

Meet Our Authors!

Go to this special page to meet the contributors to The Community Book Project:

www.MeetOurAuthors.com

Contents

January

February

March

April

May

June

July

August

September

October

November

December

January

January 1
Celebrations
Julaina Kleist-Corwin

"Celebrate who you are in your deepest heart."
~ Amy Leigh Mercree

My January 1 birthday has had pros and cons. I've learned that not many individuals I meet are born on that day. People are surprised to hear my birthdate, and, of course, I never tell the year—unless I have to.

When I was a young child, my family told me that people all over the country celebrate my birthday at midnight on New Year's Eve. I loved the fireworks and crowds cheering. I savored the joy, although I didn't believe it was about me.

As a teenager, I often received a stack of gifts at the same time as my Christmas presents. The only clues that I had a birthday were the different wrapping paper and the cake with candles next to the Christmas Yule log. My actual birthday felt like an ordinary day in the aftermath of the holiday bustle.

At this age, I don't need the people's cheers. I don't need the fireworks. I don't need the presents and cake. I feel extraordinary on my birthday. I hug the new calendar while I'm filled with excitement about the friends I'll meet and the quests I imagine. I dance with joy and gratitude for a prosperous forecast.

Julaina Kleist-Corwin is a teacher, author and writing coach. Find out more about Julaina at www.MeetOurAuthors.com.

January 2

Cowboy-Boot-Wearing Teacher
Leah Grant

"Sometimes the things we can't change end up changing us instead." ~ Unknown

All children are gifts, yet some are more special. My niece is one of those special children. Born with Down syndrome, Rayne's life has been filled with medical procedures, including an open-heart surgery. Despite being poked and prodded incessantly, her spirit has remained strong.

Every time she sees me, she runs toward me screaming, "Aunt Leah, Aunt Leah." When she reaches me, she engulfs me in the biggest and hardest hug she can give. I'm not the only one who receives these embraces. Rayne is generous with her outpouring of affection.

Unlike so many people, she's not self-conscious at all. She loves Luke Bryant and insists that she sings his songs off-key at the top of her lungs wearing cowboy boots to anyone who will be her audience. It's actually quite a show.

I gave her a multicolored top with yellow beading on it to play dress-up with, and she adored it so much she wore it to school against my sister's wishes. The smile on her face as she adorned it stretched from ear to ear.

Rayne embodies resilience, unconditional love and unapologetic expression. Witnessing her ease of displaying these truly special traits inspires me to foster them within myself.

ICF Master Certified Coach Leah Grant is a best-selling author and teacher. Weaving the practical with the esoteric, she assists her clients to live as their full, multidimensional selves. Discover more about Leah at www.MeetOurAuthors.com.

January 3

Aspire to Inspire
Sandra J. Clarke

"If you can't figure out your purpose, figure out your passion.
For your passion will lead you right into your purpose."
~ Bishop T.D. Jakes

Daily acknowledgment of what I'm thankful for provides the inspiration and motivation I need to go after my dreams. But, while reaching for stars, I discovered that gratitude is contagious. Sharing gratitude provides the impetus that inspires the same in others, and this chain reaction is a beautiful sight.

Through the gratitude others chose to share, I recognized that in every day there is an opportunity to make a difference. This is what I now strive for, and it's something that anyone can achieve.

By focusing on gratitude, I found my passion. That was the easy part—it's writing. But it took years of sitting on the sidelines spying on those who were rocking it to recognize what was missing and what was possible. My passion isn't what I do well—it's what I'm called to do with it.

If one small word or expression of gratitude I write inspires another in someone else, that's worth every minute of the time it takes to share the message.

In gratitude.

Sandra J. Clarke is a multi-award-winning and No. 1 best-selling fiction and nonfiction author and co-founder of Master Your Words—Coaching & Mentoring for Writers. Learn more about Sandra at www.MeetOurAuthors.com.

January 4
Love Begins Within
Bethany Perry

"We can't hate ourselves into a version of ourselves we can love."
~ Lori Deschene

As quickly as the holidays have passed, an all-pervasive guilt, body-shaming and self-loathing seem to follow. We don't say it to other people, but we'll say it to ourselves all day long. We join the gym, start the latest eating trend, and, in a month, we likely start another diet or simply give up. Hating parts of our body is second nature. Meanwhile, the underlying cry of the heart is asking: Could you love me as I am?

Through gratitude and loving ourselves now, you can create the "me" you long to be in the future. One baby step at a time. Slowing down. Noticing breath and hearing what the mind is saying versus what the heart is feeling. What is it I don't want to feel? Can appreciating my feelings bring ease? Especially ones I want to avoid?

Not only can it, but with practice it allows congruence between the conscious and the unconscious mind. Congruence allows trust. The serenity of mindfulness settles in, finding the comfort of home within the innermost being. My body confidently knows what it needs to eat and how to move, how to love deeply and freely receive. The wisdom of love and gratitude live within.

Bethany is a transformational health and life coach. An emerging thought leader on combining the power of neuroscience and intuition, Bethany guides you to create your desired life. Discover more about Bethany at www.MeetOurAuthors.com.

January 5

Living Out Loud With Friends
Debbie Phillips Cantin

"If you had not suffered...there would be no depth to you as a human being, no humility, no compassion." ~ Eckhart Tolle

Girlfriends! I'm forever grateful for mine! Here are some who've made a lasting impact on my life:

My childhood best friend, Donna, who offered me a safe place to stay on the weekends when my father was drunk.

My high school friend Susan, who told me I look pretty when I smile (the first time I remember anyone saying anything positive about my looks).

My friend Debbie, who told me things would be okay when I got pregnant at age 18 and my boyfriend dumped me.

My friend Jelena, who was there to give me hugs after my husband committed suicide.

My friend Coby, who recognized my pain, recommended I work on myself and introduced me to personal development—changed my life forever!

My friend Maxine, who is there to listen when I just need an ear.

I'm especially grateful for my sisters, Vicky, Wendy and Julie—girlfriends from birth!

My heart is full of gratitude for all the women whose lives have touched mine and continue to do so, for the hundreds of women who have been there through the tears, the laughter, the guilt, the joy—oh, where would I be without my girlfriends?

Deb Cantin is the designer of the Women Living Out Loud workshops, assisting women to rise to their greatest selves, and is also a financial advisor who trains women in finance. Find out how to connect with Deb at www.MeetOurAuthors.com.

January 6

Designer Genes
Darian Slayton Fleming

"No one else will ever know the strength of my love for you. After all, you're the only one who knows what my heart sounds like from the inside." ~ Kristen Proby

Blind with multiple disabilities since age 2, my strongest desire was to marry and have a family. On this day in 1985, my wonderful son, Tim, entered my world.

I left my abusive marriage, and two-year-old Tim and I moved in with my parents. One day, I remember telling my mom one thing I missed about being married was the foot rubs. My tiny son took off my shoes and rubbed my feet.

In the seventh grade, Tim competed extremely well on his math testing. We received a letter from a school official informing us that Tim had the highest math score in the seventh grade class. I remember saying, in awe, I didn't know how I produced such a smart son. My dad replied that he had designer genes.

Tim attended a technical high school. I am so proud of him. He is a journeyman in a glazier union.

Tim now has a family of his own. I have two lovely granddaughters, Sophia and Audrey. When Sophia was little, she told her mom I was her best friend forever. Tim and his family give me so much joy. When they're around, it's the icing on the cake.

Darian Slayton Fleming is a passionate disability rights advocate. She brings her own life experiences to supporting her clients as a clinical social worker and rehabilitation counselor in Portland, Oregon. Learn more about Darian at www.MeetOurAuthors.com.

January 7
To Love With Sincerity
Kamal Qumbargi

"Thankfulness is the beginning of gratitude. Gratitude is the completion of thankfulness. ~ Henri Frederic Amiel

What does love mean for you? Whatever your answer, I'm certain it's not identical to my own. Of course, there's nothing wrong with that; we are different and should love differently. However, there's a part of love we all share.

Gratitude. Gratitude for being seen and wanted for who we are. The good, bad and in between. The warmth, comfort and strength it offers is undeniable. It is the same for those that are loved by us. If you disagree, try loving or being loved without gratitude—without acceptance, recognition, appreciation or acknowledgement.

Now, I know what some of you are saying; I have given an impossible task. However, why is that? Surely, it is because those that know this task is unachievable understand that love without gratitude is not genuine love. Often, when we show our love for others, we are actually expressing our gratitude for having that connectedness and acceptance. Every kiss, hug, picture, post, gift, memory, etc. Each is an act of gratitude. As such, as long as love is shared in this life, so, too, will gratitude spread within our hearts. For it is the seed from which love grows and takes form.

Kamal Qumbargi is an inspirational writer and motivator for those on all walks of life. Share your journey with Kamal. Find out how to connect with him at www.MeetOurAuthors.com.

January 8

Gratitude Every Day

Sharon G. Teed

"Feeling Gratitude and not expressing it is like wrapping a present and not giving it." ~ William Arthur Ward

One Friday in October, there were many thoughts running through my head. Two friends living close by hadn't been honest with me for months. They felt I was wasting my time doing the activities I do. Painful as it was, I am moving on regardless of their opinions. I love to write, and I love my Toastmasters activities.

I am most grateful for my healthy family even though I can't see them now.

I am grateful for my good health.

I am grateful that I can do all the things I want to do.

I am especially grateful for my BFF in Toronto, who I have known for 48 years.

My other friends are scattered now in places like Toronto, Belleville, Brockville, Kingston and Russell, Ontario, as well as Montreal, Quebec, and some in New York State and North Carolina. We always keep in touch in various ways like emails, phone calls and actual letters here and there.

On another happy note, I am so grateful for my writing buddies on the Coffee Cooler Hour, sponsored by Donna Kozik, Monday to Friday each week since the pandemic started.

I am grateful to be alive.

Sharon G. Teed has been writing since childhood, and has also been published in "The Gratitude Book Project" series. Find out how to connect with Sharon at www.MeetOurAuthors.com.

January 9

Wanda Jean's Journey to Goodbye
Cindy Barnard Mills

"Grief is just love with no place to go." ~ Jamie Anderson

January 9, 2020, we celebrated Mother's 90th birthday. The following day, I drove her to Cedarbrook Memory Care where my brothers were waiting. In the lovely lobby, we said, "They will take good care of you…too many close calls at home. It isn't safe." Our voices kept breaking. She was never one to "make a scene." The look on her face and the ice in her voice said she believed we let her down. Guilt-ridden, we promised to visit every day and did until the pandemic hit.

No visits allowed. Through the window, she was shrinking before our eyes—too confused to converse on the phone. Guilt became terror. Would this woman who had devoted her life to her children and grandchildren die completely alone? I prayed, trusted my gut and brought her home terrified of the outcome.

I'm immensely grateful for the support of caregivers, hospice nurses and a family who knows how to circle the wagons. Four months home and bedridden, she looked scared. I said, "You're getting ready to go to heaven." Her eyes lit up. She was ready. August 20, 2020, she left us heartbroken but grateful and honored by the gift of her life.

Cindy Barnard Mills, RN, currently teaches dialysis theory and is the author of Leader for Life: Lessons Learned as a Fortune 500 Executive, a Taco Bell manager and a mom. Learn more about Cindy at www.MeetOurAuthors.com.

January 10
Honoring Madison
Christina Renee

"Being a single parent is not a life full of struggles but a journey for the strong." ~ Meg Lowrey

I had my life all figured out. Love, marriage, three children, a nice home with a beautiful backyard. Life happened, and suddenly I was a divorced single mom with a lot of anxiety and self-doubt. Raising a daughter while my world was shattered was the most challenging thing that I ever had to do. Amid my tears, perceived failures and the heavy burden of guilt, I challenged myself to find the joy and gratitude of motherhood.

I am forever grateful for my dearest Madison. I admire how confident and outspoken she is and how gracefully she handles adversity at the young age of 10. Her feistiness and wit bring me so much joy, and I am in awe of her strength. Madison often teaches me my hardest lessons and the beauty of imperfection and unconditional love.

Madison reminds me to smile more and just have fun and, most importantly, that you can have a full life even as a single mom. My baby girl, also known as my miracle, is my "shero." I am forever grateful that the universe chose me to be her mommy, and I am honored that I have her to help me light up the universe.

Christina is a life coach that believes that every woman has the power to bounce forward after any adversity. Find out how to connect with Christina at www.MeetOurAuthors.com.

January 11
Gratitude on My Mind
Karen Lynn Robinson

"A state of mind that sees God in everything is evidence of growth in grace and a thankful heart." ~ Charles Finney

A baby smiling, a toddler laughing, warm eye contact and a flirty wave. All free and heartwarming. Have you ever had the experience where you feel warm, loving energy flow through your body in radiant peace? I am sure it is the spirit who I call God reminding me to stay in the moment with deep gratitude. This could be a powerful moment with a client, with a loved one, when creativity strikes or when sitting quietly.

During these moments, gratitude is on my mind. This starts as a thought, then turns into a deep affirmation under and over the pile of limiting beliefs and self-doubt. As I evolve, it gets easier to practice gratitude. The trick is to not wait until your problems are solved or life is in order. Have gratitude in the chaos, mess and suffering.

Not easy but meaningful as our strengths are uncovered when we dust off the rubble and allow ourselves a deep breath. When struggle finds you, remember that you have all the resources you could ever need within you. Practicing moments of gratitude will get you over any mountain.

Believe. Gratitude on my mind.

Karen Robinson is a licensed clinical therapist and transformation coach for mothers desiring healing from trauma. Heal Thrive Dream, LLC is a mother-daughter company. Discover more about Karen at www.MeetOurAuthors.com.

January 12

Home Sweet Home

Dixie L. Thompson

"America is not just a country but a way of life." ~ Anonymous

I sometimes forget to be grateful that I was born in the United States of America. It never meant so much to me as when I traveled overseas while in the U.S. Army. I lived in foreign countries where I tasted new foods and learned customs that I found intriguing and confusing. Things like living in a German apartment where unfurnished meant I had to supply my own light fixtures, not just light bulbs, and the kitchen cupboards had gone with the last tenant, leaving me to put food and dishes on top of the boxes I had moved them in.

Getting a telephone in Korea meant watching someone climb a pole out by the street and attach a wire, walk across to my apartment building and climb up to the roof before dropping the wire down to my front window. He then ran the telephone line through the open window. This gave bugs and weather a small opening to invade my apartment since the window wouldn't close all the way after that.

I enjoyed my time overseas despite the oddities, but returning to the United States always filled me with joy and gratitude for what we have.

Dixie L. Thompson is a retired U.S. Army veteran, serial entrepreneur and volunteer helping others discover and reach the life they want to live. Learn more about Dixie at www.MeetOurAuthors.com.

January 13

Connecting the Dots

Sidrah Qureshi

"You can't connect the dots looking forward; you can only connect them looking backwards." ~ Steve Jobs

Looking back at the last decade of my life made it seem like a dirty canvas with scattered, random dots, whereas everybody else's life was a beautiful painting.

I was scrolling through social media posts from friends, family and people I was following. As we were heading toward the end of 2019, most reflected over the past decade and their remarkable achievements. At first, I was excited about their successes. Next, I was left with sadness and loneliness. My past decade was filled with hardships and challenges.

Fast forward; we reached the end of 2020. My heart is filled with a deep sense of gratefulness. Finally, the dots are making sense, why I had to go through these health, relationship and financial challenges. It was to help others with the same life adversities, as my own wounds have now healed.

In 2019, I could only see my life struggles, the gaps between the dots, and not the life learnings, the gains. I now know to focus on the gains, not the gaps. Although my current life painting is unfinished, I am grateful for my dots. I have faith one day the painting will become a masterpiece connecting all the dots.

Sidrah Qureshi is a neuroscientist, brain trainer and brain performance coach. To get your brain into its best shape, connect with Sidrah at www.MeetOurAuthors.com.

January 14

Passing on the Love
Heidi Miller-Ford

"I'm the girl that wants to bring every stray animal I see home just so they can feel loved and safe." ~ Unknown

From as young as I can remember, pets have always been a part of my life. When I was old enough to go play in the neighborhood, it wasn't unusual for me to bring back a stray, which I would beg my parents to keep. Heaven forbid a neighbor's dog had puppies! When I was sixteen, one of my first jobs was working at a pet store. Of course, I purchased the little Cocker Spaniel that I couldn't bear to leave there every night.

As a parent, I have passed on that love for pets. We've had everything from ferrets to a chicken my girls pushed on a swing at our house. These animals bring such joy to us. Yes, they're a lot of work! And at times, can be messy.

But they become family members who hold a special place in our heart. I still tell stories about some of the crazy pets I had growing up. One of which was a crow that would land on my dad's car every night when he pulled into the driveway. I hope my children will have fond memories of their animal friends to pass on to their children someday as well.

Heidi Miller-Ford is a wife and homeschool mom of three who runs a blog helping families homeschool with confidence. Find her www.MeetOurAuthors.com.

January 15
Grateful for My Struggles
Cate Cook

"Some of God's greatest gifts are unanswered prayers."
~ Garth Brooks

I am grateful for my struggles, for without them, I would not have found my strength. We all would prefer to live a life free of adversity, but it is only in times of hardship and struggle that we find out what we are made of.

Divorce, having a child with a birth defect, bankruptcy and many other situations have brought me to my knees. I would have preferred an easier road. But, looking back, I see that these experiences are exactly what has shaped me into the strong, confident woman I am today. I am so different from the person I was 30 years ago.

Growth happens while conquering the path we are put on. We each have the ability to overcome whatever comes our way. Adversity is not meant to break us but to shape us into the best versions of ourselves.

Now, when faced with a "lifequake," besides praying constantly for guidance and help, I try to look at the bigger picture to see what I am supposed to learn during this time. My struggles have always rerouted me onto a new path, actually, a better path, than the one I was traveling on.

Cate Cook is the creator of Posh & Pure Styled, a blog that encourages inner growth as much as styling outer beauty. Find out more about Cate at www.MeetOurAuthors.com.

January 16

Ian's World, My World
Warren L. Henderson Jr.

"Love is of all passions the strongest, for it attacks simultaneously the head, the heart and the senses." ~ Lao Tzu

We all have some person or event that comes to mind when we think of gratitude. Likewise, there are those who warm our heart with pleasure when we hear their name. For me, one of those is Grandson Ian! Ian Thomas Cummings energizes a room with his smile, his personal magnetism and his thirst for knowledge.

Picture this: Our living room has a large window overlooking Puget Sound in Washington. The patio door (on the opposite wall) opens facing east. One particular evening, everyone was in awe of the striking sunset. Three-year-old Ian noted that the sun was going to sleep. He promptly informed us that it wakes up by the patio door in the morning.

Using his baseball and soccer ball, I illustrated the rising and setting of the sun as he experiences the events. Ian not only confidently grasped the concept, he began explaining it to anyone who was in the house at every sunset. Before danders flare, remember his age. He can enjoy his Ian-centric world for a bit before introducing rotating planets. In my case, I am grateful for the opportunity to fill his mind with marvels and then watch his dreams grow.

Warren L. Henderson Jr. is a college professor and the author of *Make-It-New Journal: Transform Your Outlook; Rekindle Your Life*. Find out how to connect with Warren at www.MeetOurAuthors.com.

January 17
You Are Divine by Design
Joanne Pearce

"Everyone has been made for some particular work, and the desire for that work has been put in every heart." ~ Rumi

As you travel along the road of life, you are in for a very exciting adventure. It starts out like an uncharted map, full of possibilities and potential with many lessons to be learned along the way.

On your journey, you will come across some detours, potholes and areas that seem to be under constant construction. One day, I ended up completely derailed from the road I was on. In hindsight, it was the best thing that could have happened.

I discovered we all have a spiritual GPS! It had been alerting me for years, telling me I was headed in the wrong direction. It had been speaking through feelings, the language of the soul. I had deviated from my life's purpose, and I was on the wrong road.

Your spiritual GPS has sacred coordinates that, when plugged in, will guide you to the good you desire. It's called gratitude. It's through the inherent power of gratitude that your dream life unfolds.

Whatever road you're on, begin each new day by filling your tank with gratitude and your heart with joy. Then, watch in awe as the power of gratitude transforms your life into one of magic and miracles.

Joanne Pearce is the founder of Sacred Healing Lotus and a certified Proctor Gallagher Institute consultant. Find out how to connect with Joanne at www.MeetOurAuthors.com.

January 18

Whose Words Are They Anyway?

Bonita "Joy" Yoder

"There is no time like now to to remember your inner joy and follow your passion." ~ Bonita "Joy" Yoder

When I was at a family reunion at about five years old, my older cousin Clinton put a wooden doll named Woody upon his lap. They talked to each other. People laughed.

What was happening? I later learned that they were doing "ventril-o-quism," a big word for a youngster. That image of wooden Woody speaking was imprinted on my mind.

At 16 years old, I checked out a book from the library on ventriloquism and spent hours in front of the mirror practicing talking without moving my lips. I began doing magic and ventriloquism shows. At age 22, I graduated from law school.

Shortly before graduation, a Kansas City talent agent offered me a contract performing at school assemblies, and I said, "But Dave, I'm about to be a lawyer." His response? "If you can hold the attention of children, you can hold the attention of any jury." He was probably right, but I declined. Thus, the jury is still out!

Years later, I dusted off my dreams. Now I use the presence of puppets to bring humor into inspirational speaking. Puppets are playful truthtellers and joy bringers. Thank you, Cousin Clinton, for inspiring me with this expression of joy so I can help others find theirs.

After practicing law over 25 years, today Bonita "Joy" Yoder emcees, speaks and "edutains" with humor and ventriloquism. Connect with her at www.MeetOurAuthors.com.

January 19

Gifts of a Tennessee Decade

Carol Brusegar

"The mind, once stretched by a new idea, never returns to its original dimensions."~ Ralph Waldo Emerson

Spending the last decade in Tennessee after living primarily in Wisconsin and Minnesota for the previous 60 years has been a mind- and spirit-stretching experience.

Regional differences are striking. Civil War monuments, battlefields and cemeteries. Plantation tours, some adjusting their narratives to reflect the enslaved people who labored there. Family cemeteries in corners of new housing developments that include those enslaved. Deep southern drawls. Southern gospel music and groups. Meat- and-three restaurants, country music and celebrities. Festivals like Mule Day. The pervasive influence of very conservative churches, theology and politics. So much is different from my Midwest roots.

Tennesseans enjoy the exquisite beauty of rolling hills and nearby mountains, many waterfalls, caves and parks and the Cumberland River flowing through downtown Nashville. Travel opportunities abound as Tennessee shares borders with eight other states.

Beyond all of that, the highlight of this decade is deep involvement in a progressive faith community. We built a community of inclusion in this conservative atmosphere that now includes virtual members from across the country. Great friendships forged during that process will endure regardless of distance and time. I treasure it all—history, culture, beauty, change and relationships—and will never be the same.

Carol Brusegar is the author of *Create Your Third Age: Steps to Making Your Years Past Fifty Fulfilling and Joyful* and related books. Discover more about Carol at www.MeetOurAuthors.com.

January 20

Be and Feel Grateful

Vicki Peel

"A basic law: The more you practice the art of thankfulness, the more you have to be thankful for." ~ Norman Vincent Peale

Although I am grateful, I haven't always felt grateful. I have been blessed with a wonderful family, a fulfilling career and a comfortable home that is my refuge from the chaos out there.

For a long time, I felt guilty for failing to feel grateful when I had so much to be grateful for. So, about two years ago, I started a gratitude journal. Just before bedtime, I would write five things for which I was grateful, beginning each with "I am grateful for."

Sometimes I had difficulty coming up with five things. And sometimes I questioned my sincerity when I realized some statements included things I owned, which made me feel shallow and undeserving. But over time, I slowly realized something almost magical. I began to feel a sense of well-being and contentment to a depth I had never known. And throughout my day, I began to notice simple things that gave me joy that I would write about in my journal. I recognized that the key to feeling grateful was simply taking the time and making the effort to be aware of my circumstances.

To feel grateful, be aware, and take time to reflect. It will change you.

Vicki Peel, Ed.D., reimagines home economics by encouraging and supporting people with home, lifestyle and food hacks through her blog. Discover more about Vicki at www.MeetOurAuthors.com.

January 21
The Day We Met
Angela I. Schutz

"Love is composed of a single soul inhabiting two bodies." ~ Aristotle

For Juniper (January 21, 2014)

Today is my granddaughter's birthday. I know it is supposed to be a special day for her, but it's a special day for me too. It is the anniversary of the day I met her. I share in the wonder of that day. The moment I saw her, so pink and perfect, I picked her up, held her close, whispering, "You are born for greatness!"

I will always be grateful that she is my precious granddaughter and honor her presence in my life. I loved teaching her throughout her formative years, and now, when I look at her, I am proud of the kind, generous, brilliant being she has become. I can look back on all the times raising her and smile as I recount the happy, goofy, poignant memories.

I am grateful that, despite life's challenges, I didn't quit on her. I am so glad that I was given the chance to create a close and loving relationship with her. So today, I am proclaiming this day as the anniversary of the day I met my favorite girl on the planet. Today, I am celebrating grandmotherhood and all its resplendent joys.

Angela Schutz: founder of Driven To Succeed Consulting LLC, published author, professional speaker, adjunct professor and career coach dedicated to helping others empower their lives. Learn more about Angela at www.MeetOurAuthors.com.

January 22

Gratitude Leads to More Choice!
Alberta Fredricksen

"None is more impoverished than the one who has no gratitude. Gratitude is a currency that we can mint for ourselves and spend without fear of bankruptcy." ~ Fred De Witt Van Amburgh

I have often shared with friends and clients that conflict is a gift that just keeps on giving. This usually produces an animated response that leaves little room for being or feeling grateful when conflict arises. If conflict is only seen as a spoiler, a negative or something to be avoided at all costs, you lose the power of choice! Truthfully, we have good reason to choose to be grateful when conflict appears in our lives.

Gratitude is a gift and a powerful antidote to conflict or feelings of disempowerment or having no choice. If we choose to be grateful when differences arise, we can avoid engaging in power struggles.

Gratitude for what we are about to learn through exchanging information is empowering. The expansion of choice or the opportunity to decide or influence is what motivates people to go beyond their powerlessness into competence and then from competency and confidence into achievement.

The gift of gratitude is actually a transfer of energy—of illumination, options and opportunity! We can motivate ourselves and others and offer relief from tension and inner turmoil by choosing gratitude for opportunity and then providing choices for all.

Alberta Fredricksen is passionate about helping others transform the presence of conflict in their lives into communicating more effectively and forging stronger, more fulfilling relationships. Learn more at www.MeetOurAuthors.com.

January 23
The Love of a Friend
Angela I. Schutz

"No person is your friend who demands your silence or denies your right to grow." ~ Alice Walker

I often think of the many joys I have in my life: the joy of a close family, a warm home and a beautiful garden, the joy of laughter and the twinkling eyes of the one who told the latest joke with such flourish that everyone in the room is laughing—either as a result of the joke or the sight of the jokester!

When I think of one of my greatest joys, I think of my friend Bob. Bob is the kind of guy you instantly love. He is the one who makes me laugh when I need a bit of silliness and shelters me in his arms when all I want to do is cry. He'll look at me and say, "Come on, you can tell me," and before I know it, I am pouring my heart out.

Gifts come in many forms, but one of the greatest gifts a person could have is the unconditional love of a true friend. So, if you are reading this on the 23 of January, think of Bob; wish him a virtual happy birthday, and then go out and call your best friend, and tell them you love them.

Angela Schutz: founder of Driven To Succeed Consulting LLC, published author, professional speaker, adjunct professor and career coach dedicated to helping others empower their lives. Find out more about Angela at www.MeetOurAuthors.com.

January 24

On Any Given Day
Joyce Mills Blue

"The smallest act of kindness is worth more than the grandest intention." ~ Oscar Wilde

On this day many years ago, my first son was born. He was eight weeks early. When my water broke, I called the doctor and we rushed to the hospital. They were supposed to stop my labor but hooked me up to the monitors wrong and swore I wasn't in labor. They were also supposed to give me a steroid shot to help mature my son's lungs, but that didn't happen either. Things were not as they seemed. Things were in a flurry. I was scared and confused.

None of the things that were supposed to happen happened, and my son was born just after midnight, January 24. I'm grateful he was healthy! I searched to find the meaning and the cause of the events of that day. Ultimately, I had a decision to make. A decision to enjoy my new, healthy baby boy or to continue to torture myself over the events of that day.

Be grateful for your blessings. Let go of the stories of your past. On any given day, you have a choice to make. A choice to be happy, excited and grateful or a choice to be scared, sad or angry. Choose wisely.

Wealth strategist Joyce Blue helps empower others to financial security even in today's economy. Have your money work for you instead of for the bank. Learn more about Joyce and her offerings at www.MeetOurAuthors.com.

January 25
The Divine Mirror
Abraham Joseph Ajenifuja

"The thief's purpose is to steal, kill and destroy. My purpose is to give a rich and satisfying life." ~ Jesus

Have you ever looked at yourself in the mirror and didn't like what you saw? If so, you are not alone. I have information that what you were looking for was your divine mystery. Without mystery, there is little or no value in life. It creates an unpleasant feeling of un-fulfillment within. The reason we enjoy reading books or watching movies is because they reflect parts of what is missing in our lives.

Divine self is your gateway to ultimate brilliance—a life well ful-filled. It's your unique, creative birthright, and somewhere, some-time in your past, something happened, and it was stolen from you and hidden in an electromagnetic spiritual dungeon.

I am grateful to God that what seemed to be lost since my child-hood has now been revealed to me. The answer was always there, but I missed it. I went from looking at my divine self from a dis-tance for many years until we became reconciled.

If you are experiencing discontent with life in any form, I want to encourage you that the answer is not far from you. I can show you how to discover your divine self and live the life you've always desired.

Abraham Joseph Ajenifuja is the visionary, advocate and pioneer of the revolutionary Vision, Intention, Purpose (VIP) Concept—the formula for authentic wealth abundance. Learn more about Abraham at www.MeetOurAuthors.com.

January 26
Journals, Jesus and Coffee
Sheryl Lynn Siler

"Fill your paper with the breathings of your heart."
~ William Wordsworth

I'm grateful for journals, Jesus and coffee. I know, it sounds like one of those T-shirt sayings. I treasure my mornings as I grab a cup of roasted goodness and pull out my journal. My journal is a place to have a conversation with God, dump the spinning thoughts and do a bit of dreaming.

The day is just better when I pause and focus on God. Putting pen to paper to write a love note creates a focus and connection. It becomes a time of thanksgiving for all that I have, a place to share dreams, express ideas and a diary of all I have to be grateful for.

There is power in recognizing the remarkable but also the ordinary blessings. The ordinary sweetness of my husband bringing me coffee. The ordinary bird hanging out at the feeder. The ordinary trip to get groceries.

There is also power in recognizing the very ordinary YOU—well, not so ordinary but a treasure. Do you feel treasured? Journaling has brought me to that discovery that I'm treasured by God, family, friends and—seemingly important but often overlooked—treasured by myself, which is a very special gift from journals, Jesus and coffee.

Sheryl Siler has a passion for learning, enjoys teaching and inspires others with her heart of service. Get her encouragement, journals and resources to make home life sweeter. Find out more about Sheryl and her offerings at www.MeetOurAuthors.com.

January 27

Kindness...I See It Everywhere!

Karen Hannon

"Stay the course. Face the storm. Do it afraid. Go for the dream."
~ Rich Boggs as Captain Jack

In February 2019, during a laughter-filled visit, my brothers, Richard and Stephen, and I were talking about the future. We are all in our 70s, but we still have goals and dreams that we want to realize, a legacy to leave for our children and grandchildren. Among other topics, we brainstormed my dream of writing a book and launching a kindness movement.

I am beyond grateful for the gift of my brothers—for their friendship, unconditional love and acceptance, kindness and encouragement. In times of doubt, I hear their voices. When needed, I can borrow their belief in me and continue to move in the direction of my dreams. And the results? *The Kindness Handbook* and *Destination: Kindness!* They are dreams realized!

I encourage you to do the same. Who are your people? Listen to them. Believe in their belief in you until you believe in yourself. Ask, What can I do now with what I have? And do it! The possibilities are limitless. Start small. Start Now.

P.S. Sadly, Richard died suddenly in August 2019. We are working to honor his memory with the *Kindness...I See it Everywhere!* book and events. Story submissions are welcome.

Karen Hannon is a certified dream-builder coach, author and entrepreneur. She would be delighted to hear from you. Find out how to connect with Karen at www.MeetOurAuthors.com.

January 28

Birthing Magic

Mary McCallion Dempsey

"We are all meant to be mothers of God, for God is always needing to be born." ~ Meister Eckhart

After a late New Year's Eve, I woke to Beineán's excited announcement!

Beineán, Rhys and Rhuadhán, our young grandsons, had a sleepover, and we welcomed in the New Year with a firework display nearby. I was still sleepy when I heard Beineán's excited words. "Granny, my sister is here!"

Beineán's mam, Karen, our daughter, was due with her baby but not till the end of January! As my confused mind tried to make sense of his words, within seconds the happiest photo popped on my phone backing his story.

Rhys reported that "Granny screamed so loud, I thought every pane of glass would shatter."

Karen had just got up and was about to put eggs on the pan for breakfast when she got a strange sensation. Within 20 minutes, little Roisin made her appearance.

Karen delivered her little baby girl by herself on the kitchen floor as hubby, Liam, spoke to the midwife and ambulance men on the phone. All was over by the time they arrived and eggs were still on the pan!

And she arrived at her magical divine time—first of the first at 11 a.m. This most beautiful, grace-filled day is etched into our hearts.

Mary McCallion Dempsey is a spiritual guide to inspiring women who seek to uncover their true worth and value to the world and future generations. Discover more about Mary at www.MeetOurAuthors.com.

January 29

Life Is a Gift

Davina Louise Adina

"Life is a gift, a journey to uncover our true essence as love."
~ Davina Louise Adina

We did not create ourselves, but a force far above and beyond our understanding blessed us with a sojourn in this earth. Through this journey, I have learned to appreciate the miracle of my body, the systems that work within it that keep me alive, my heartbeat, my lungs, my legs that move me from place to place.

I marvel at the gift of sight to behold the sea washing against the shores, the stars that shine at night, the colors of the rainbow.

I am grateful for the gift of touch to feel the softness of silk, the coolness of ice. I am grateful for the good times that I remember with a soft smile and the times that were not so good, where I cried and my heart was broken. The gift of emotions.

So many blessings and trials that stretch us come our way, but we grow like the root pushing through the earth to the sunlight.

I am grateful that I was created. I am learning the beauty of who I am. Love, that is who I am and you and the person next you. That is what we came here to learn. Love one another.

Davina Louise Adina is an up-and-coming writer. Having had a career in the business arena, she moved to writing as it's a desire that she has always dreamed of. Discover more about Davina at www.MeetOurAuthors.com.

January 30

My Service Helped Me Grow
Diana L. Keeler

"Live, love, laugh, and never stop learning!" ~ Diana L. Keeler

I am immensely grateful for the United States Air Force and everything it taught me. Before entering, I was shy and had no self-confidence. I wouldn't go anywhere without a friend or family member, and I never stepped outside of my comfort zone. Sadly, I was destined to never leave California.

I grew up in San Diego, but my first duty station was in Louisiana, which was so far from home that it may as well have been in another country. I had no friends or family close by, so I was forced to make new friends. Out of necessity, I grew up fast and began doing things for myself and on my own. My confidence and self-esteem grew as each day passed.

The Air Force taught me discipline, self-confidence and leadership skills. They instilled a strong code of ethics and the desire to learn. While serving, I grew to love helping others learn and succeed. Because of this desire to serve others, I created Self Development Insights, where I share my knowledge through my blogs, books, courses and mentoring.

Aim high! I did, and I am so grateful for it!

Diana Keeler is an Air Force veteran, wife, mother and grandmother. She holds an M.A. in management and leadership and is a chief editor, certified holistic nutritionist and vegan nutritionist. Discover more about Diana at www.MeetOurAuthors.com.

January 31
A Deep Dive into Gratitude
Ellen Watts

"Sometimes, what we need the most is some quiet space
and a new perspective." ~ Ellen Watts

I sit, staring into my coffee, feeling unsupported, let down, weary.

I decide to change because this pity party is a thought, and a thought can be changed. So I begin my descent into gratitude, starting with what's right in front of me. "I'm grateful for this coffee—grateful to the server who brought it to me and the barista who made it for me."

I dive deeper still. "I'm grateful to the person who first discovered coffee, and that roasting and grinding it makes it taste so good. I'm thankful that I wasn't the one who had to grow this coffee plant, tend it, protect it, harvest it."

I visualize all the people working long hours in many conditions to roast it, sort it, bag it, pack it in huge containers and drive it to the docks. The pilot who flew the plane, the attendants, the drivers who transported it to the stores, the café owner who bought the coffee and trained her staff. And I realize just how many people have served me, to bring me this one cup of coffee and allow me this moment of rest. "Thank you all."

I feel deeply supported, uplifted and inspired.

Ellen Watts is the award-winning author of *Cosmic Ordering Made Easier: How to Get More of What You Want—More Often* and the founder of The Co-Creator's Club. Discover more at www.MeetOurAuthors.com.

February

February 1
Homemade Gratitude
Debra Varsanyi

"You cannot do a kindness too soon, for you never know how soon it will be too late." ~ Ralph Waldo Emerson

Click, click. Mom's at it again. She holds her tool like a pencil and wraps a pre-cut piece of yarn at the top of a hook. Then, she inserts the hook through a square of mesh canvas while she follows a colored pattern. Wonder who this one's for.

Due to Mom's craft of hooking rugs, family and friends have been blessed with picturesque carpets in various shapes and designs. Her handmade rugs became an exquisite manifestation of her love. My mom, Elizabeth, expressed homemade gratitude.

Mom went to heaven unexpectedly in July 2016. Her smile remains locked in my mind, and my feet are greeted every morning by a cushy hooked rug. As I glance at the carpet in forget-me-not blue, dandelion yellow and sage green, it reminds me of the colorful love she poured forth. Even though four years flew by, when the bedroom window is open and a breeze wafts in, I can still catch the floral essence of her perfume.

I'm grateful my loving mom used her talent to hook rugs and grace family and friends with her homemade gratitude.

Debra Varsanyi writes short stories. Two of them, "The Door to Paradise" and "Moving Targets," were published in anthologies by Sunbury Press. She is currently writing an inspirational novel. Discover more about Debra at www.MeetOurAuthors.com.

February 2
A Heart of Gratitude
Sandra D. Munoz-Harlow

"A joyful spirit is evidence of a grateful heart." ~ Maya Angelou

I'm always focused on things that bring me joy; I want my life to be joy-FULL! One of the best ways for me to do this is to begin each day with a grateful heart. Having a heart of gratitude means focusing on the best and most blessed areas of my life. Doing so keeps me open to receiving the messages of good that await me as I go forth into my day and, hopefully, to sharing that goodness with others.

When I lose focus, I miss the joy. Have you lost your grateful heart? In your darkest hours, turn your thoughts to those things that bring you joy, no matter how small they may seem in comparison to the worries that lie heavily on your mind.

If you live your life from a place of joy, it is easy to fill your heart with gratitude, and conversely, if you have a grateful heart, you will always find something to be joyful about.

Isn't it amazing how your heart and mind are so connected? When you pursue joy, gratitude follows. When you have a grateful heart, joy abounds. May you have both in overflowing measure!

Sandra D. Munoz-Harlow is a life coach and family law attorney who loves helping people live their life with joy. Connect with her at www.MeetOurAuthors.com.

February 3
Little Guarana
Katie De Souza

"A loving friend often has a furry body and four paws."
~ Katie De Souza

You were tiny and apprehensive as you slowly walked across the soft blanket on the floor, wondering why you were outside of the gated area and your bigger brothers and sisters were still watching you from inside. Your little, tan legs with white socks and lilac body slowly made your way toward us. You shook a little as we picked you up to say hello.

Your pretty, green eyes looked into ours, and our hearts melted. Yes, you are our little Guarana, who we had been waiting to find for years. We both knew we should be together. Your small, bunched-up face with white markings on your muzzle snuggled into our arms as we held you. You were happy. You came home with us later that day, cuddling with Gabby and Leo.

You learned the word "food" the quickest. You know "come here" but only do so when you want, which is typical of a bulldog. Saying "food" gets you here immediately.

At 8 months, you love to go out on walks and say hello to everyone you meet, even if that means breaking into a jog to catch up with runners who pass by.

You are our loving companion.

Katie De Souza is an author and entrepreneur who inspires couples to achieve their dreams and live a happy and fulfilling life together. More at www.MeetOurAuthors.com.

February 4
Retirement Tribute to My Dad
Luma Poe

"My life is my message." ~ Mahatma Gandhi

Of all the things that I am grateful to God for, the one thing that I am most grateful for is my father, Apelu Poe's, much-deserved retirement from the ordained ministry in July 2021. Originally from Samoa, South Pacific, Dad has been serving in the ordained ministry in both the Congregational and the United Methodist churches in the United States for over 20 years. His areas of expertise also include academic teaching and evangelism.

Dad received a diploma of Theology from Malua Theological College, Samoa. He did postgraduate work in the United States and earned a Master of Divinity degree from Pacific School of Religion, Berkeley, California, and a Master of Sacred Theology from Yale Divinity School, New Haven, Connecticut. He also earned a Master of Arts and a Doctor of Philosophy from Vanderbilt University, Nashville, Tennessee.

Now living in LaVergne, Tennessee, Dad is dedicated to sharing his passion in helping people live according to God's time. His goal is to decipher the Bible code so that people may be able to discern God's path for their lives and how it is that God wants them to live to best receive his blessings and to best shine his holy light.

Luma Poe is one of the top sort managers at the FedEx Nashville hub. She is a product of Trevecca Nazarene University in Nashville. Find out how to connect with Luma at www.MeetOurAuthors.com.

February 5

I Heart Symon
Ann Elizabeth O'Keife

"It's so dark right now, I can't see any light around me. That's because the light is coming from you. You can't see it but everyone else can." ~ Lang Leav

"You've had a heart attack, Mr O'Keife. It's lucky you are here now," said the senior cardiologist at Worthing Hospital. The words rang in my ears as myself and Symon, my husband of 13 years, looked at each other in shock.

It had been a difficult few years. My parents had died within nine months of each other, I had changed my job in social work, and we had been asked to move from our rented flat. Symon always loves and supports me.

When February 2020 arrived, it was wet, grey and dull. Symon was recouping, and the pressure of being a full-time caregiver hit me. I needed a lift-up. Fortunately, I have lots of personal development tools, but my key one is gratitude. I re-ignited the Gratitude Group Sussex page on Facebook. Within months, it grew from just 20 people to over 440 members. People from all over the world wanted real connection, joy and hope. It gives me an enormous sense of purpose and pride.

Finally, I am so grateful to the National Health Service (NHS)—the jewel in the crown of the British Welfare State. They have literally saved my husband's life and saved our marriage.

Ann O'Keife is a wise woman, writer, teacher, counsellor, laughter yogi and hypnotherapist. She has written for national and local publications. She founded The Gratitude Group Sussex on Facebook. Discover more about Ann at www.MeetOurAuthors.com.

February 6

Unblock Gratitude with Tiny Appreciation

Colin Ellis (pen name Q.C. Ellis)

"Don't get me wrong. I admire elegance and have an appreciation of the finer things in life. But to me, beauty lies in simplicity."
~ Mark Hyman

Mary was still grieving her husband's death. She told me, "I've nothing to be grateful for! My mind refuses to be positive. I cannot stop being negative constantly!"

People experiencing chronic stress and anxiety often say this. It is helpful to keep it real and in the present moment. Appreciation is about what you can see, hear, smell, taste or touch right now. I asked Mary to look around and find something to which she can say, "That's OK." At first she declared, "I cannot find anything!"

On digital cameras, there is a macro button, which zooms into the target area—say, a flower. In the same way, find something small. It could be a tiny, shining glimmer of light on a surface (or through the curtains) or an interesting shape (maybe cast by a shadow), a colour or texture. I suggested doing this at least 12 times a day.

Months later, Mary told me, "I was surprised at how quickly 'appreciation' got my mind back on track. When I decided to not just do it when my mind was being negative, that's when my life began to change dramatically!"

Mary bubbles with gratitude, and I'm grateful to be a part of her journey to wellness.

Colin coaches and writes (pen name QC Ellis) on mindfulness, meditation, and personal development. He supports people to awaken and embody their true nature and greatest potential. Find out more about Colin at www.MeetOurAuthors.com.

February 7
Gratitude Is Clarity
Matt Nguyen

"He is a wise man who does not grieve for the things which he has not, but rejoices for those which he has." ~ Epictetus

Flash back to three years ago as I nervously went to my mailbox. The mail arrived that sunny afternoon. With much anticipation, I opened up the envelope with my blood test results, scanning for quick reassurance that everything was fine. Suddenly, my legs felt like lead. It was official. "I am pre-diabetic," I moaned. Just a year prior, my father, a Type 2 diabetic, almost died of a heart attack. By a miraculous event, his chest pain the night before averted an overseas trip that would have been his last.

Steel determination took hold. I will not go down that road similar to my father. A new chapter in my life began. The reversal of my pre-diabetes three years later brings new clarity and gratitude I have not experienced before. Life has new meaning and sparkle with my desire to help end Type 2 diabetes in a million pre-diabetics professionals.

My mission to share the five essential keys that helped end my own struggle with pre-diabetes was born. There is no greater joy than having the opportunity to help others avert a life of pain. Gratitude is clarity of purpose to be in service to others.

Matt Nguyen, DPM, is a holistic diabetes health coach and podiatrist on a mission to help pre-diabetics reverse and end their Type 2 diabetes. Learn more about Matt at www.MeetOurAuthors.com.

February 8

Zoxzox
Darian Slayton Fleming

"Being deeply loved by someone gives you strength, while loving someone deeply gives you courage." ~ Lao Tzu

On my birthday today, I reflect on the symbolism of February—valentines and love.

Blind with multiple disabilities, I expected to spend my life single. Then, my soul mate, John Fleming, entered my world. After seven years of friendship, John proposed. We had 10 happy years of marriage when John succumbed to lung cancer. He'd given me three special gifts.

The first was laughter. One day, when the movie we were watching ended, we simultaneously high-fived each other. We shared many jokes like that.

John gave me adventure. Once, we attended a skydiving boogie on the Oregon coast. I surprised John, saying that if I was going to try skydiving, I wanted to discover if I could see the ocean from the air. John found the best tandem master with whom to entrust my life. I jumped and could see the ocean and even Haystack Rock. Like falling in love, that skydive was a scary and thrilling adventure.

John gave me unconditional love. I never had a nickname until we discovered that our computer speech software pronounced "xoxox" as zoxzox. Whenever John called me Zoxzox, I knew he was feeling happy and loving toward me.

Darian Slayton Fleming is a passionate disability rights advocate. She brings her own life experiences to supporting her clients as a clinical social worker and rehabilitation counselor in Portland, Oregon. Learn more about Darian at www.MeetOurAuthors.com.

February 9
The Hidden Treasures of Travel
Mary Jo Gregory

"It is never too late to be what you might have been." ~ George Eliot

I am grateful to my parents for allowing me, at age 13, to go off on a six-week grand tour of Europe with my aunt and uncle. Why? It began my lifelong love affair with travel and eventually became my future career.

Many, many trips and years later, at the age of 40, travel rescued me after a divorce that resulted in a devastating blow to my personhood. The solution—pack up my big-girl pants and go off on personal growth treasure hunts. I had a person to find: me!

Leaving my daily routine and worries at home, I learned to joyfully experiment with life. I could let my guard down and learn to become the real me. Also, from a distance, I often came up with the answers to my burning questions of the moment. I always returned home with new insights, enthusiasm and already planning the next trip.

Most importantly, I experienced the goose bumps of a new love affair as I embarked on each new treasure hunt. Today, still striving to become a better person, may I never stop traveling. I am grateful to be able to repeatedly fall in love—with a new country, that is.

Mary Jo Gregory is a 30-year travel professional and soon to be author of Traveling with Zest, a four-step system to follow through life for both here and there. Discover more about Mary Jo at www.MeetOurAuthors.com.

February 10

The Impossible Became Possible
Lynette Chandler

"Freedom is not just ours to enjoy but to treasure, protect, and pass on to future generations." ~ Os Guinness

In my childish mind, going to university after school was a given. It never occurred to me there were enormous boulders in my way. Then I learned the truth. Where I come from, there is a limit on local university enrollment for minorities. Limited seats meant those who got in had stellar grades. People like me had to leave the country for higher education. That required gobs of money my parents didn't have. There was no student aid or other option.

It was a crushing defeat. I remember thinking, "Is this how it will be for my children?"

Years later, by divine intervention, I met my husband, and he moved me to the United States. Suddenly, all those things that were prohibitive for me became possible. I could go back to school and get help to do so. I could also start my own business with relatively few hoops to jump through. It was like having to walk a dirt path for years and suddenly being given a car to drive on a four-lane highway.

I cannot put into words the gratitude I feel, and I thank God regularly for this country and the opportunities she gives me.

Lynette Chandler creates planners, workbooks and journals that help entrepreneurs gain leads and grow their businesses. Discover more about Lynette at www.MeetOurAuthors.com.

February 11

Planting the Gift

Margaret Jackson

"Now is the season to know that everything you do is sacred."
~ Hafiz

Last April, the one-hour journey to collect plants kept being delayed for reasons I no longer remember. Plant pots needed washing. Assembling water, buckets, hoses and scrubbing brushes kept being put off for another day. October is repetition. Finding a spade, locating the bulb planter, digging holes, collecting wood ash (daffodils love it), purchasing compost and bulbs—all demand time.

All this gardening effort takes time. Time away from what? Away from chasing various chores and dramas of the day. But if I set the aim—today I am going to do it—then it happens.

Right now, striking red geraniums are in various stages of bloom. Pungent chives, heady oregano, tiny, blue Thai basil flowers, sturdy Italian basil and mint lean east for the morning sun and turn south following the light as it travels. The display constantly changes as the weeks pass by. Soon, the daffodils will peep through the earth, showing up every year like clockwork.

I reflect that my effort is required to invite a hoped-for display that provides appreciation for the turning of time, and my feeling of gratitude is the reward for witnessing each unfolding cycle.

Margaret Jackson is a personal coach bringing positive enhancement to the lives of her clients. Find out how to connect with Margaret at www.MeetOurAuthors.com.

February 12
Just Want To Say Thanks
Tiresa Poe

"We make a living by what we get. We make a life by what we give." ~ Winston Churchill

Have you ever experienced what it feels like not being able to express your sense of gratitude to the people whom you love the most? I have. Every now and then, I try to tell my mom, my dad, my brothers and my sister just how much I am grateful to them, how much I love them and how much they mean to me. But I don't always find the words to express my sense of sincere gratitude and unconditional love for them.

If you are a parent, couple, relative or a close friend and you are reading this, you probably understand what I am trying to say. That's why I am profoundly grateful to Donna Kozik for giving me this opportunity to say thanks to my family.

I feel overwhelmingly grateful to my father, Apelu, and my mother, Faapio Poe, who have always supported me and are always there for me. I also thank my brother Eli and his girlfriend, Natalie, my brother Josiah and his wife, Alyssa, and my sister, Luma, who have always believed in and inspired me. My niece, Kelianna, and my nephew, Micah, bring laughter to my heart all the time. May God bless you all.

Tiresa Poe is CEO and founder of Task Mai, an online on-demand service platform specializing in helping people with their everyday needs. Find out how to connect with Tiresa at www.MeetOurAuthors.com.

February 13
What's Your Favorite Day?
Kamin Samuel

"You're constantly surrounded by signs, coincidences and synchronicities, all aimed at propelling you in the direction of your destiny." ~ Denise Linn

For many decades, I have had a favorite day. It's not my birthday or Christmas. It's today, February 13. You see, on this day, I got into college, and then six years later I got winged as the U.S. Navy's first African-American female helicopter pilot. From that moment on, today has been my all-time favorite day.

Imagine my surprise when, on an early date with my amazing husband, I asked him his birthday. His answer was February 13! I squealed with delight. His response? "Who has a favorite day? And who has a favorite day that's not their birthday or a holiday?" Of course, I did take it as a sign from above that we were meant to be together.

I do have other favorite days—almost every day. This one just happens to be the pinnacle of days. For this day has led to momentous expansion in my life beyond my wildest dreams. And for that, I am immeasurably grateful.

So, what's your favorite day? For me, we can't have too many favorite days where we can tap into deep gratitude for all that day has brought us and for who we get to be because of it.

Kamin Samuel is an international rapid transformation business coach who specializes in helping people reinvent themselves and transform stuck beliefs and behaviors to accelerate growth, performance and wealth. Find out more about Kamin at www.MeetOurAuthors.com.

February 14

Romance on Valentine's Day

Holly Pitas

"When the angels ask me to recall the thrill of them all,
I will tell them I remember you." ~ Johnny Mercer

Romance filled the air as Mom reminisced about dating Dad. He liked to hear her sing when they sat and listened to the radio. Often, he brought a flower corsage for her hair. She told how her heart would jump when he helped her with her coat, then lifted her long hair from the collar.

A favorite story was the phone date on February 14, 1946.

While on the call, her mother handed her a giant heart-shaped box that had been delivered earlier. She was thrilled for the beautiful box of candy and opened it right away. They chatted about the different chocolates.

He asked her to sample some. "Is there an orange cream? A caramel?" Find this kind and that kind as he named his favorite flavors.

He asked about a solid chocolate in gold foil, but there were none. Dad said, "Maybe it's on the bottom layer. Take a look." She lifted the light cardboard divider to reveal the lower layer. There in the center was an engagement ring!

Decades into their marriage, each Valentine's Day, Dad gave Mom a giant box of fancy chocolates. She would retell the story in dramatic fashion as they celebrated the anniversary of their engagement.

A Valentine coincidence: In 1992, on February 14, mutual friends introduced Holly to John. They married in 1993.

Author of *Don't Get Caught Naked*. Certified emotion code practitioner. Discover more about Holly at www.MeetOurAuthors.com.

February 15
The Power of Gratitude
Melody Juge

"There is a calmness to a life lived in gratitude, a quiet joy."
~ Ralph H. Blum

Each February 15 signals the anniversary of my career. I'm reflecting on the past 38 years with a smile and a happy heart. This day is an annual reminder of the contributions I have made to the well-being of others while I care for myself. I am full of gratitude for the people I have met and the experiences I have had.

Little did I know, at the beginning of my journey, what the ensuing years would bring and how all these experiences would shape my life. Looking back, I find that I have a respectful and humbling appreciation for the exchanges that provided the most dramatic contrasts.

It was from these encounters that I learned the most valuable life lesson of all: Everything does indeed happen for a reason and for the highest good. No matter its physical-universe labeling of good or bad, another miracle is in process.

Through appreciation and gratitude of all people, success took hold. I am genuinely grateful for the lives I have touched and for the contributions that each encounter has made to my life. I believe strongly that the appreciation and gratitude of all things is the key ingredient to being happy.

Melody Juge is the founder of Life Income Management™: Creating Income for Life and creator of RetirementSense™, a proprietary retirement planning process. She is an investment advisor registered with fiduciary status. Learn more about Melody at www.MeetOurAuthors.com.

February 16
Power of a Sister's Love
Shealing Young

"It's a funny thing about life; once you begin to take note of the things you are grateful for, you begin to lose sight of the things you lack."
~ Germany Kent

My sister is a testament of how powerful love can be. That love can heal, and that love can be enough. For years, I have carried the pain of abandonment and felt incomplete because I did not have the unconditional love of a mother and father.

I have realized the love I was missing in my life my sister has been giving and showering me with this whole time. All these years thinking no one really, truly saw me or could understand how lonely it was to be an orphan. Xiaoling knew. She understood the loneliness, and she sees me; she always saw me. She helped me heal from a broken heart. She was there when I succeeded and failed. She stood beside me at my wedding, for the birth of my children. Every corner I look, she has been there, loving me, supporting me, sometimes carrying me. Always believing in me. What I thought I would never have, I received in love from my sister.

Gratitude changed how I see myself and my place in the world. It taught me to see beauty in everything. When I was able to see beauty, I opened myself up to allow love in.

Shealing Young teaches women how to use meditation, gratitude and affirmations as powerful spiritual tools that can help you heal. Her mission is to empower through self-care and meditation. Find out more about Shealing at www.MeetOurAuthors.com.

February 17
Ripples of Kindness
Linda Berry

"No act of kindness, no matter how small, is ever wasted." ~ Aesop

I believe thoughts are real.

These energetic morsels are behind all our actions. When thoughts originate in our heart as love, they create a beacon of positivity that can transform people's lives, even those you may never meet.

Today, and the rest of the week, gives everyone an opportunity to flex their heart muscle and send this high-vibration energy to others. Throughout the world, in mid-February, we are dedicated to kindness, taking the extra conscious step to brighten someone's life. The positive deeds done during Random Acts of Kindness Day and Week become contagious as the receiving individuals get inspired to do an act of goodness for somebody else.

Every thoughtful gesture of kindness counts, no matter how big or small. It amazes me how they can unfold exponentially like a ripple on a pond. For example, singer Gloria Estefan says she transfers this love energy with every fan autograph signed and believes she instantly changes their lives.

Learn to use this energy of thought as you help others around you. Whose life can you instantly change? What impact in the world can you make? Get started now and keep the ripples of kindness flowing all year long!

Linda Berry is an angel whisperer and the owner, consultant, coach, and reader for the Spiritual Discovery Center. She's also an international astrologer, podcast host, and spiritual and metaphysical book author. Learn more about Linda at www.MeetOurAuthors.com.

February 18

Colour Your Day with Curiosity

Stephanie Duckworth

"Mere colour, unspoiled by meaning, and unallied with definite form, can speak to the soul in a thousand different ways." ~ Oscar Wilde

Stained glass has always been one of my favourite things. I enjoy the vibrant colours, the beauty of the images, and appreciate the skilled workmanship. Stained glass can show up in churches and Victorian front doors. There is so much to love about this art form; however, I believe that the best part is the way in which my appreciation of the flat blue, intense cranberry, burnt amber and white opaque glass etched in uniform fleur-de-lys led to an awakening of joy in my life through the power of curiosity.

I wonder what prompted someone to change plain glass into stained glass. It must have been curiosity!

I started noticing the way in which my daily commute to work on a red London bus included being in a daydream, admiring the stained glass on some of the Victorian front doors.

You see, I felt like I had discovered a way into expressing myself, being more visible and creative. And I was curious how to bring more of this self-expression into fruition through experiences in my daily life that intrigue me, just like noticing the stained glass.

Stephanie Duckworth is a women's life empowerment coach, hypnotherapist and therapist. Discover how to unlock your resources and renew hopefulness with a clear map for creating the life you really want. Find out more about Stephanie at www.MeetOurAuthors.com.

February 19

Mom

Theresa Scandale

"Life doesn't come with a manual. It comes with a mother."
~ Unknown

My first memory is a pair of cowboy boots I got when we lived in the shelter. You said, during our stay there, whenever you prayed for something, God provided it—like when we needed a toaster, and the next morning there was one outside our door. You didn't know where we were going, but you trusted He would lead us there. My childhood memories are wonderful because you carried the weight of every burden. After my father died, I can imagine how alone you felt raising us kids, but you never let it show. You've always been both parents to me and allowed me to love my father despite the pain he caused you.

Growing up, I didn't know we went without. I never knew about the housing assistance, paycheck-to-paycheck living or food stamps. What I remember are piano lessons and trips to buy school clothes, not knowing you afforded them by testing shampoo products.

I am humbly grateful for everything you've done for our family and saddened by how much you sacrificed to make everyone around you happy. I only hope that this essay will show the appreciation and admiration that I've for so long wanted to put into words.

Theresa Scandale is a writer, teacher of English as a foreign language (EFL), aspiring linguist and genealogy enthusiast. She travels with her dog, Topanga, and runs a blog and YouTube channel. Discover more about Theresa at www.MeetOurAuthors.com.

February 20

My Friend, The Field

Carol Caffey

"God is an infinite sphere, the center of which is everywhere, the circumference nowhere." ~ Hermes Trismegistus

Once upon a time, there was a man who was digging in a field. He had heard there was a treasure there and had decided to find it. He dug and dug, day after day, digging and more digging. One day as he was digging away, his intuition led him in a certain direction, and he unearthed a surprise.

There before him in the dirt lay the most spectacular, the most splendid jewel he had ever seen. It seemed to glow with its own internal light. It felt alive. The color was indescribable.

Right then and there, right that moment, he decided to buy the field. The treasure he had come upon, the most beautiful sight he had ever seen, would be his. The great jewel and the land that had housed it would be at his disposal forever--whenever he needed them. He would not need permission to experience the presence the jewel and the field gave off, the intrinsic help they radiated. It would all be his. Available now.

Thank you, LIFE!

Carol Caffey has been a lifelong seeker of the jewel of great price, spending much time in the field digging. Connect with Carol at www.MeetOurAuthors.com.

February 21
A Soul Journey to Happiness
Lauren A. Ebbecke

*"Happiness is when what you think, what you say
and what you do are in harmony." ~ Mahatma Gandhi*

It is Friday afternoon, and I have cabin fever. I usually don't get cabin fever, but it has been a long six months of not socializing because of COVID. I craved real connection with people. So, I took myself out on a date night!

I found a wonderful café with a wild-caught Chilean sea bass and a flourless chocolate cake that even my mother would love! As the bartender poured a glass of wine, a gentleman came in and sat one seat over from me for social distancing.

We chatted about COVID, jobs and life as sounds of laughter, clinking glasses and chatter all flowed to Billy Joel's song "My Life." He compellingly told me his life was in transition and that he was not happy in spite of all of his material wealth and success. Over the next 15 minutes, I compellingly shared with him what I was intuitively observing.

He emphatically stated, "Wow, you are way more evolved than most people." Those words hit me like a cosmic time-out! I smiled and replied, "I have worked on myself so that I can assist others on their soul journey to happiness. Happiness comes from the inside out."

Lauren A. Ebbecke is a life coach who works with people stuck in drama, trauma and chaos to create happiness, peace and confidence from the inside out. Find out more about Lauren at www.MeetOurAuthors.com.

February 22

Expressing Gratitude: Count the Ways!

Alberta Fredricksen

"If the only prayer you say in your whole life is, 'thank you,' that would suffice." ~ Meister Eckhart

Many people are held back from their desires by their inability or unwillingness to express gratitude. This can be a major obstacle for anything we desire—abundance, love, acceptance or a higher level of consciousness. Thanksgiving and expressions of gratitude can become the fastest means of reaching our goals.

The more gratitude and thankfulness we feel and express, the more opportunity we merit by cosmic law. The more we give to God, and to God in others, the more we can receive. Perhaps we take for granted many divine blessings as though they were just our natural right. We may be grateful for the outer appearances in life but have less appreciation for spiritual things.

We can form the habit of expressing gratitude for every small blessing that comes to us multiple times daily. We can put our attention on the small details of life, saying thank you to others—and to God. It is a mistake to take our prosperity or well-being for granted. We can expect blessings because God wants us to have the fullness of His care for us, and we can choose to express gratitude for each gift of life as we receive it.

Alberta Fredricksen is passionate about helping others transform the presence of conflict in their lives into communicating more effectively and forging stronger, more fulfilling relationships. Discover more about Alberta at www.MeetOurAuthors.com.

February 23

Gita
Kate Smith

"Burdened by knowledge but unwinged will be those who are heartless." ~ Heart 1932

Little did I know, when I met Gita in the '90s, how much of an influence she would become in my life. Creating the culture of peace was her "work," her life's work, about which she was laser-focused.

I became a co-worker. Despite many lapses from the work, she never gave up on me. She led by example—gentle, caring for all living things, nonjudgmental and determined to cultivate peace. She taught me to think with the heart, spiritually, and not just the mind. I now understand a heart-based decision is the right one.

I am still learning.

She was witty, hospitable, generous and wise. Friends and strangers alike were welcomed with a cup of tea on the veranda and a chat. She was a great storyteller, often based on her own experiences, of both plenty and struggle.

I will be forever grateful to Gita for her teaching, her patience and her dedicated friendship. Even though she is no longer physically with us, her presence and guidance are still felt. I am a better person for the time I spent with her—more tolerant and compassionate with a deeper spiritual understanding and practice.

"Thanks" is not nearly enough!

Kate Smith is a lifelong learner and educator who aims to help others using her skills and experience. Learn more about Kate at www.MeetOurAuthors.com.

February 24
How to Begin Again
Leslie Shelton Walters

"Acknowledging the good that you already have in your life is the foundation for all abundance." ~ Eckhart Tolle

When I got divorced, I felt covered in deep shame, hurt from the sum of the circumstances. I had failed—failed my family, myself and God. But, despite the mire of discouragement and the stink of failure, there was an ever-beating heart still full of hope.

There is a word I learned in French class that has an English counterpart. The word is quotidian. Quotidian is the embodiment of the normal, day-to-day life we go through. If something is quotidian, it is routine, monotonous, met on the daily.

Even though they may seem anything but exciting, I am immensely thankful for the monochrome days of resolve that fit into the term "quotidian." Though they pass like beads on a string, it's in those days of inner perseverance where determination and healing slowly turn to triumph.

It is in the day after day of trying, of failing, of hoping and not giving up. It's in the day after day of picking yourself up to do it all over again even if you don't feel like it. The day, after day, after day.

And slowly, finally, the wounds stop hurting so deep. And healing begins in those quiet moments of the quotidian.

Leslie equips fempreneurs of faith with God-given vision, helping them get unstuck and inspired to achieve their goals in 10 days or less. Learn more about Leslie at www.MeetOurAuthors.com.

February 25

The Magnificent Seven Rides Again
Deborah Louise Brown

"Let us be grateful to people who make us happy; they are the charming gardeners who make our souls blossom." ~ Marcel Proust

We dubbed ourselves the Magnificent Seven. As volunteers in an international service organization, we pledged allegiance to the ideals of achievement, integrity, friendship, dignity, community and making a difference. We raised funds for scholarships for abused women seeking to pursue their education and improve the lives of their children.

I grew into the person I am today because of the Magnificent Seven. They asked me to lead at our local club level, then encouraged me to lead nationally and internationally. I am a happier, more confident and fulfilled woman as a result.

Donna, Maureen, Susan, JeanAnn, Louann and Terri have helped me tend my garden for over 30 years. I am grateful for the safety net my friends and I created. We have loved each other through marriages, divorces and the untimely deaths of beloved parents, husbands and children.

The light shines brightly when the Magnificent Seven convenes, even just a silly string of texts replete with emojis and bad jokes and ridiculous GIFs. I am most grateful for the laughter. We are a delightful gang of funny women wondering where all the time and elasticity went. My soul blossoms as I thank my charming gardeners for the sunflowers of 1994.

Deborah Louise Brown has over 30 years' experience as a coach, publicist, marketer, editor, publisher, author and speaker. She designs and illustrates coloring book journals for adults and children. Find out more about Deborah at www.MeetOurAuthors.com.

February 26
Grateful for My Superpower
Monica Morgan

"When I have a camera, I know no fear." ~ Alfred Eisenstaedt

As a little girl, I remember a wide array of fictional superheroes—men, women and sometimes even children—who were endowed with some amazing talent or quality that they were able to invoke for the good of mankind or some noble cause.

I later realized that I had also had a special ability—to see things that others did not see or to see things differently than others saw them. Be it color or contrast or context or perspective or angles or positions, I could use an ordinary camera to capture the images that I saw.

My superpower has allowed me to travel the world photographing world leaders, both famous and infamous, from Mandela to Ghaddafi, from Sophia Loren to Prince, from Aretha to Ali to the Million Man March to the greatest honor of all—serving as the personal and official photographer to the immortal Rosa Parks.

My superpower is not just for celebrities; it has allowed me to make people realize their superpower, to help little girls see the power within themselves and little boys see their greatness. I am forever humbled and grateful for God's indescribable gift to me—my special lens—my superpower.

For over 30 years, Monica Morgan has been "living life through the lens" of her camera, and now she's speaking about it. Discover more about Monica at www.MeetOurAuthors.com.

February 27
Living Gratefully
Adrienne Cooper

"Just don't give up trying to do what you really want to do. Where there is love and inspiration, I don't think you can go wrong."
~ Ella Fitzgerald

My initial dream was to teach. I wanted to help others learn. When I got a job as a tutor, it just reinforced my decision. In college, I graduated with a degree in mathematics education. I was ecstatic.

In my second year of teaching, I walked into the classroom and realized I hated it. I loved the children, designing projects and lesson plans, but I hated being in front of the class every day. So, I quit. For years, in each job I held, I became the unofficial trainer. I loved the role but always felt like something was missing. Eventually, I would move on again.

I was between jobs when I tried instructional design. I loved it. I design lessons and projects without having to talk in front of people. Yet, each day is a new challenge. There are new clients and new things to learn. Sometimes, I make mistakes. Big ones, but I don't give up. I have amazing support and people who encourage me to keep trying. Every day I'm grateful I kept trying until I found what worked for me. The bonus: I'm living my dream every day.

Adrienne Cooper is a mindset and confidence coach who partners with people to help them discover and achieve their dreams. Find out how to connect with Adrienne at www.MeetOurAuthors.com.

February 28

The Relevant Grandmommy

Robyn Passow Fisher

"This very moment is the perfect teacher, and, lucky for us, it's with us wherever we are." ~ Pema Chödrön

"Okay, Grandmommy," my 3-year-old grandson, Henry, yelled. "I'm on Uranus! You're on Neptune!"

When the pandemic lockdown began, my daughter asked me to isolate with them and help care for Henry while she and her husband worked from home. Of course, I said yes. For five months, while the world around us raged with uncertainty, I played planet hopscotch, made up stories and songs on the ukulele and jumped on the trampoline. And I took a nap every day.

I became a widow when my grandson was only 7 months old, and before this time, I had been struggling to find my relevance in his life. The other side of the family teemed with doting grandparents, step- and great-grandparents. Over here, there was just me, a grieving widow who had trouble controlling emotions. I wasn't very much fun.

But just like when I was caring for my husband in his final days, I did my best to stay in the moment, knowing these were special times. Henry and I bonded! I learned quickly that I may not be the bootie-knitting grandma, but I am most certainly the playmate grandmommy, very grateful and very relevant indeed!

Robyn Fisher is a writer, pilgrim, blogger and podcaster who writes about life reinvention after loss and hiking the trails for healing. Discover more about Robyn at www.MeetOurAuthors.com.

February 29
Unexpected Blessings
Carrie Berkebile

"It is always the simple that produces the marvelous." ~ Amelia Barr

Unexpected blessings sometimes show up as obstacles. Until the day my family computer died, I harbored a secret from my husband. I had built a small online business as a virtual assistant.

My husband had a definite opinion on what family electronics should be used for, and working from home was not on his acceptable usage list. I knew if I bought a brand-new computer, the same rules would apply.

With plans for a laptop lifestyle, I searched the local yard sale sites for a decent used laptop. None met my criteria. I found a large desk and a rebuilt Dell computer tower and monitor for $45.

The lifestyle I currently have is so much better than the laptop lifestyle I was striving for. I work from home. My husband no longer works the night shift. I have friends and colleagues in other states and in other countries. My daughters have grown a love for everything from vintage fashion to Japanese anime, video editing to website coding. I am deeply grateful as we sit by my computer to discuss, laugh and love much.

Carrie Berkebile is a tech virtual assistant, course creator, digital marketer and WordPress website developer. Discover more about Carrie at www.MeetOurAuthors.com.

March

March 1

Your Shortcut to Fulfillment

Marcelle della Faille

"Gratitude is the fairest blossom that springs from the soul."
~ Henry Ward Beecher

Often, we find it difficult to welcome the blessings that come our way. "It's too good to be true." "Who am I to deserve this?" We express so many unconscious sentences that close the doors of abundance and well-being on us.

To become a conscious and deliberate creator again, accept to receive the abundance offered to you by the Universe, and make it your usual way of operating and living. When someone presents you with a gift, just say, "Thank you." Feel the wave of gratitude that overwhelms you, and realize how much joy you get from receiving this gift.

This includes welcoming money. The Universe is abundant. It sends us everything we ask for. The Universe orchestrates prosperity according to our requests and our capacity to receive.

Be careful what you ask for. Do not limit yourself. Think big. As you develop your capacity to receive bigger amounts of money, you amplify your ability to receive the Universe's largesse, and you attract more of it.

Decide that, as from today, you will receive everything that comes to you with an open heart and a peaceful soul. Being grateful daily is the shortcut on the path to fulfillment!

Marcelle della Faille is a writer and trainer of financial abundance coaches, helping them develop their love and passion into a profitable and fulfilling business. Learn more about Marcelle at www.MeetOurAuthors.com.

March 2
Old Stuff/Dr. Seuss Day
Beth Munro

"Don't ever be ashamed of loving the strange things that make your weird little heart happy." ~ Elizabeth Gilbert

Who knew? Old Stuff Day and Dr. Seuss Day are the same day—March 2.

It's called a day to celebrate by honoring old stuff or getting rid of it or repurposing it. (A fabulously flexible holiday to have, as Dr. Seuss might say.) I call it my way to approach stuff—old and new.

I'm grateful to accept my weird little heart and to never again fear that I'd force myself to discard things dear to it: my sweet, little coin purse, a gift before my mom passed; the silk scarf (now a backdrop for art) from my stepmom for my first costume in a play; or the Thing-One-and-Thing-Two, Red-Fish-Blue-Fish postcards (now art) from my sister. The coin purse got its third zipper at a repair café that I'm grateful to be involved in organizing. I'm thankful for a new vase leading me to release all the vases I'd saved to decorate someday. I appreciate the space reclaimed from items sold, donated or "regifted." (I'm grateful for Seinfeld, but he can wait for his own holiday.)

What are you grateful for today? What thing-one or thing-two might you honor, release, repurpose or repair?

With Beth Munro, you won't throw away the things you love most. You'll learn to keep your weird little heart happy—in the space you have. Learn more about Beth at www.MeetOurAuthors.com.

March 3

I Am Alive. What's Next?

Susan Miller

"Believe in your heart that you're meant to live a life full of passion, purpose, magic and miracles." ~ Roy T. Bennett

It was January 2, 2020, and I was seeing a cardiologist in my local hospital. For over a year, I had been experiencing a lot of breathlessness periods, so this was just part of the exploratory process. After the routine tests, and whilst I was still buttoning up my blouse, he said, "I'm afraid your aortic valve is nearly closed, which is severely restricting the blood flow to your heart. You will need to have it replaced as soon as possible."

Two months later, I was checked into the hospital for open-heart surgery. It was meant to be a fairly straightforward procedure, and after four hours, I would be in recovery. However, after 13 hours of multiple life-saving operations, I was left in a medical coma.

When I was brought out of my coma and eventually made it home, I accepted my life was a blessing. I have spent months recovering and vowing that the next years of my life will be spent making a difference. When I look at the multiple scars on my body and grimace, my daughter says, "Mom, those scars saved your life."

I realise now that gratitude is more than just a word—it's a way of life.

Susan Miller is an expat Canadian living in Wales, United Kingdom, with her husband and three children. She is the founder of Team Author UK, which publishes books for indie authors. Discover more about Susan at www.MeetOurAuthors.com.

March 4

Let the Good Times Roll!

Ginny Lang

"Mardi Gras is the love of life. It's the harmonic convergence of our food, music, creativity, eccentricity, neighborhoods and joy of living. All at once." ~ Chris Rose

I love Mardi Gras! I lived in Houston for three decades, so a weekend road trip to New Orleans became a spring treat for my husband, Frank, and me. We used to stay in the French Quarter at a hotel where Simon, a talking cockatoo, meowed and called, "Here, kitty, kitty!" whenever anyone arrived. We'd dump our bags in our room, put on our walking shoes and carnival masks and hit the streets.

The rich, French traditions of New Orleans' Mardi Gras include lavish costumed feasts and balls, king cake and parades, all steeped in the smoky, music-filled ambiance of the southern coast. Fat Tuesday moves with the date of Easter each year, and it has been celebrated as the last day to eat and drink before the fasting of Lent begins.

Rio, Trinidad and Quebec are famous for their Carnival celebrations, and some places you might not expect, like Australia and Senegal. Any city that hosts a giant annual street party is my kind of place!

Mardi Gras isn't celebrated where we live now, but you'll still find me in purple, green and gold beads on Fat Tuesday. Laissez les bons temps rouler!

Ginny Lang is a veteran management consultant, coach, trainer and facilitator to nonprofit organizations as well as an accomplished speaker and teacher. Discover more about Ginny at www.MeetOurAuthors.com.

March 5

Celebrating Life
Alberta Cotner

"Success is not final; failure is not fatal. It is the courage to continue that counts. Never, never, never give up." ~ Winston Churchill

I have experienced several challenges throughout my life. Through sheer determination and will, I am a living example that you can overcome anything. However, when I faced the challenge of losing my son, I wasn't sure if I would ever recover from that. While I always felt that I was a strong person, this showed me what true strength I held within me.

My son was my best friend and someone who genuinely cared about people. I'm proud that I raised such a wonderful young man, and I am thankful he was in my life for at least 24 years. He loved life and lived each and every day to the fullest! I love and miss him dearly.

Early in my grief process, I met Ms. Ena Griffin from New York. She had also lost her son at the young age of 19. She has been there for me in so many ways. I appreciate and love her like a sister. I'm very grateful to have her in my life. Although we grieve for our children, we must remember to be grateful for each and every day we are given. Nothing is granted, and life is precious.

Originally from Texas, Alberta Cotner has faced her share of challenges throughout her life. By sharing her stories and experiences, she hopes to help others navigate similar challenges. Find out how to connect with Alberta at www.MeetOurAuthors.com.

March 6

The Miracle of Appreciation

Anne McLeod Ryan

"Gratitude is when memory is stored in the heart and not in the mind." – Lionel Hampton

Years ago, I found myself paralyzed by sadness, lying on the floor, trapped in a thick, black goo of depression. As I lay there, I heard a small voice say, "Remember this time; you will use it to help others."

I climbed out of that cold, deep well of depression through gratitude. I learned to be thankful for every little thing: walking in sunshine, wind gently sweeping my hair. I began to notice things people did every day to make my life easier. I learned to say "thank you" in each moment. Every expression of appreciation became a handhold to pull myself up the slippery wall, out of that dark well of depression.

Eventually, I began to make one-of-a-kind thank-you cards and hand them out. What joy! Then I thought, "Why not spread this joy across the world?" I gathered a community of talented women living in gratitude every moment of every day. Together, we are creating the Do-It-Yourself Thank-You Cards Project. With our card kits, co-creators experience the magic of appreciation in the moment and spread it forward, lifting one another to walk in sunshine, wind gently sweeping our hair.

Anne McLeod Ryan is the Leader of the DIY Thank-You Cards Project. Find out more about Anne at www.MeetOurAuthors.com.

March 7

Gratitude for Life's Synchronicities
Mary Choo

"Whether we name divine presence synchronicity, serendipity or graced moments matters little. What matters is the reality of our hearts has been understood." ~ Nancy Long

By synchronicities, I mean those opportunities that drop into your life uninvited, and only if you have time to notice them do you realize they are exactly the help you need at this moment to make your life work.

It happened again when I was putting together my monthly newsletter. I had shared a guest post from a teacher who uses a 10-minute mindfulness quiet time exercise to get her students to be present and focused each day before class.

Wanting to balance this with some support for stressed-out teachers themselves, I decided to take a break and check my email. I opened it, and there it was. An invitation to register for a free online mini course with Eckhart Tolle on "Awakening Your Inner Light"!

It was an aha moment, and the warm feeling of relief I felt as I read it made everything feel so much easier. Just another gentle synchronicity from Universe reminding me that we all have this inner light within us, and synchronicity works like magic when we feel grateful and allow it to heal our hearts.

Mary Choo is an occupational therapist, kinesiologist, mindfulness practitioner and published Amazon author of *Reclaiming Ourselves*, a self-help guide about energy healing therapies. Find out more about Mary at www.MeetOurAuthors.com.

March 8

Thankful for the Unexpected

Pamela James

"Unexpected events can set you back or set you up. It's all a matter of perspective." ~ Mary Anne Radmacher

"The airport is dark. The borders are closed," said my husband, calling from Ecuador. We didn't know it then, but it would be almost six months before he came home. During that time, my primary companion was #MightyMaximo, our new puppy. It was Maximo who got me out of the house, who introduced me to our human and doggy neighbors down and around the block. New friends for us all.

Here's the thing. We lost our first fur baby quickly and very unexpectedly just a year prior. It was so devastating that we were done with dogs. Yet one day my husband decided, out of the blue, we were getting a puppy after seeing a picture my mother sent. I still wasn't sure for the first several weeks. Of course, now I wouldn't give Maximo up!

Now, as Maximo and I walk our neighborhood, I often say a silent thanks for Maximo, for the life force and love he provided while Carlos was gone. I'm also thankful that somehow my husband knew, was guided, to make a decision that seemed strange at the time. Maximo filled a gap in our lives, and I'm thankful for him and for my husband every day.

Pamela James is a health/wellness and life coach who helps stressed, professional women take control of their lives so they can have success, health and happiness. Find out how to connect with Pamela at www.MeetOurAuthors.com.

March 9
Angel on Earth
Heather Aquilina

"Wherever your journey in life may take you, I pray you'll always be safe, enjoy the ride and never forget your way back home."
~ Vicki Reece

Dear Son,

I am thankful every day that, of all the souls waiting for a place on Earth, it was you who picked us. Mid-career, past littered with dysfunctional relationships, having a child was a giant leap of faith. You were an experiment without a control. I diligently researched pregnancy health, followed advice carefully to combat any age-related risks. We tried for years until, when I was 40, you were born. Every day I give thanks for you. Naturally happy, you only cried to tell us something wasn't right. So bright, everywhere we went your curious eyes and engaging smile fixed onto strangers and drew them to your side.

Every day I've rejoiced in your company—first as you showed me how to care for you, then as I slowed to join your curious watching of tiny, wondrous moments, normally a blur rushing by. You've taught me about letting go, releasing the delightful you I know to embrace the new you you're becoming, a new relationship with new experiences to share. With adolescence in full swing, you challenge me now to become my best self and keep our relationship strong for as long as the future grants us.

Heather Aquilina is a habitual learner working to balance running a management consultancy with communicating authentically through her writing and art in the hope of inspiring others. Learn how to connect with Heather at www.MeetOurAuthors.com.

March 10

Connecting to Purpose
Dena Crecy

"People who use time wisely spend it on activities that advance their overall purpose in life." ~ John C. Maxwell

It was July 1995. My divorce was final after a 15-year marriage. As I attended counseling, I began to search for my life purpose. A mother of two and no longer a wife, I knew there was a call on my life to do more.

After much searching, I found a 12-week life purpose class, where I discovered mine. As I embraced being fearfully and wonderfully made, I recalled common themes in my life, connected to my passion, discovered my personality preference and spiritual gifts and even learned that my first name means "peaceful." At the end of the class there was a graduation where we declared our life purpose. My life purpose is to glorify God by connecting women of God to the purpose of God for their lives.

It was so impactful that I started facilitating groups and became a certified life coach and, in 2010, started a 501(c)(3) called Relationships God Style. I am grateful to have purpose in life. It keeps me focused and minimizes distractions. I am grateful to be able to help women find what they, like me, are desperately searching for: purpose in life. I am grateful for the connection to purpose.

Dena Crecy, DTM 2, is a life coach who helps women connect to purpose by connecting to God's plan for their lives. Learn more about Dena at www.MeetOurAuthors.com.

March 11

The Diagnosis That Changed Everything

Sarah Dew

"And in the end, it's not the years in your life that count.
It's the life in your years." ~ Abraham Lincoln

The day I was told I had breast cancer is a day I will never forget. Sitting there, trying to process everything the nurse was telling me, I kept thinking, "It can't be true." But it was. Just 36 years old; my world as a wife and stay-at-home mum to my 5-year-old son had been turned upside down in the blink of an eye.

For 18 months, I fought as hard as I could to beat the disease that had invaded my body. A mastectomy, reconstructive surgery and six rounds of chemotherapy later, I'm thankful to say that I made it through to the other side.

My fight showed me that no matter how devastating something might be at the time, good things can come of it. Cancer taught me that life is precious, and that it goes way too fast. It made me realise that it was time to stop just existing and start living. And I wanted to help others do the same.

I retrained as a life coach, and now, thanks to my experience, I have the privilege of helping others every single day to become their best selves and live their best lives.

Sarah Dew is a transformation life coach who helps other women step out of a life on autopilot and into one of purpose. Learn more about Sarah at www.MeetOurAuthors.com.

March 12

The Gift Arrived with Pain
WaiSin Tong-Darbonne

"The deepest pains of our lives are always the greatest gifts if we find a way to use them and we don't let them use us."
~ Tony Robbins

Born in starvation times in China, I was sold as an infant to a childless couple who forbade me to have friends, wanting a provider when aging and a mini-servant until then.

At 8 years, one task was to clean the stinky sewage ditch below our house. One day, I felt a painful bang to my head. The naughty boys uphill targeted me with a big onion! I took it home and planted it in a pot.

I was so excited as it grew! It became my first friend. Soon, a big, beautiful pink amaryllis bloomed! One stormy day, I worriedly watched it from the window. It was so beautiful, yet it resiliently withstood the assault of the wind and rain, becoming even stronger and more beautiful. That was the moment I received the gift that has served me all my life.

My lovely plant-friend had taught me if it could survive and grow stronger through struggles, then surely I could! That gift has gotten me through immense struggles, from starvation, servitude, isolation and abuse to now having an amazing life, full of joy and friends and an incredible soulmate husband!

I always appreciate the gift in pain.

WaiSin Tong-Darbonne is an internationally collected painter, and she coaches women to boost self-confidence through art. Find out how to connect with WaiSin at www.MeetOurAuthors.com.

March 13

Disappointment on Our Honeymoon

Dr. Allen Darbonne

"The mind is its own place, and in itself can make a heaven of hell, a hell of heaven." ~ John Milton

Hiking up a gorgeous mountain trail with breathtaking views! On one of the most spectacular tropical islands in the world! Overlooking sparkling ocean hundreds of feet below our trail! A honeymoon made in heaven!

So, why was she muttering right behind me, not smiling or talking about how wonderful it was? She was clearly unhappy with me. My heart was heavy with sadness. Had I made a mistake marrying her? My mind was spinning.

We stopped at a safe spot. Sitting in sad silence. Biting our tongues. Both near tears. Finally, she broke the silence. I learned something about our minds that day. I thought she was experienced on mountain trails. Actually, it was her first time. She was terrified! She thought I didn't care deeply about her since I should have known why she was unhappy without her having to tell me. Opening our hearts, we realized we simply missed information needed to perceive the experience very differently.

Twenty years into our extraordinary soulmate relationship now, we're still grateful to have learned not to question the love but to question the argument. True love is safe and always deeper than a misunderstanding.

For over 50 years, clinical psychologist Dr. Allen Darbonne has helped couples and families all over the world to build deep soul-mate relationships. Find out how to connect with Dr. Darbonne at www.MeetOurAuthors.com.

March 14

Thank You, Giardia!

Patricia Jean Smithyman-Zito

"Right this moment, you have all the resources you need to make a masterpiece out of your life." ~ John Assaraf

I have been promoting health and wellness since a parasite in my intestines almost killed me. I lost 25 pounds in a week. My organs were shutting down because of severe dehydration.

We need to be our own doctor, paying attention to everything within the whole body, mind, spirit, self. Paying attention and choosing a healthy lifestyle opens our world to new moments of feeling fully alive. Once specific routines are in place, we can discover and enjoy our new self.

Recognize and honor the healthy you inside. Your body will thank you by responding positively. Listen to your self-talk, and speak of the positive changes taking place. Become aware, more focused, and be honestly disciplined.

Want to feel healthier and have more energy? Decide on small, healthy choices. You will quickly understand that being fit, positive, happy and living with passion is something you gratefully choose to implement.

I'm grateful for that invasive parasite over 35 years ago! I have lived a healthy life, encouraging others to bring about change on purpose.

Right here, in your abundant now, you are capable! The choice is yours. Live well, my friend.

PJ Zito is a loving wife, mom, grandma, retired teacher, interpreter for deaf friends, musician, composer, music video creator and published author. Find out more about how to connect with PJ at www.MeetOurAuthors.com.

March 15

The Healing Power of Pets
Daphne Bach Greer

"Until one has loved an animal, a part of one's soul remains unawakened." ~ Anatole France

Where would I be without my Pixie the pig, Buck the sheep, Marty and Rex my adorable dogs? Animals bring a smile to the heart and are a blessing to the soul.

Arriving just in time while overwhelmed with grief, my six week old yorkie Marty, became a godsend. Never leaving my side, now eleven years later, the bond and unconditional love exchanged has been priceless. Over the years, I've learned that life feels complete with furry companions. They can fill an empty heart with over-flowing satisfaction and wholeness. That compassionate look in their eyes connects you on an emotional level with an understanding beyond our comprehension.

On days when tragedy strikes or when life seems unbearable, dogs bring music to the heart when your flesh is telling you there's nothing to sing about. Cuddly canine companions can restore your spirit, ease your tears, while conjuring up sparks of hope buried within, spreading sunshine to the darkness in our world.

Want to rev up your life and ignite that joy that feels forever lost? Get a pet! You just may find yourself smiling when you'd least expect it, giving your heart the healing balm it so desperately needs.

Daphne Bach Greer is the author of *Barely Breathing: 10 Secrets to Surviving Loss of Your Child*. She writes about faith and finding hope after loss. Find out more at www.MeetOurAuthors.com.

March 16

Happy Panda Day

Anne Hunter Logue

"I thought the secret of life was obvious: Be here now, love as if your whole life depended on it, find your life's work and try to get hold of a giant panda." ~ Anne Lamott

Pandas are such fun and playful animals. I chose Happy Panda Day for that reason. A panda brought me a meaningful message for a special client through my intuition. In a healing session, my client saw a vision of a panda, and the next day I found a book entitled *Zen Shots* with the exact image she described. The synchronicity of that event proved our work was valid and anchored our experience. I have learned so much from the healing work I have done with many people, and I continue to spread my message through writing my books.

Interpretation and perception are significant ways to construct our reality. If I have an experience (or a dream) that is uncomfortable or confusing, interpretation is the way I find my path through that experience.

Intuition helps me strengthen my connection with Source. I am able to find meaning and direction in my life with the understanding I have gained. If people face fear, grapple with their place in the world, struggle with health issues or whatever, finding our path through a strong relationship to Source is our way home. My gratitude is for that strength, the unending tapestry of life.

Anne Hunter Logue is a healing practitioner and children's author of *The Story of the Sun* and *I Once Had a Tiger*, published by Westwood Books Publishing. Find out more about Anne at www.MeetOurAuthors.com.

March 17

Coming Home Where I Belong

Jordan Bernal

"The best part of traveling is finding yourself." ~ Ken Poirot

When my technical writing job of 11 years was outsourced to a foreign country, and work-related injuries left me in constant pain and unable to find employment, I was devastated. A decade passed. I still had no definitive direction for my life and no idea who I was. I began writing what I loved to read—fantasy.

I set my first novel in Ireland so I could research my Celtic heritage. As I stepped from the aircraft, the feeling that washed over me was profound. I'd found my cynefin—my one place of true belonging. Yet I'd never been there before. What little I knew of the Emerald Isle amounted to "wearing o' the green" on St. Patrick's Day.

Each day, as I explored the countryside, I grew more at peace, more anchored. My wanderings took me to centuries-old stone circles and monuments, tidy villages, vast peat bogs, ancient ruins, and windswept cliffs.

As I traced the crosses atop St. Declan's Well, my novel came alive. It was then I realized, though not the land of my birth, Ireland is truly the land of my heart.

Today I celebrate St. Patrick's Day knowing who I am, and I'm grateful.

Jordan Bernal is the author of *The Keepers of Éire*, *The Keepers of Alba*, and *Reluctant Paladin*—dragon fantasies that encourage readers to let their imagination take flight. Discover more about Jordan at www.MeetOurAuthors.com.

March 18

Sunshine on My Shoulder

Nancy J. Haberstich

"O, Sunshine! The most precious gold to be found on Earth."
~ Roman Payne

What a difference sunshine can make in my mood, creativity, productivity and my health. When the sun shines, I feel special, like there's a spotlight on me demanding my best performance. Are people that I meet on my walk friendlier on a sunny day? Do words come more easily when I write with the afternoon rays streaming into my office? Are phone calls more pleasant and my voice more cheerful on a sunny day? It seems so.

Sunshine is a source of vitamin D. Flowing from the cosmos, it is absorbed by my skin and then converted by my body into a mood elevator and bone builder. But managing this asset requires direct exposure, so I must get outside to collect my daily dose of the sunshine vitamin.

My mother used to say, "When you can't find the sunshine, be the sunshine." She encouraged me to wear bright colors and a big smile on cloudy, dismal days. Sunrises and sunsets are special moments in time that put things into perspective. I am grateful for the abundant sunshine that nourishes all life forms on this planet—the plants, animals and even a gazillion photosynthetic microbes capable of cleansing environmental waters.

Nancy J. Haberstich, RN M.S., creates STEAM resources featuring the nanobugs to help people of all ages understand microbiology and infection prevention. Find out more about Nancy at www.MeetOurAuthors.com.

March 19

Exit Stage Left

Julaina Kleist-Corwin

"All the world's a stage / And all the men and women merely players / They have their exits and their entrances / And one man in his time plays many parts." ~ William Shakespeare

My only child, Adrian, was born on March 19, 1971. He had a life-long love of theater that began when he was 5 years old. He'd stand in his backyard tree house, dressed in different pieces of clothing he had put together, and say, "I'm a carpenter." On another day he'd say, "I'm a painter," or, "I make movies." His little one-man shows worked. The Suzuki violin lessons he had from preschool through his elementary years set the path for experimenting with sound and music. Adrian's choices were his own. I always wondered what he'd want to do next.

In college, he became an audio designer/tech for their theater. His best friend was the lighting guy and his fiancé, the stage manager. The producer of the plays trusted Adrian with the keys to the buildings so the three of them could work after hours to meet performance deadlines.

Then tragedy struck. Late one night, I received a call from the hospital. Adrian and his two friends had been alone in an accident at the theater. The brick ballast for the curtain fell 40 feet down on my son's head. Adrian had made a stage exit. I'm grateful for the 26 years he was in my life.

Julaina Kleist-Corwin is a teacher, author and writing coach. Find her books *Written Across the Genres*, *The Choice Matters*, and *Captivate Audiences* on Amazon. Learn more about Julaina at www.MeetOurAuthors.com.

March 20
Mikey (K.Q.)
Theresa Scandale

"Some people cross your path and change your whole direction."
~ Unknown

You said you entered my life to teach me something. When your job was done, you'd leave. We're five years older now, and you've taught me more than I dreamed you could. We were opposites. I cannot imagine anyone else so unlike me. You were cold and calculating where I was sensitive and emotional. You were headstrong and confident, and I'd sometimes wither in your presence.

But you showed me a love that uplifted me. You taught me patience and resilience while holding a mirror (or several) to my flaws. You showed me what to change inside myself to properly love someone else. Sometimes, your approach was gentle; sometimes, it tore my heart out. But I've always learned from you.

"Money is transient," you said as we boarded the plane. "It's the experience that matters." That trip to Morocco wasn't what I was grateful for. It was that you cared about my childhood dream. And in Bulgaria—that you walked with me for hours in the snow. And it wasn't our life in Spain. It was that you wanted to share your life with me.

I cherish our memories. But it's the experience of loving you that I'm forever grateful for.

Theresa Scandale is a writer, teacher of English as a foreign language (EFL), aspiring linguist and genealogy enthusiast. She travels with her dog, Topanga, and runs a blog and YouTube channel. Discover more about Theresa at www.MeetOurAuthors.com.

March 21
A Vehicle and a Husband!
Lesa Dale

"And my God will supply every need of yours according to his riches in glory in Christ Jesus." ~ Philippians 4:19

My husband and I have been married for almost 10 years, more than my first two marriages combined. I was waiting tables to support my two boys. After some complicated relationships, I had given up on dating and turned everything over to God.

At this same time, I needed a new vehicle. Honestly, my van acted possessed. While driving, interior lights flickered. Doors locked and unlocked and came open; we had to weld the passenger door in place so it would close.

One Sunday, a missionary spoke at church, and with the closing prayer, God flashed a number in my head—most of the money I had saved to purchase another vehicle.

"Really, God?"

I wrote the check and gave it to my pastor. A couple of weeks later, John asked me for my number. Shortly after, I agreed to a date. That first night, I told him about giving the money. Not realizing I had already done so, he says, "You need to write that check." I knew then. He was the one! Within two months, he bought me a van. A year later, to the day, we were married. He is truly the husband God intended for me.

Lesa Dale is a Christian life coach and founder at Life Walk GPS: Make better life decisions by understanding your gifts, personalities and strengths. Learn more about Lesa Dale at www.MeetOurAuthors.com.

March 22

God's Precious Gifts

Roslyn Rajasingam

"We can do no great things, only small things with great love." ~ Mother Teresa

We could not conceive. We tried for seven years. Raj suggested that we adopt. I thought, "Am I capable of loving someone else's child?" We were informed that international adoption takes four years. "What? Four years?" He pleaded gently, then I agreed. Midway, I wanted to pull out our application. He convinced me to be patient.

After waiting for four years, we were allocated a 20-month-old boy. He had to attend medical tests and needed to recover before being allowed entry to Australia. A few months later, Rafael joined us, and we became a family! Due to our age, we had to decide quickly if we wanted a second child. We agreed and started the process again.

Another four years of waiting! The process had to be followed in accordance with the Hague Convention. Four years later, we travelled to the Philippines with Rafael to welcome his new little brother, Roque. The boys are now 20 and 14 years old, respectively. They love each other like blood brothers and fight like real brothers!

I am extremely grateful to God for making us a family. We love these young men. They are God's precious gifts to us!

Roslyn Rajasingam is a coach who shows people how to discover and live their calling and purpose. Discover more about Roslyn at www.MeetOurAuthors.com.

March 23

Remembering My Mother and Father

Katrina Willis

"Gratitude is the memory of the heart." ~ Jean-Baptiste Massieu

If not for a mistake in my father's travel booking, my parents might never have met. However, as fate would have it, one sunny day in the late 1950s, on the tiny-but-picturesque Lord Howe Island, the charming boy from the bush met a shy, city career girl. And, as they made happy, holiday-mode conversation that day, they had no way of knowing that their lives had been changed in an instant.

My mother thought nothing would come of it. But, as the saying goes, true love always finds a way. They were married as soon as my mother graduated as a nurse. Together, they formed a formidable team; their shared goal was to create the best life possible for their little family. And create the best life, they did!

We lived modestly, but our home life was always rich with guidance, wisdom, love and laughter. Always love and laughter. I'm so grateful for the sacrifices they made, the struggles they hid and the challenges they faced (and conquered) together.

I'm grateful for many things. But, mostly, I'm grateful for the privilege of sharing my life with these two amazing and wonderful people. Thanks, Mum and Dad. I miss you.

Katrina Willis is a writer, digital creator and wellness blogger. Discover more about Katrina at www.MeetOurAuthors.com.

March 24

A Yogini In A Bikini

Tara Myers

"Gratitude is the wine for the soul. Go on. Get drunk." ~ Rumi

I tried something new today. Beach yoga. The idea always seemed so sandy to me, but break out of my comfort zone I did. The simplicity of it all was awakening and empowering. The instructor and only other participant had uplifting, infectious energy. Me, I like the elements, so I was in my element.

One of my least favorite things about studio yoga is the artificiality of it all—imported soundtracks of waves, made-in-China statues of fish, birds and the like, toxic candles scented with "ocean breeze." Air conditioning always puts a kink in my zen too.

The beach provided the antidote to all that. We flowed to nature's soundtrack—waves and wind. We balanced our poses to the natural horizon. We grounded our sit bones in forgiving white sand, not vinyl flooring. We gained inspiration from flying fish, soaring gulls and a pair of crabs I couldn't stop watching. As if out of respect for our practice, they crawled clear of our colorful beach towels. Best of all, there was the sun. The hot, shiny sun over the Gulf of Mexico. In gratitude, I flowed through my sun salutations.

Tara Myers is a lifelong writer who splits her time between the Gulf Coast and the West Coast. Learn more about Tara at www.MeetOurAuthors.com.

March 25
The Magic Of Life's Lemons
Bethany Perry

"When life gives you lemons..." ~ Unknown

Today is the birthday of a man I have loved for 19 years. He's Canadian and I'm American. COVID kept us apart for his 60th birthday, but it didn't keep us from celebrating.

We spent the evening on Zoom listening to music, lighting birthday candles, dancing together from afar—creating music between the notes.

I wanted to order his favorite pizza for delivery, but the restaurants were closed. The world was in an unknown we've never experienced. I realize even more has happened since you are reading this a year later. But I want to ask you: What do you do when the unexpected shows up? When things are difficult, hard or traumatic?

Sometimes we can't "pull ourselves up by our bootstraps." Our brain literally doesn't allow it. Many of us have felt so alone, angry, divided, yet the desire and need for love and touch remains.

So, how do we find gratitude when our outer world is spinning? We choose! While not always easy, we can decide. Almost magically then, a flickering light begins to appear deep inside even if ever so faint. Notice your heart; see the light within. You'll discover gratitude will grow and love will blossom.

Bethany is a transformational health and life coach. An emerging thought leader on combining the power of neuroscience and intuition, Bethany guides you to create your desired life. More about Bethany at www.MeetOurAuthors.com.

March 26
Rock Bottom to Rock Solid
Bonnie S. Hardie

"If you dream it and you believe it, then you will be able to achieve it." ~ Liz Hancock

Due to a series of unfortunate circumstances, the summer of 2016 I found myself homeless, living in a tent in the woods in Central Florida. Christmas Day 2016 and New Year's Day 2017, I woke up on a bus stop bench.

I had to use my mindset during this time to stay positive and reframe my negatives into positives. It seemed that I was swimming upstream all the time and was unable to make any progress. One negative was that I was sleeping outside every night, dealing with the weather, noise, etc. However, I turned this into a positive and said, "I'm getting fresh air, seeing the moon and stars every night, learning about astronomy."

I am a resilient and resourceful person and was able to use the resources around me to survive. I tapped into my inner resolve and knew that there was a lesson for me to learn, and I could use my experience to help others. My favorite mantra is: "Make dreams happen."

I'm pleased to say that currently I have a business with international clientele, helping others improve their mindset and grow their personal development, and I was able to spend over two weeks in England in January 2019. There's power in positivity!

Bonnie Hardie is a mindset and business coach/consultant in Florida. She shows people how to reframe negatives into positives and appreciate what they have while not dwelling on what they don't have. Find out how to connect with Bonnie at www.MeetOurAuthors.com.

March 27

Journeys of Perseverance

Larisa Lambert

"There is no way I could save myself and not save the people I love." ~ Nighisti Negasse

Tears swelled and dripped, then flowed down her cheeks and off her face. Lois rubbed her right hand up and down her left arm as she cried, showing us how her friend Nighisti, refusing to give up on Lois's life, gently coated her arms with anointing oil and prayed for her to be healed as Lois lay in her bed terrified. She had developed an allergy to the only medicine that could save her life from an invasive strep A infection.

We heard the astounding tale of Nighisti's bravery in preserving many other lives by getting them out of war-torn Eritrea, a small African country, in the late '70s in spite of impossible obstacles. We heard of Nighisti's travels across the globe that brought her to Alabama and into Lois's life.

I was hooked. I instantly wanted to tell the story of this unlikely, unknown hero and honor her bravery and perseverance as badly as Lois wanted it told.

Nighisti's perseverance in rescuing many is something Lois and I have adopted and incorporated into our 10-year journey of sharing Nighisti's incredible trek in the book, *Many Hidden Things: The Story of An Unlikely Hero*.

Lois Bankston and Larisa Lambert invite you to celebrate their friend's faithfulness and strength. Find out more about Lois and Larisa and their community at www.MeetOurAuthors.com.

March 28

Lucky
Katie De Souza

"The best luck of all is the luck you make for yourself."
~ Douglas MacArthur

I am lucky you were born.

Growing up in the Amazon is like a whole other world to what I knew in England. Having wild monkeys to play with and seeing baby sloths in the trees. Fishing on the Amazon River, not for fish but for alligators. You camped in the jungle and captured the *Atta tanajura* ants so you could fry their bottoms and eat them!

You said you brought home lots of wild animals, and especially monkeys, to be your pets until your mum found out, then you had to return them to their natural homes.

Thankfully, you found jiu-jitsu at age 12—something you loved and which kept you occupied and out of trouble.

Having to work from age 13 to help support your family, you decided to leave your Amazon home at 21 and see what other opportunities there were for you in the world.

Lucky for me, you chose England, and within weeks of arriving, we found each other.

I'm very proud of the man you have become, a loving father to our beautiful daughter and son, a caring husband and an amazing jiu-jitsu fighter and instructor —with our own business, living a life we love.

Katie De Souza is an author and entrepreneur who inspires couples to achieve their dreams and live a happy and fulfilling life together. Find out more about Katie at www.MeetOurAuthors.com.

March 29

Lockdown Silver Lining

Carol Anne Cooper

"Enjoy the little things, for one day you may look back and realize they were the big things." ~ Robert Brault

Is it possible to appreciate the impact of a pandemic? Deaths and fear running around the world, lockdown occurring in country after country. But, every cloud has a silver lining; you just need to believe and look for it.

Looking back over the last year, a world that stopped, and time stood still, I see moments that warm my heart. My writing workshops moving online, opportunities popping up for networking, speaking events—talks and interviews online—all from the comfort of my own home.

A treasured memory of my daughter and I sharing Monopoly for the first time with my grandchildren—ages 21, 15, 11 and 9. Their delight with it, playing it over and over again. So many lessons learned, plus a deeper bonding of siblings taking place.

Jigsaw puzzles, all sizes from 200 pieces to 1000, out for all to share. Skills of focus, determination, patience, collaboration, coming into play and getting them completed, including, to my amazement, a Wasgij!

Out of job loss and time off school grew two successful businesses, a jewellery one for the eldest and a cake one for the 15-year-old. Both girls learning so much from the experience. I wonder. Did Monopoly help?

Carol Anne is The Writing Facilitator, assisting women with getting their books written. She is the creator and leader of the seven-step programme, Let's Write. Learn more about Carol Anne at www.MeetOurAuthors.com.

March 30

Rebirth

Lynne Turbie Menon

"This is a wonderful day. I've never seen this one before."
~ Maya Angelou

Today and every tomorrow is a day to be thankful. I woke up in the hospital 40 years ago, angry that I'd not made an ascent to Heaven. Today, I am eternally grateful for my life. I could have been a statistic of teen suicide. Now, I shout from the rooftop that parents should speak with their children about feelings; anxiety and depression are not typical teen behavior. It could save your child's life.

My mom wanted nothing more than to see me happy. In her final days, I moved into her three-story house to care for her. One morning, I took our pup for a walk, and we came upon a guy that he decided to sniff; apparently my little sheltie-shepherd realized something special about this man. Not only was he a dog lover, he also turned out to be a loyal friend and poetry lover and, to my surprise, lived in the apartment above Mom's.

A courtship ensued, and four years later, we had a fairy-tale wedding in India. Today, I treasure every sunrise and sunset I get to share with my husband and two amazing children. I am eternally grateful for my happy-ever-after.

Lynne Menon, MFA, is a freelance writer and blogger. She is a wife and mom, editor of the California Writers Club, Tri-Valley Branch website, and is working on her memoir. Discover more about Lynne at www.MeetOurAuthors.com.

March 31

Gratitude No Matter What

Barbara Farfan

"You don't become what you want; you become what you believe."
~ Oprah Winfrey

I've been nothing but grateful for getting older ever since I delivered my sister's eulogy on what would have been her 50th birthday. After that, birthday gratitude was a logical choice. I've orchestrated life-affirming birthday adventures since then—New Zealand biking, Grand Canyon hiking, Portuguese cliff-walking and Slovenian pet-sitting. My 60th birthday tour of exotic Asian retreats promised to be my best adventure yet.

And then there was COVID.

Alone in a locked-down Mexican Airbnb efficiency, the most adventurous part of my 60th birthday was giving Google translation delivery directions and waiting for my soggy, lukewarm pizza to arrive.

While gnawing on an ever-expanding wad of dough, it occurred to me that birthday gratitude was my conscious choice for over a decade. I decided at that moment that this birth-demic day would NOT be the exception.

So, on that March 31 birth-demic day, for no good reason, under no good conditions, with no discernible justification, I chose to be grateful. Because that's the kind of person I wanted to be.

My one and only 60th birthday surprise was the gift of unconditional gratitude. And every day since, unconditional gratitude has enabled me to truly feel free. Happy birthday to me!

Barbara Farfan is an unconditionally grateful full-time international pet-sitter, the founder of thanksthoughts.com and an ebullient 60-something citizen of the world. Discover more about Barbara at www.MeetOurAuthors.com.

April

April 1

For Pure Merriment
Roberta Gold

"The first of April, some do say / Is set apart for All Fool's Day.../ ...
But on this day are people sent / On purpose for pure merriment." ~
Poor Robin's Almanack, 1790

The eggs came out perfect—over easy, yolks a bright orange. The potatoes, crispy and golden. The raspberries were small but a dazzling bright purple. I set the plates on a cheery spring tablecloth and put a vibrant succulent in the center. For extra effect, I scatter some of the shiny, colorful rocks I used with the succulent around the base of the planter.

I call the kids in for breakfast. I am not disappointed as they praise my handiwork. They take their first bites and look up at me with those perplexed eyes that quickly begin to sparkle as they break out into fits of laughter.

I did it—this was my best April Fool's breakfast to date. Being able to fool them with gummy eggs, chopped up "apple" potatoes and hard candy raspberries was brilliant. Oh, and the planter rocks were candy-coated chocolate. I wish I could have bottled up the joy that poured out of my children that day. Their excitement at dinner, telling how they shared the story of their breakfast meal surprise with school friends, had me blushing with pride. I truly love a good-hearted April Fool's Day prank.

**Roberta Gold, RTC, CHP, created Laughter for the Health of it
and Laughter Rocks! She's an inspiring speaker, author and an
attitude adjustment coach. Find out more about Roberta
and her offerings at www.MeetOurAuthors.com.**

April 2

Honoring Justice Ruth Bader Ginsburg

Lynne Turbie Menon

"My mother told me to be a lady, and for her, that meant be your own person, be independent." ~ Ruth Bader Ginsburg

As the director of the Women's Rights Project at the ACLU, Ruth Bader Ginsburg, aka Notorious RBG, passed five landmark cases in the 1970s. One of these laws, the Equal Credit Opportunities Act of 1974, allowed my newly divorced mother and many others like her to gain financial independence, affording them the right to open their own bank accounts, establish credit in their names and apply for mortgages.

Other landmark cases passed by RBG helped raise women and men up to a more equal playing field. These laws include: allowing women to be jurors, giving women admission to schools reserved for men, barring discrimination for women due to pregnancy, and entitling men to the same caregiving rights as women.

RBG's work as a staunch defender of women and minorities propelled her to the U.S. Supreme Court in 1993, where she used the Equal Protection Clause of the 14th Amendment to ensure protection for all. The 5'1" legal leader became a center of power that was larger than life, and RBG will be remembered as she wished: "as someone who did the best she could with whatever talent she had to make things a little better for people less fortunate."

Lynne Menon, MFA, is a freelance writer and blogger. She is a wife and mom, editor of the California Writers Club, Tri-Valley Branch website, and is working on her memoir. Discover more about Lynne at www.MeetOurAuthors.com.

April 3

Silent Voices

Sarah-Jane Watson

"Unless someone like you cares a whole awful lot, nothing is going to get better. It's not." ~ Dr. Seuss

Seven hundred thousand children are abused each year. In 2020, resources for a child's "grown-ups" are limited, making prevention crucial to the well-being of children globally.

In eighth grade, my best friend did what I couldn't, or didn't think I could, do. He spoke up. One day, he visited and witnessed a first-hand account of my stepmother's loss of temperament. He confronted me about what he saw. I had never told anyone. He learned I had been enduring physical and verbal abuse from my stepmother for as long as I could remember. He listened to my every word. He encouraged me to tell my mom. He even told me that if I couldn't and didn't tell her, he would. I was frightened, but he gave me the strength I needed to talk to my mom.

I don't know where I would be if it wasn't for my childhood best friend. He helped me find my voice. My gratitude will last a life-time. He saved my life. He is the reason I am a survivor.

If you see something that doesn't seem right, reach out. Say something. If a 12-year-old boy can speak up, so can you. You could save a life.

Sarah-Jane Watson: creative professional in wild and wonderful West Virginia, with more than 16 years of experience in photography, design and marketing/advertising. Find out more about Sarah-Jane at www.MeetOurAuthors.com.

April 4

Always Paws
Katie De Souza

"Cherish every moment; you don't know when it's your last."
~ Bruiser the Bulldog

You were always there for me. A little pitter-patter of paws would come to be by my side when I entered the room.

Always ready for a cuddle, especially if I was sad. Your favourite was sunbathing in the warm sun out on the grass in the garden. We would sit for hours, your head resting on my legs, and just watch the world go by.

Sometimes, we'd go to the beach for a little walk. We never went too far, as you didn't like exercise too much; chilling was more your thing, as expected from a beautiful bulldog.

My constant companion. I'm grateful for the beautiful puppies you gave me and how caring you were looking after them. Although, we could tell you were happy by the time that they had grown and found their new homes.

We were so lucky you lived to almost 10 to share so much love and happiness with us.

You taught me to always "paws" and cherish special moments spending time with loved ones. You are forever in our minds. You live on in the stories I have written about your adventures, so children can love and know you as we did.

Katie De Souza is an author and entrepreneur who inspires couples to achieve their dreams and live a happy and fulfilling life together. Learn more about Katie at www.MeetOurAuthors.com.

April 5

Why Wait to Be Free?

Julaina Kleist-Corwin

"That's the thing about pain. It demands to be felt." ~ John Green

April 5 is my Day of Freedom anniversary. I celebrate it as if it is a birthday, and it is, of sorts. When one is restricted and then released, new life begins.

I didn't think I was hurt from a fall when I went ice-skating one winter. However, in a year, pain in my hip told me otherwise. Each year it intensified and tested my tolerance. I ignored its warnings and kept working. I didn't want recovery from surgery to take me away from my commitments.

"I'll help you carry that," my assistant and friend, Eileen, would say as I struggled with the folders and items I carried to and from the classes I taught. Any extra weight added to the agony. Seven years later, I couldn't walk farther than from the front door to the car.

I finally scheduled a hip replacement for April. The evening after the surgery, the nurses had me walking arm-in-arm with them down the halls, and I felt like I could climb Mt. Everest. Renewed since then, I walk three miles every morning and have increased energy. I am grateful I'm free from hip pain, and I celebrate every April 5.

Julaina Kleist-Corwin is a teacher, author and writing coach. Find her books *Written Across the Genres*, *The Choice Matters*, and best seller, *Captivate Audiences*, on Amazon. Discover more about Julaina at www.MeetOurAuthors.com.

April 6

Exchanging Places With My Mother
Connie Ragen Green

"Everything we experience in life is preparing us for something we will be called upon to do in the future." ~ Connie Ragen Green

My parents separated when I was 3, and memories of my father faded away. I was the only child of a now single mother who was doing the best she could.

Twice we found ourselves homeless, sleeping on the floor of a laundromat or in the empty room at church. By age 11, I began earning money from babysitting, mowing lawns and other odd jobs. This was when we exchanged places, and I began caring for my mother.

Little did I know, during those turbulent years of scraping together money for the rent and struggling to have enough to eat, that I was developing skills that would enable me to care for my mother during her final years.

The relationship that had been tumultuous during my formative years transformed into one of mutual respect and unconditional love. I showered her with gifts and took her shopping for new clothes. She listened to my ideas with an open mind. We laughed together and reminisced about our past. Secrets were shared and beliefs debated.

I'm grateful for the life my mother made for me and how I was able to use those experiences to repay her for bringing me into this world.

Connie Ragen Green works with new authors and entrepreneurs and mentors them on how to create massive passive income streams with a joyous online business. Learn more about Connie at www.MeetOurAuthors.com.

April 7

Forever Grateful

Shirley E. Kennedy

"When life shouts, 'Give up,' hope whispers, 'Try it one more time.' Embrace life with deep gratitude." ~ Shirley Kennedy

Geez! Just one morning I'd like to be on time. Is that really too much to ask? Every school day, I struggle to get my daughter to the bus on time, and today is no exception. She believes time waits for her and cannot be convinced otherwise. It's so frustrating.

I have an appointment, and I'm late. Again. Then, I have a long walk to wait for a lift home. Walking is painful, so, among the multitude of emotions I feel, gratitude isn't one of them.

I grab my keys and rush out the door. As I approach the sharp corner, glare bursts through the treetops above, and dappled light blurs the vision ahead. I am blinded until a dark shape looms from the shadows. My car and a large tip truck are on a collision course. Head-on.

Then, the steering wheel jerks to the left, propelling the car out of harm's way. I am shaken and speechless, for I know I didn't turn that wheel, and I'm saved by God's divine intervention. I pull off the road, cast my eyes and hands to Heaven, and, with deep gratitude, thank God.

Always live a grateful life.

Shirley E. Kennedy writes prose and poems with heartfelt gratitude inspired by life experiences, nature, visual and literary prompts and inner thoughts. Find out how to connect with Shirley at www.MeetOurAuthors.com.

April 8

A Woman in Sobriety

Ali Stewart

"I am at a place in my life where peace is my priority.
I make deliberate life choices to protect my mental, emotional
and spiritual state." ~ Unknown

Today is the day that my life was changed forever. One decision that sent my life's path in a new direction. The day I decided my life came first, before alcohol and drugs—today is my sobriety date. My actual sobriety date is April 8, 2013. Before this day, my addictions dictated my emotions, decisions and ultimately ran my life. I could not cope with life on life's terms without them.

As I look back on the past seven years, I am full of gratitude today. Today, I am a strong, independent woman, a loving single mom, a successful small-business owner, and now, a published author. I have my Higher Power to thank for the strength to get sober, go back to school at 39 years old, open my own business, end my unhappy marriage, be a strong role model for my son, and, finally, put myself on the line to pursue becoming an author.

Could I have done this on my own? Absolutely not, and for that I am forever grateful! Recovery has given me a second chance at life. I am proud of the woman I have become when I look in the mirror.

Ali is dedicated to her sobriety/spiritual growth. She has a young son, who is her heart and soul. She is a spa owner by day, author by night. More at www.MeetOurAuthors.com.

April 9

My Heart Flows in Gratitude

Ruthie Urman

"The greatest thing we'll ever learn is just to love and be loved in return." ~Unknown

Gingerly, I step over, around and through the beyond-hoarded, cluttered mess inside Nick's front door and wonder, Why am I here, again? The obsessive collection of plastic to-go beverage cups, the six-foot-long cords, dangling like a snake's den. Paper piles knee-high.

The hole in the kitchen ceiling: the light ripped, torn apart with wires listlessly hanging like sad, wilted flowers. Nick says it's like the cobbler's children who go barefoot. His electrician fingers so beautifully sculpted and now so idle.

The grungy, filth-collecting, 30-year soiled carpeting that cries to be freed from its nails because it's seen enough, memories stuck in the stains. Cards clutter every stair. A danger zone, an accident waiting to happen. Am I in danger being there with the opening of my heart?

And when we lie down in bed, all miraculously goes away, for me; safe and snug in his cradled arms, I know how Nick feels about me. Not verbally, not in words. His sensual kisses, electric touch (an electrician's fingers?) woo me beyond the mess. And all I see is Nick, is us, is beauty beyond beautiful. The mystery clears. My heart flows in gratitude.

Popped out from my mother's womb with pen and paper, I began writing early. We heal and are empowered through our stories. I would love to be your writing anchor. More at www.MeetOurAuthors.com.

April 10

Lifetime Inspiration

Kiya Immergluck

"Be ashamed to die until you have won some victory for humanity."
~ Horace Mann

At my graduation from Horace Mann Grammar School over six decades ago, our principal shared this quote, and I'm grateful for the lifelong inspiration it has given me!

I have celebrated many victories in my life large and small: being a teacher, joining an Israeli Peace Corps, being part of the early feminist movement in the 1960s, marching for civil rights and women's rights and anti-war, getting my very shy baby nephew to smile, earning a Ph.D. and becoming a psychotherapist, whispering permission for my daddy to die during his final illness, appearing in a play, surviving cancer, loving friends unconditionally and continually striving to be the best person I can possibly be.

I'm proud of all those victories, public and private, and the mantra still booms in my head: "Be ashamed to die until you have won some victory for humanity!" Perhaps it is enough to continue to strive for that ultimate achievement, and it might inspire me to stick around as long as my beloved grandfather who lived to be 104!

Kiya Immergluck's magical name means: "Because of God, I'm always lucky!" in Hebrew and German. She is a psychotherapist, writer and artist living in Chicago. Find out how to connect with Kiya at www.MeetOurAuthors.com.

April 11
Grateful for the Seasons
Tara Alexandra Kachaturoff

"Live each season as it passes; breathe the air, drink the drink, taste the fruit and resign yourself to each." ~ Henry David Thoreau

I was born in Southern California. It wasn't until I left behind the "endless summer" lifestyle that I really experienced nature's cycle.

Now living in the Midwest, I enjoy the full palette of seasons. Like a play in four acts, I witness their beauty, enjoying the full sensory experience of temperature, weather, light and shadow. Each reflects a different aspect of myself and all that's beautiful in life.

My favorite season is summer. It's hot and occasionally humid. It's a perfect stage for outdoor meals, cool lemonade and a stack of novels guaranteed to entertain. Nights are equally enchanting with swirls of fireflies that punctuate the inky darkness.

Autumn welcomes the crunch of leaves beneath my shoes. Their vibrant hues of red, orange and yellow tickle my eyes. Shorts and T-shirts are replaced by warm coats and mittens as year-end holidays sneak up well before I'm ready. Soon thereafter, winter's frosty beauty makes its debut.

And, just when winter feels like it will never end, I see the tender sprouts pushing through the soil and tiny buds appearing on trees. Spring rains invite rainbows, and, with them, the hope for a new season and anticipation of what's to come.

Tara Alexandra Kachaturoff is a business coach and the creator, producer and host of "Michigan Entrepreneur," a weekly television talk show featuring businesses from startup to stellar. Learn more about Tara at www.MeetOurAuthors.com.

April 12
Turn Off the Flash
Sarah-Jane Watson

"A sister can be seen as someone who is both ourselves and very much not ourselves—a special kind of double." ~ Toni Morrison

My little sister, Katherine, was born on April 6, 1999. I had been not-so-patiently waiting for her arrival. My heart shattered when I didn't get to hold her right away. Instead, she was placed in an incubator. Her breathing was off. She didn't sound like a newborn baby. She made moaning sounds reminiscent to that of Casper the Friendly Ghost.

The doctor acted quickly with plans to ship her to a larger hospital. After waiting 15 years to become a sister, there was no way she was going anywhere—not until I had taken a photograph. I did what any photographer-to-be would do!

Snap! I clicked the shutter! Wince! Flinch! Her body froze momentarily, and she clenched her tiny fists. I had forgotten to switch off the flash! I will never live that down. Today, Katie likes to joke that I am responsible for her poor eyesight.

Her birthday is April 6, but April 12 is Best Sister in the World Day. That is the day we got to bring her home from the hospital. Katie and I celebrate BSITW Day on the 12 of every month. Simply because we are sisters and because we can.

Sarah-Jane Watson: creative professional in wild and wonderful West Virginia, with more than 16 years of experience in photography, design and marketing/advertising. Find out more about Sarah-Jane at www.MeetOurAuthors.com.

April 13

Choosing Love and Joy Energy
Richard LoveJoy

"We can change our lives. We can do, have and be exactly what we wish." ~ Tony Robbins

Thirty years ago, I found myself on a Philadelphia hotel rooftop, looking at a 10-foot-long strip of 1,000-degree hot coals. I glanced to my left and caught sight of this beautiful woman in the next line. My soul leaped with joy, and immediately I knew she was my soulmate. Despite Tony Robbins' transforming "UPW" four-day event, I was disappointed to not meet her!

Fortunately, I signed up for Tony's next event, "Date with Destiny," in San Diego. There, standing in the registration line, I saw her! I deliberately found a seat next to her and said, "I have been wanting to meet you. I saw you at the fire walk last month!" Trisha responded, "Wow, I'm glad you found me; let's get to know each other!"

In separate groups, we both crafted mission statements that chose the energy of love and joy as our purpose. After four days of deep inner explorations, it was like we had known each other for 20 years. We have been together every day since and added LoveJoy as our new last name.

We traveled 3,000 miles to meet when we lived 60 miles apart. I am grateful divine energy guided me to meet my soulmate!

Richard and Trisha LoveJoy are soulmates, consultants, certified professional success coaches and mentors who inspire simple solutions for clients to live in love and joy and inner freedom. Discover more about Richard and Trisha at www.MeetOurAuthors.com.

April 14

Never Met in Person

Dr. Joanna Lynn Faulk

"Make your weird light shine bright so the other wonderful and witty weirdos know how to find you." ~ Unknown

I know that there are friends who have known each other forever! Those friends are incredible and rare. However, there is not a word yet for old friends whom you have never met. This sentence best describes my new friend Jodi.

Where do I even begin? How did this happen? I have never met her in person but already find myself celebrating life, laughing constantly and building memories.

Friendship is not about who you have known the longest. It is about who comes into your life and demonstrates through actions (not only words) that they are here for you.

I am not sure who used this analogy before, but my friend Jodi is just like my favorite bra (yep, a bra). It was hard to find but super supportive and comfortable. It always lifts me up, makes me look better and is close to my heart. (My mom will hate this analogy, but Jodi will laugh. She gets my humor, even my stupid humor.)

So, to summarize, this Texan has a New Yorker for a new best friend. Who knew that, during the 2020 pandemic, I would gain such a beautiful soul as a friend? Incredibly grateful.

Dr. Joanna L. Faulk is an education consultant, motivational speaker and author of The *Wealthy Educator—Wealth Is a Mindset.* Follow your soul; it knows the way. Find out more about Dr. Faulk at www.MeetOurAuthors.com

April 15

The Beauty of You

Sabrina Jones

"O God, help me to believe the truth about myself, no matter how beautiful it is." ~ Macrina Wiederkehr

If you were asked to think of someone beautiful, would you consider yourself? Beauty is typically regarded as a feminine characteristic, but, in my opinion, it is genderless. It is the art of being, loving and accepting yourself and inspiring others to do the same.

Your reflection in the mirror is stunning. It is miraculous. No one has the exact reflection as yours. It represents you and all of your life experiences. Setbacks and heartbreaks are opposite to accomplishments and love. Yet, they're all necessary for the full appreciation of life and self. I encourage you to love your reflection. Physical beauty is wonderful. However, it does not encapsulate the word completely.

Because you know yourself most intimately, your perspective may be skewed in comparison to others. They see the outer, but you know your inner. They witness the successes, but you know your secrets. Meanwhile, disappointment one day could adversely be the excitement of winning on the next. It is the yin and yang of life. Please grant yourself grace to appreciate the entire picture. The good and the bad are creating a stunning view. Embrace all of it. Think of beauty and consider yourself.

Sabrina Jones is a women's empowerment coach. Her passion is encouraging clients to pursue their desires to flourish. Find out how to connect with Sabrina at www.MeetOurAuthors.com.

April 16

Rise Up! Reclaim Your Value!
Judi G. Reid

"Be joyful always; pray continually; give thanks in all circumstances, for this is God's will for you in Christ Jesus."
~ 1 Thessalonians 5: 16-18

On Friday, March 13, 2020, the governor ordered that, beginning Monday, the state would be under lockdown to prevent the spread of COVID-19. Only essential services would be allowed to continue operating.

I panicked! I prayed! What would that mean?

Every Monday for the last 19 years, I drive to a medical center for life-saving therapy to retard deterioration of an incurable lung disease. Would I be allowed to continue? Coronavirus was still new with innumerable unknowns.

Over the weekend, I decided to keep my Monday appointment amidst the lack of clarity. I understood, with Alpha-1 being a rare disorder and with my years of self- and professional education, I held the key to authority in the chaos.

As I expected, administrators approached me about possibly terminating my infusions. After I presented a strong, credible case, we agreed to contact experts during the next four days and reach a professional conclusion.

My procedure qualified. The first three months were disconcerting, almost depressing. I prayed continually to focus on the blessing rather than the masks and excessive regulations.

Every night, I continue to celebrate the gift of extended life and my value in God's eyes. I rejoice in the dawn of a new day.

Judi G. Reid is a No. 1 Amazon best-selling author and certified life breakthrough coach. She helps women transform their lives, move forward and flourish. Learn more about Judi at www.MeetOurAuthors.com.

April 17

Moving Freedom Forward

Jamie Massey

"Set a goal, and in small, consistent steps, work to reach it. Get support from your peers when you start flagging. Repeat. You will change." ~ Seth Godin

After 16 years, Kristie is now free from addiction. Tony is thriving in spite of past debilitating suicidal thoughts and anxiety. Melissa's life of fear and self-condemnation is behind her.

Grateful? You bet! Still working on the residue that trauma, disappointment, hurt and unwise choices leave behind? Absolutely. Each of these amazing people overcame mindsets and behaviors that destroyed relationships, robbed them of peace and joy and crippled many areas of their lives. And now, they walk in freedom! Hallelujah! Hooray!

They don't continue to move forward in their life of freedom alone. People from all walks of life, cultures and backgrounds with a wide spectrum of hurts, habits and hang-ups come together to take daily steps with each other as part of the online Freedom Forward program.

Kristie's goals are different from Tony's, and Tony's are not like Melissa's. They are each in different small groups within the program. Tony's trademark is communicating positivity and wisdom. Melissa's impact is through strong empathy and kindness. Kristie's practical voice of reason motivates her group. They, and many like them, know they are not alone in their quest for lifelong freedom, for they now have camaraderie, true friends, unconditional love and immense gratitude.

Freedom Forward offers online, faith-based accountability and encouragement for those with hurts, habits and hang-ups, including addiction. Learn more about Jamie Massey and Freedom Forward at www.MeetOurAuthors.com.

April 18

My Better Half

Dr. Robyn MacKillop

"You are not my better half, girl, you are the best of the complete me." ~ Bader

A fall day in Oregon, when the weather was just beginning to turn, the most amazing man to grace this world was born. The universe knew I was coming. I say this because there is no one else who fits me like a perfectly cut puzzle piece. He knows my reactions, keeps up with my extroverted impulsiveness (he's an introvert) and always warns me when there is a food I will not like.

Donovan entered this world differently than I did. Solid and thoughtful from his first breath, he didn't fuss and squirm or drive his mom crazy. Me, well, I drove my mom bananas. I wore a leash as a toddler because I would escape any stroller, high chair or other restraint in a flash.

Circumstances brought us together early and made sure we circled back to each other. His demeanor allows me to be who I am without apology. Our core values are aligned, so disagreements are few. He is dependable, strong and brimming with integrity. We believe in each other and together make a formidable team.

As partners in crime and life, he makes my world worth living in. He is my better half.

Dr. Robyn MacKillop, Ph.D., is an online course writer; savvy business owner; fiercely independent; a lover of cats, dogs, skulls, husband; pro-education; fun; and unstoppable. Find out more about Robyn at www.MeetOurAuthors.com.

April 19
Whispers in the Wind
Vicki Dobbs

"If the only prayer you ever say in your entire life is 'thank you,' it will be enough." ~ Eckhart Tolle

I was awakened by a cacophony of birds blaring in through my open window. I was grateful for the cool morning and the soft breeze blowing through. I wasn't ready to wake up. I closed the window and lay back down. But sleep would not come.

The birds got louder. Getting up, I slipped on my sandals and wandered out in my jammies to investigate. I encountered only silence.

Looking up, I walked under the four ash trees shading our house but found no birds. Turning back, I stumbled, drawing my attention down to the ground. There, just a few feet away, lay two feathers. One a crow, the other a blue jay. Bending, I picked them up, spotting two more by the next tree. They, too, were crow and jay feathers. Intrigued, I searched between the last two trees and found two more. Four trees, three identical pairs.

Making a feather bouquet, I pulled a hair from my head and gifted it to the trees, speaking aloud my gratitude. Having just begun my spiritual journey, I welcomed these feathers as a gift from Spirit acknowledging the call to attention, for listening that morning and not going back "to sleep."

Vicki Dobbs is an author, teacher, mentor and spiritual coach. Gathering in small, intimate circles, she helps you connect your heart's desire with your soul's fire. Discover more at www.MeetOurAuthors.com.

April 20

Focus on Friends
Ruth Strebe

"There is no fragrance in April breezes till breathed with joy as they wander by." ~ William Cullen Bryant

I read an article in the Post that started: "T.S. Eliot wrote, 'April is the cruelest month,' and April 20 stands out if you want to zero in on a specific date besieged with bad news." I had been joking about the 4/20 curse for years, but the article solidified the darkness surrounding my special day in an uncomfortable way.

I resolved to build a better relationship with April 20. Like Bryant said, to capture the fragrance of April, we just need to notice it.

One year, I got roller skates. Zoom!

In high school, I found a hamburger cake and bouquet on my desk. Later, friends lured me away for the surprise of lugging a piano from our garage and up two flights of stairs just so I could practice in warmth.

I picture my colleagues wrapped in car blankets, braving wind and sleet for "Ruth's Birthday Picnic Surprise."

Recently, I was serenaded by famous Facebook singers. "You've Got a Friend."

One April 20, we met a Swedish couple standing in line for a cruise. This meeting became years of worldwide travel together, language learning, heartbreaks, laughter and lifelong friends.

Friends make your day, and this day is truly wonderful!

Ruth Strebe is just an interesting gal—choosing, for the time, to observe what life has to offer and focus on personal development. Find out how to connect with Ruth at www.MeetOurAuthors.com.

April 21
Seeds for Your Harvest
Larisa Lambert

"No soul that seriously and constantly desires joy will ever miss it. Those who seek, find. To those who knock, it is opened."
~ C.S. Lewis

Kathy's heart was clearly broken and her sorrow deep. She laid out the shattered pieces before us as she shared the horror of the day her son was killed. It was excruciating to experience this glimpse of her grief.

I didn't know Kathy until she sat beside me in our women's study group. She made me laugh while her sweetness and encouragement made it easy for us to become friends. Her vulnerable transparency gave us all courage to trust each other and share our fears, disappointments and questions about our lives, relationships and faith.

One night, Kathy began to share how, in the midst of her grief, it seemed every song, every sermon, every verse, strangers, random daily happenings and people she loved seemed to be bringing up the topic of joy. It felt like a joy conspiracy! But how could she experience joy in the midst of the chaos and questions in her mind and the numbing agony in her heart?

Miraculously, joy has become the byword of Kathy's life, although the circumstances of hurt, anger and disappointment did not change. She has begun to harvest joy from the simple seeds God planted in the midst of her sorrow.

Kathy's experience inspired *Joy Harvest for Women: A 90-Day Devotional Prayer Guide & Journal to Reap the Benefits of Joy in Your Life*. Find out more about Larisa and about Kathy's experience at www.MeetOurAuthors.com.

April 22

Circle Back to Good
Cris Rominger

"Some people talk to animals. Not many listen though. That's the problem." ~ A.A. Milne

(Words of wisdom told from the perspective of "Hanky the Horse")

Life is like a circle. As you go along, there are pockets of wonderful, happy times, parts that get a little wobbly and times when it's challenging and difficult. But if you stay in the circle and keep going around, things naturally get better and come back to good. Sometimes real good people get kind of square heads and stop going around in the circle. They get stuck in the corners.

But if you can stay in the circle, things always smooth out. If you find yourself stuck somewhere, instead of letting the challenges take over or fighting the bad things, try to offset it with something happy. Think of something that's good — something to be grateful for. When you're grateful, you take your mind off the sad parts, and it lets the happiness in. Laughter helps too.

Gratitude, happiness and laughter are always healing. So, next time it gets a little wobbly, remember to go back in your happy circle. Life doesn't go in a straight line. It goes in a circle. And it always comes back to love.

P.S. Remember to be patient. The best things take time.

Love, Hanky

Hanky (a one-of-a-kind horse who always looks on the bright side) and Cris write for BellaRoseandFriends.com, a collection of original children's stories and messages focusing on love, happiness, kindness and bravery. Find out more about Hanky at www.MeetOurAuthors.com.

April 23

Embrace Fear from Within

Melissa Rowe

"Fear is the cheapest room in the house. I'd like to see you in better living conditions." ~ Oprah Winfrey

I was in my 60s when I was shaken by a number of awakenings, which revealed to me that I must first love and take care of myself before helping and giving to others. First, I had come to understand fear as a natural and continuous process of growth and change.

Second, I had done the work and faced the fact that the only way to get rid of my fear of doing something was to just do it.

Third, I realized that the only way to feel better and stronger about myself and my capabilities was to "feel the fear and do it anyway."

Fourth, pushing through fear is less frightening than living with the underlying feeling of helplessness.

Fifth, I recognized that the problem is not fear itself but rather how I identified and handled it. In the past, I allowed fear to dictate most of my life decisions.

This awakening carried a different type of fear, a consciousness of my deeper sense of knowing.

Melissa Rowe is a life coach who supports women in supporting themselves and recognizing their strength, power and greatness from within. Find out how to connect with Melissa at www.MeetOurAuthors.com.

April 24

The Moment

Leah Grant

"There is love in holding, and there is love in letting go."
~ Elizabeth Berg

I had never been present when someone died. Being there when my father took his last breath proved to be more moving than any other spiritual phenomenon I'd previously witnessed.

It happened on day four of him being home from the hospital. My mom and I, who were taking care of him in their living room turned into a makeshift bedroom, knew he didn't have long.

His kidneys had stopped functioning six days earlier, and he'd lost the ability to communicate two days ago. His breathing was labored, and, when awake, his eyes stared sadly, seeming to beg to put him out of his misery. We did our best to comfort him and keep him medicated for the pain.

The moment he passed away, I was beside him. I sensed he was about to go despite no visible changes. Frozen, I watched as his chest fell for the last time. His spirit left his body and slipped into an invisible hole. From it emanated the most peaceful, blissful waves of energy. I felt pulled toward the pure love feeling of it, but it was only open for the briefest moment.

I'm grateful to know he is in a beautiful place.

ICF Master Certified Coach Leah Grant is a best-selling author and teacher. Weaving the practical with the esoteric, she assists her clients to live as their full, multidimensional selves. Learn more about Leah at www.MeetOurAuthors.com.

April 25
The Gift of Serving Others
Kim Zilliox

"You can have everything in life you want if you will just help other people get what they want." ~ Zig Ziglar

Early in my career, I worked in sales. At that point in my life, I was very focused on winning. My want in life was to have the most money and "things." I was very successful and had everything I wanted.

Or, so I thought. The problem was I didn't. I didn't have fulfilling long-term friendships, a partner to share life with or any sense of meaning from my work. I was winning in terms of what I thought I wanted but was losing at having a truly rich and abundant life.

Fortunately, I had a wake-up call 22 years ago. I hired a coach to help me review my values and create a mission statement. In an instant, I found my true calling in life. I realized my real want is actually to help others get what they want. As I leaned into the gift of serving, supporting and contributing to others, I felt complete abundance and joy. To see people succeed and shine is the greatest gift and want that I could ever have. I am eternally grateful to that coach and for discovering my mission, which is "to inspire, lead and contribute to others leading great lives."

Kim Zilliox, M.A., MBA, is an executive coach with over 20 years of experience helping others to enhance their leadership skills, increase results authentically and reach extreme joy and satisfaction. Find out how to connect with Kim at www.MeetOurAuthors.com.

April 26

Marie, I Love You

Bettina "Sparkles" Obernuefemann

"Love your neighbor as yourself." ~ Matthew 22:35-40

I was a nervous wreck when I was introduced to my future family. But "Mother Marie" immediately turned toward me with open arms and gave me a friendly hug that lowered my anxiety level from ten to one.

Over the years, sweet, spiritual Marie's affection for me always made me feel welcome. I appreciated being part of many family gatherings, highlighted with delicious dinners and hours of recalling funny family escapades.

I was sad for Ma when I found out she was orphaned at the age of 3 and grew up like the mistreated Cinderella. On top of that, born on December 25, her birthdays were seldom celebrated.

A short time before Ma went to heaven 12 years ago, she surprised me by looking into my eyes saying, "You don't believe I love you." I said, "Of course, I do."

These words kept ringing in my mind. Soon it came to me that she was referring to the truth that we must know who we are and love our inner selves before we can genuinely love others.

I keep feeling Ma's spirit around me and often burst out singing joyously, "Marie, Happy Birthday to you. I love you."

Bettina "Sparkles" discovered her self-worth and self-realization while healing PTSD. It is her passion to share and to inspire others with her three self-published books. Find out more at www.MeetOurAuthors.com.

April 27

After the Bitter, the Sweet

Dr. Brenda L. Nielsen

"You're imperfect, and you're wired for struggle, but you are worthy of love and belonging." ~ Brene Brown

There he was, a bundle of joy in my daughter's arms, so tiny, so new. I could hear those oh-so-charming clicks and clucks of the newborn, my first grandchild. He was all pink and puckered in his face and had a shot of bright red hair. When I held him in my arms and cooed, he opened his eyes, dark and deep, and looked up at me. Angels passed through the room.

My grandson will be celebrating his second birthday soon. Each week changes him as he grows from an infant into a little boy. When he sees me, he smiles, says, "Gam'ma," and gives me a hug.

Almost five years ago, I went through a rough cancer treatment, lying in the hospital in intensive care. I danced with the angels then, hovering in and out of life for five days. Finally, I was given the choice to stay with them or to come back, knowing that the surgical damage was permanent. I chose to hope.

When I see my grandson's smile, look into his eyes and hear his voice, I am thankful that Grace gave me the choice, and that I chose to live!

Lady Brenda (Brenna) Nielsen, Ph.D., is a radiographer, clairvoyant, naturopath, master aromatherapist and 25th generation shaman. She helps people find joy in life, especially after a large trauma. More at www.MeetOurAuthors.com.

April 28

Blessing M'Lady's Nobility

Warren L. Henderson Jr.

"If one needs something substantial, something infinite, something that makes one feel aware of God, one need not go beyond a grandchild to find it." ~ Eidelon Cipherest

Gratitude is feeling blessed and honored to be Scarlett's "Ampapa." I have an opportunity to aim at setting a Christian example before her each day. Ah! M'Lady! My joy. She blesses my life in every way. She smiles at me ever so sweetly. Like her mother before her, she is the light of my life. I love her dearly. Feeling her arms around my neck whenever we draw each other near is like heaven.

We have our own parting, or bedtime, prayer: "Good night and God bless you. Sleep tight. See you in the morning. I love you." As with most little girls, Scarlett is enamored with the royalty of fairy tales. Feeding that fantasy, I refer to her as M'Lady. That's my shot at the chivalrous "my lady."

Recently, during one of our weekly video calls, she asked why I call her M'Lady. When I said, "Because you are my princess, and I am your prince," she said, "No, Ampapa. Daddy is my prince, and I am his princess." My eyes filled with tears, and my heart swelled with joy that my three-year-old granddaughter understands the notion and that she experiences that relationship with her father.

Warren L. Henderson Jr. is a college professor and the author of *Make-It-New Journal: Transform Your Outlook; Rekindle Your Life.* More at www.MeetOurAuthors.com.

April 29

Mom, I Chose You

Danielle F. Romer

"I'll love you forever. I'll like you for always. As long as I'm living, my baby you'll be." ~ Robert Munsch

The doctor said, "We all are wearing gloves. This clearly shows that you are the first person in the world to touch your son," placing Ari on my chest. He said it with a smile while both of us, baby and mommy, experienced the touch of our bare skin. I was beaming. I did not want to let him go to the nurse for his first outfit. I was screaming in my head, "I am so grateful, so thankful and so blessed." I wanted to feed him right now.

That was the most exciting and rewarding time of my life.

Fast forward 30 years after this moment. I am living in Florida, and Ari has been in Seattle, Washington, for almost five years. That day, when he called, I could easily notice the anxiety in his voice. "Mom, are you okay? Is everything all right?"

I reassured him, "I am fine."

"Are you sure?"

(I just had a terrible fall at work.) Before I tell him about anything, he would already sense it when something happened to me, and vice versa. High mother-son connection.

Yes, from the day he was born, this grew stronger. No mother could have more gratitude in her heart than me for the love, the relationship, the caring we shared over the years. Nowadays, he jokes, he can eat his food on top of my head while holding me on his chest.

Danielle Romer, founder/CEO of DaRo Life Coach, serving survivors of abuse in regaining peace of mind and emotional wellness. Find out more about Danielle at www.MeetOurAuthors.com.

April 30

The Anchor for My Soul

Gwyn Goodrow

"Your love keeps me afloat but will remain the anchor in my soul."
~ Rabindranath Tagore

When I accepted the marriage proposal, I knew my fiancé had extraordinary friendships from his U.S. Navy career. These deep, life-long bonds became apparent on my wedding day—the day I met the United States Navy.

Our wedding ceremony venue was a historic bed-and-breakfast inn in Grapevine, Texas. We exchanged vows in a spectacular garden overflowing with flowers, family and friends. As the event concluded, my husband and I departed in a horse-drawn carriage for a quiet conversation. We soon returned to the inn, and the horses retired for the evening.

Surprise! John's military friends and their spouses were waiting. These patient friends had traveled long distances—from the east coast and west coast—to be reunited after more than 20 years. They reminisced for hours with laughter as they told and embellished their shipmate tales. The stories conveyed how their friendships expanded as they endured hardships and thrived in diverse circumstances. Their laughter raised my frame of reference about the caring, generous, honorable and trustworthy man that I had married.

Life shifted on my wedding day, but I rely on my ever-present anchor to keep my love afloat and soul secure through our years together.

Gwyn Goodrow is co-founder of www.CabinsOrCastles.com, where she blogs about hospitality destinations and the personal transformation benefits of journaling. Learn more about Gwyn at www.MeetOurAuthors.com.

May

May 1
Mayday—Dancing or Sinking?
Ginny Lang

"The earth laughs in flowers." ~ Ralph Waldo Emerson

I love May. The month was marked for this New England girl by the local pool opening the last weekend in May, right after my birthday, by lobsters appearing in tanks at seaside markets, iced tea tinkling on the dinner table and pink cherry blossoms everywhere. My Irish grandmother helped me make a May basket full of flowers to hang on the front door for my mother—ring the bell and run away!

May Day traditions flourished in Britain for more than 700 years, crowning the May Queen, celebrating the antics of Morris dancers and bringing in the May to encourage everything to grow. Then, within photographic memory, the maypole became a more genteel pageant for young ladies and children.

For my Dad, a WWII vet, Mayday meant something entirely different. The National Maritime Museum in Cornwall tells us that the Mayday distress signal originated in 1923 from the French "m'aidez," or "come help me." For Dad, "Mayday!" prompted immediate action to save lives.

Here's hoping that your May Day associations are like mine, blooming flowers and dancing in the spring sunshine, grateful that the storms are far away.

Ginny Lang is a veteran management consultant, coach, trainer and facilitator to nonprofit organizations as well as an accomplished speaker and teacher. Find out more about Ginny at www.MeetOurAuthors.com.

May 2

I'm Grateful for the Struggle

Cassandra Martin-Himmons

"A lot of what is most beautiful about the world arises from struggle."
~ Malcolm Gladwell

What am I grateful for? I'm grateful for struggle. Why? Because, without struggle, there cannot be true gratitude.

Over the past several years, I've experienced struggles such as lay-offs, caregiving for aging relatives and an autoimmune disorder diagnosis. And although these experiences haven't been fun, they've helped me become the person that I am today.

Today, I am a woman who successfully made a career transition becoming a stress management coach, facilitator and instructional designer. I am a woman whose life was enriched by an even deeper relationship with my loved ones. I am a woman who is taking control of her health and gaining a better appreciation for the strength of her body and all that it can do. For all of this, I am grateful.

"It's always darkest before the dawn." For me, those words ring true. Be grateful for the struggle, for those moments when you feel like you can't go on. Dig deep, find your grit, and once you make it out of the valley, you, too, may be grateful for the struggle that led you to become the person you've always wanted to be.

Cassandra Martin-Himmons is a facilitator, stress management coach and author of Yes, I'm Grateful, a journal to increase gratitude. Find out how to connect with Cassandra at www.MeetOurAuthors.com.

May 3
Reflecting in Gratitude
Josiah Poe

"In the darkest times, hope is something you give yourself." ~ Iroh

Let me, first of all, say congratulations to my father, Reverend Dr. Apelu Poe, pastor of Bethel-Woodlawn United Methodist Church in Clarksville-Woodlawn, Tennessee, on his 65th birthday today, May 3. I personally feel that during challenging times, much like this period of the global coronavirus pandemic, reflecting on our blessings can be a great comfort.

In regard to my relationship with my father, I am grateful for so many aspects, from the life lessons he taught me growing up to his spiritual guidance as a man of faith. As a missionary, my father's work would often require our family to constantly relocate, sometimes to areas around the world stricken with poverty.

Having to live in such environments granted me a new perspective on life, and I am now grateful for things many people take for granted. I would not be the person I am today without his presence in my life, and for that, I will always be grateful, and I will hold fast to that no matter what the future may bring. I would encourage others to take time to reflect on the good in their lives and celebrate the things that bring us gratitude.

Josiah: 31-year-old from Samoa, currently residing in Murfreesboro, Tennessee, with his wife, Alyssa, and 2-year-old son, Micah. He works for an organization that cares for dialysis patients. Find out more about Josiah at www.MeetOurAuthors.com.

May 4

Grown-Up Kids
Dale Troy

"A mother's job is to teach her children not to need her anymore.
The hardest part of that job is accepting success." ~ Anonymous

"They grow up so fast; enjoy it." I remember those words clearly. My mom liked to remind me to cherish every moment with my three daughters as I was raising them.

Now that all three are grown and flown, I often wish I could relive those early years. The best I can do is study the piles of photographs and dozens of photo albums now hidden in a hall closet. All the vacations, birthdays and adventures are captured in those pictures. I know I can't go back; images are the next best thing.

The last time my three daughters spent the weekend at our house, my heart was filled with joy. Seeing them cook together, laugh together and play together brought me back to those childhood days. I'm comforted knowing they have a sisterly bond that can't be broken. They will always be there for each other.

My mom often says, "The best thing I did in my life was raise three great kids." I learned from the best, and on this day, her birthday, I appreciate my mom for showing me the way.

Dale Troy, college success coach, teaches students the skills and habits needed to thrive in college. Dale and her three daughters graduated from Yale. More at www.MeetOurAuthors.com.

May 5
Unconditional
Ron Forte

"Blessed is the influence of one true, loving human soul on another."
~ George Eliot

I woke up very anxious. As if it wasn't enough to suffer from agoraphobia, I now had to go across town during early morning traffic with my girlfriend. Getting out of this was impossible. She noticed how stressed I was (although I was desperately trying to hide it) and offered to drive.

When we arrived, she casually changed into something more comfortable, and I was amazed at how calm she was. My anxiety began to dissipate as we spoke and became focused on what was happening and how our lives would never be the same again.

A few hours later, we were joined by professionals who would help make this experience seem less scary for both of us.

The moment had come. Everything I had accomplished in my life until then had suddenly become futile. The selfishness of my personal goals for the future disappeared and were replaced by indescribable pride and unconditional love.

As I watched my son being born that day, I realized what true gratitude really was. Watching him grow up and seeing his personality and independence develop continues to be a great source of pride, love and gratitude for our family unit.

Ron Forte is a positive psychology life coach who uses empathy, humor and specific, scientifically based interventions to assist his clients through their journey of positive change and well-being. Find out how to connect with Ron at www.MeetOurAuthors.com.

May 6

An Attitude of Gratitude

Tola Gbadebo

"The unthankful heart discovers no mercies; but the thankful heart...
as the magnet finds the iron, will find, in every hour, some heavenly
blessings!" ~ Henry Ward Beecher

The complications of the modern world can make one forget the amazing little things in life to be grateful for. Gratitude helps people refocus on what they have, not what they lack.

2020 was a tough year, and it was difficult to be grateful amid a pandemic, a global cry for justice and fear of recession. I experienced symptoms of the coronavirus and triumphed. Once I recovered from the symptoms, I was immediately on to the next challenge: an 80% salary reduction. Somehow I maintained a gratitude attitude and commenced on a 14-day gratitude challenge. In the middle of this gratitude challenge, I had an almost fatal freak accident.

Post-accident, maintaining gratitude was an attitude that required discipline. It was in those moments I appreciated the saying, "Is your glass half empty or full?" Yes, I was in excruciating pain but not dead or maimed. I was extremely grateful for a roof over my head, food on my table, clothes on my back, family, friends and a glorious future. There is always something to be grateful for. Cultivate the habit. Count your blessings daily.

Tola Gbadebo is a success coach who inspires people to achieve optimal success aligned with their purpose by nourishing their body, empowering their minds and nurturing their spirit. Discover more at www.MeetOurAuthors.com.

May 7

I Married My Best Friend

Steve Sponseller

"Our wedding was many years ago. The celebration continues to this day." ~ Gene Perret

May 7 is an important day for me. It's the day I married my best friend. My wife, Beth, and I met in college on a blind date. Three years later, we got married on May 7 and have been sharing life's adventures for 32 years.

I'm so grateful that our paths crossed in college. We are proof that blind dates really can work out. Since we met, we have traveled throughout the United States and other countries. Our travels included backpacking on remote islands, cruises to tropical places and spending lots of time at Sea Ranch, California. I'm happy that we have shared those trips together.

Our family has changed over the years. We adopted twin girls from China when they were 13 months old, and we have enjoyed the companionship of several cats and dogs. Through these changes, we have remained best friends.

Each year brings new adventures and a chance to experience new things. A 45-pound backpack is not quite as comfortable these days, but we still love exploring the world's natural beauty.

We all need friends in our lives, and I can't think of anything better than marrying my best friend. I love you, Beth!

Steve Sponseller is an intellectual property attorney who helps entrepreneurs and business leaders identify and protect their innovative ideas. More at www.MeetOurAuthors.com.

May 8
Grateful for Personal Development
Neal Abramson

"No one is born in any less glory or goodness than you or I."
~ Desmond Tutu

I'm grateful that we can all change and improve our lives.

When I was 16 years old, I went to prison because I broke the law. But it wasn't just that I broke the law. It was that I was an angry kid who decided my outlaw friends were better role models than my parents.

I learned from going to prison that the Department of Corrections could take everything away from me but one thing—my knowledge.

So even though I had been a high school dropout, I decided I was done with being stupid. I read every book I could get my hands on in the prison library. I also took the GED while incarcerated and got the highest score of anyone who had ever taken it in the institution I was in.

Today I have three degrees, published a book titled *You Can Choose Your Life: A Guide to Experiencing More Peace, Freedom, and Happiness Right Now* and started a business around my heartfelt belief that we can all turn our lives around. We just have to be committed to our personal growth and willing to create a future that is different from our past.

N.G. (Neal) Abramson is a best-selling author, life-coach and owner of *You Can Choose Your Life* books & empowerment programs. Find out more at www.MeetOurAuthors.com.

May 9

I Am Known by God

Michelle Winfield Fuqua

"Let gratitude be the pillow upon which you kneel to say your nightly prayer. And let faith be the bridge you build." ~ Maya Angelou

I have lived on the edge of dark despair that calls me into the abyss. The call was unsuccessful because I am known by God. I am not an accident, and I have a specific purpose for living in this season. When depression, despair and doubt attempt to derail me, I hear my name whispered on the air. God knows my name; He knows everything about me. Therefore, I can rest in who I am and what I am called to do.

Each of us must come to terms with our own identity. We must learn to love ourselves, knowing that we are already loved unconditionally. Spirit calls our name, calls from a deep place. The call gives us fuel to release our fear of failure, our sense of lack, and our self-doubt. Therefore, we are able to rise on our knees.

I am grateful for the rise. I am grateful for the faith that pushes me to soar, that elevates me to the height of purpose. The faith that gives me a clear assignment, path, and destiny. My life is not in vain because I am known by God and called to His purpose.

Michelle Fuqua is a pastor, author, and life coach who helps women to walk out their God-given destiny and become their best, divine self. Connect with her at www.MeetOurAuthors.com.

May 10

What Does May Bring?

Marguerite Senecal

"I thought that spring must last forevermore; for I was young and loved, and it was May." ~ Vera Brittain

Autumn was long, gentle and lingering; no violent storms stripped flaming colours from trees and rudely turned leaves to mush. Willingly I obeyed the urgent call; make time, make time! Walk in the woods. Inhale crisp air. Stand in awe at maples ablaze in reds. I never want summer to end. Fall was a consolation prize.

On winter's edge, the days darken at 4:30. Too early. I push against the loss of light. But I know I must look for subtler joys. Birds swoop by in massive squadrons, move as one, prepare to escape south. I stop. I watch. Something in me soars with them.

First snow steals in overnight. Dull gray streets and rooftops turn to bleached sheets by morning.

Winter demands respect. Cold can freeze us; ice can break our bones. We must get along with it. Its kinder side brings a pensive quiet, a restfulness, the warmth of a fireplace.

In the long darkness, a promise.

In time will come first signs; melting, earthy soil smells, first chirps, fragile sprout of buds.

Winter teaches me to be with what is, to notice, to hope, to be grateful.

May brings blooming, the coming of the light once more.

Marguerite Senecal is an executive coach in communication and leadership and an award-winning video producer, passionate about history. Connect with her at www.MeetOurAuthors.com.

May 11

Scatter Extra Love and Joy

Trisha LoveJoy

"There is no beautifier of complexion, or form, or behavior, like the wish to scatter joy and not pain around us." ~ Ralph Waldo Emerson

The month of May represents spring, exalts the moon and supports the joy of life! If you are passionate about living, May is a difficult time of year for anyone to leave behind.

May brings an explosive energy of vitality and is the perfect time to scatter love and joy. Positive energy abounds as new projects begin, and old projects are dusted off to be renewed. There is a well-known saying that April showers bring May flowers. Being my birthday month, May is my favorite month of the year!

I was born under the astrological sign of Taurus, and being born under this sign indicates a life designed to inspire and empower others. I am blessed that the sign of Taurus is the anchor of the Universe, belonging to the element of Earth. I am honored to be born to display strengths of reliability, practicality, responsibility and stability with patience and devotion. I am also blessed to be born with the ruler being Venus, planet of love, attraction, beauty, satisfaction, creativity and gratitude.

Let us feel the love ruled by Venus and express the joy in Spirit. This is my celebration day to scatter lots of extra love and joy!

Trisha LoveJoy is a consultant and certified professional coach and speaker who inspires and empowers others to live their dreams in love and joy. Find out how to connect with Trisha at www.MeetOurAuthors.com.

May 12

Gratitude's Healing Power

Mary Choo

"Gratitude opens the door to the power, the wisdom, and the creativity of the Universe." ~ Deepak Chopra

What I love is the way gratitude gives me the feeling that someone cares and I'm not alone. As it opens my heart, I feel my body chemistry changing, and I start to feel more encouraged and happier inside. It gives me an inner strength to tackle whatever setback I have experienced and helps me to work out a plan B to keep me moving forward.

Gratitude for me is associated with feelings of care and kindness. It can feel like a gentle reminder to check in with myself, come back to my center and remember I don't have to do everything on my own. Maybe it's time to give myself the same care and kindness that I have received from others. Create some "me time" and practice mindfulness to calm my overwhelm and anxiety. Then I can use this space to notice the synchronicities in my life and recognize that they are silent offers of help from the Universe.

Messages that show me the Universe is always there waiting patiently to co-create with me. I just need to remember to ask, and it will bring me the help I need, often in ways I could not have imagined possible.

Mary Choo is an occupational therapist, kinesiologist, mindfulness practitioner and published Amazon author of *Reclaiming Ourselves,* **a self-help guide about energy healing therapies. Contact her at www.MeetOurAuthors.com.**

May 13
This Is My Life...And His
Dr. Robyn MacKillop, Ph.D.

"The best way to navigate through life is to give up all of our controls." ~ Gerald Jampolsky

I wake up in the morning ready to jump out of bed and meet the day. I swing my legs over the edge and realize quickly things aren't as I expect. My legs won't swing. My body won't sit up. I can barely move. This is my morning every day now. This is my life. This is multiple sclerosis.

I struggle to find gratitude in a life weighed down by anchors I can't control, so I try to focus on the floats. My biggest life preserver is my husband, Don, who has stood beside me through our new normal. When I struggle to get out of bed, he immediately awakens to help me. When I can no longer type, he'll take the keyboard while I dictate. He's had to take on most of my responsibilities around the house while navigating his roles as husband and caregiver.

I gave him the chance to cut the line, but he said the captain stays with the ship. He doesn't mind being the lifeboat in a stormy sea, paddling whatever direction will lead to calmer waters. He is the beacon that leads me ashore to safety. He is everything and I am eternally grateful.

Dr. Robyn MacKillop is an online course writer and savvy business owner. She is technologically advanced, fiercely independent, a lover of cats-dogs-skulls-husband, pro-education, fun and unstoppable. Find out more at www.MeetOurAuthors.com.

May 14

I Am Enough
Gabriela Awad

"I exist as I am; that is enough." ~ Walt Whitman

A challenging and intense year, COVID-19 and general lockdown in most of the world, everything seemed to stop. Suddenly it was all too much. I couldn't breathe. Darkness seemed to overtake it all.

And then, unexpectedly, a little light switched on inside. A little voice saying, "I want to live. Even if no one else cares, I care. And that is enough."

And then miracles started happening.

I found a renewed sense of freedom and hope from within, an unwavering love and support, no matter the times. I started smiling at the sun, the birds singing, the leaves moving in the wind. Appreciating every second I could spend with loved ones, in person or online. It all went from the worst year to the best year yet, in the blink of an eye.

I felt connected to everything and to everyone. The rivers cleared; the skies became bluer. People started being more mindful; solidarity and appreciation sprung everywhere. We all took a collective breath, realized what is truly important, went back to basics.

A year of awakenings, deep transformations, rebirth, reconnection with what is essential in life. Reconnection to self.

A miracle year. I'm SO grateful to have lived it!

Gabriela Awad is the creator of Upliftment University. She's a transformational coach and an intuitive healer. Discover more about Gabriela at www.MeetOurAuthors.com.

May 15

My Gratitude Prayer

Peggy Lee Hanson

"The grateful mind is constantly fixed upon the best. Therefore, it tends to become the best. It takes the form or character of the best, and will receive the best." ~ Wallace D. Wattles

Dear God, Angels, Saints, Universe, and anyone else up there who runs this crazy world down here from up there: Thank you, thank you, thank you for all the blessings and events you've given me during this life of 61 years, 3 months and 2.5 days as I pen this piece.

I thank thee all for the times, as an adult, when life presented the challenges of financial strife, disappointment in knowing firsthand of miscarriage, not understanding the early death of my dad, and many more instances of heartbreak.

For in not having the privilege of knowing the pains of loss, I would not know the joy of abundance, the happiness of the memories before suffering the taking away of what I held so near and dear to my heart.

Thank you, thank you, thank you for allowing me to connect with women and men from across the globe—who share their stories and prayers of gratitude with the world those which heal hearts, calm the soul, and inspire the mind. Through my work they have permission to be who they truly are to reach those they were sent to heal, calm, and inspire.

Peggy Lee Hanson is creating the most significant worldwide online resource for aspiring writers to share their wisdom, expertise, and strategies in book form. Find out more at www.MeetOurAuthors.com.

May 16
Driven with Gratitude
Phillip D. Woolfolk

"I would maintain that thanks are the highest form of thought, and that gratitude is happiness doubled by wonder." ~ G.K. Chesteron

Looking in the rearview mirror of my life, I hear stories of me, as a child, guzzling gasoline from a Coca-Cola bottle left by a neighbor working on his car. Had I not survived, there could be no forward reflections.

Then I was part of a 10-car pileup on the parkway in 1988. The employees of the auto shop where my car was towed were astounded when I stopped by to pick up items from the car. From the looks of the mangled car, they assumed the driver didn't make it and if so, shouldn't be walking around unscathed. Pockets filled with glass was the only evidence I was even in the car.

Then in 2012, while coming home in an ice storm, part of a tree fell on the roof of my car, with one branch protruding into the driver side windshield near the steering column. The rear window imploded. As I slowed down I could hear an eerie sound. It was the tree seconds before falling and just as I hit the gas, in what seemed like slow motion, I could see the remainder of the tree, just missing the car by inches.

Even with the loss of my mother, father-in-law, aunts, an uncle, sister-in-law, cousins, extended family and very good friends, I remain monumentally grateful for this journey called life.

Phillip D. Woolfolk is a profitability advisor, working in a variety of industry sectors, providing expense reduction, focused class action settlements, and tax incentive services to improve profitability. Find out more about him at www.MeetOurAuthors.com.

May 17
My Attitude of Universal Gratitude
Chineme Noke

"Stand up straight and realize who you are, that you tower over your circumstances." ~ Maya Angelou.

I express Universal gratitude for the strength and fortitude to overcome many barriers and obstacles throughout my life. Thereby, I have fulfilled goals that I determinedly pursued while advancing what I now believe to be my life's purpose.

I once assumed that my reason for being began with my beautiful daughter, who was born with a congenital, chromosomal condition called Williams Syndrome. However, I was already a highly qualified corporate lawyer leading large, professional teams. Looking back, surely this must have been part of my life's purpose, because, as a Black woman working in the male-dominated, corporate legal world for over 20 years, I learned to deal effectively with the challenges, barriers, obstacles and opportunities with which my rapid progression was presented.

My experiences prepared me for the essential role as advocate for my daughter's many needs—medical, educational, social, adulthood, while also successfully challenging the unjust and unlawful. I spent many late nights preparing court cases; through it all, I have set important legal precedents that now help many others with similar perceived barriers and obstacles.

Despite post-traumatic, chronic health conditions, I continue to help people overcome their life challenges, and for that, I remain eternally grateful.

Chineme helps people with obstacle/challenge obliteration with ease by following the action plan in her success guide, *There Is No Time Like the Present to Create Your Future*. Find out more about Chineme at www.MeetOurAuthors.com.

May 18
Mindful Gratitude
Dawn Eileen

"Gratitude is twofold; it is both appreciation and that it is freely given." ~ David Steindl-Rast

I am grateful for many things. It is about acknowledgment of the things we have. The mindfulness in our daily lives that allows us to see the small things in a bigger way. The accident was avoided because you stopped to pick up the penny. The fact you woke up this morning whether you have pain or illness. The ability to walk, talk, see, live, cry, feel, touch are all taken for granted, but others do not have these things. The fact that we have shoes, clothes, a roof, or food. It may not be what we want, but we have more than something. Be grateful with grace.

Being mindful has taught me to see so much more than the bright side of life. I have been through trauma, abuse, accidents, death, near death experiences. I am humbled and learned to be grateful for all I have. Having gratitude has raised the level of happiness in life and it can yours. Start a gratitude journal for a week and see how much you find to be grateful for.

If you woke up tomorrow with only what you were grateful for today, what would you have? Be mindful of your gifts.

Dawn Eileen is an inspirational writer, artist, traveler, deep thinker and lover of life who believes in celebrating moments. Check out more about her at www.MeetOurAuthors.com.

May 19

Brutus and His Tent

Patti Bakewell

"We may have pets, but when it comes to unconventional love, they are the masters." ~ Donald L. Hicks

In a very colorful tent in my living room lives a shar-pei named Brutus.

I can't always see him, but I hear snores coming from it. Sometimes I can see his sweet face poking out or his normally curled tail unfurled and relaxed. Other times the tent will be shaking as he rearranges his sleeping bag. I've found treats he's hidden, toys he loves and, if I'm missing a shoe, it's probably in the tent. (Brutus takes my shoe so he doesn't miss a car ride. He knows I can't go without it.)

Most tents don't fit the theme of a living room. That's true at my house too. It is definitely a statement piece. I may have gone too far when I added twinkle lights inside it, but it looks so cute all lit up with Brutus peeking out the door. Brutus makes us laugh every day, whether it's the way he sits and quietly watches traffic or the way he runs through his tent when he's playing. He just makes you smile when you see that little black wrinkled face.

We are hoping he doesn't decide we need another tent—it's supposed to be a living room, not a campground!

Linda Berry is an angel whisperer and the owner, consultant, coach, and reader for the Spiritual Discovery Center. She's also an international astrologer, podcast host, and spiritual and metaphysical book author. Learn more about Linda at www.MeetOurAuthors.com.

May 20
Worthy Four-Legged Friends
Linda Berry

"Shelter dogs are the most loving, wonderful, sweet pets in the world. They understand being rescued, loved and protected."
~ Faith Hunter

There are several days during the year that celebrate dogs, but this holiday expands my heart the most. Today, National Rescue Dog Day, not only brings awareness to the 3.3 million sheltered dogs waiting for adoption but also encourages spaying and neutering. An additional benefit involves fostering dogs to assist their socialization in finding just the right homes.

Going a step further are the dog networkers who've hit the scene, evolving from social media. Rita Earl Blackwell professionally photographs rescued dogs, sending photos to appropriate animal shelters for adoption and highlighting them on her Seen = Saved Facebook page.

Sharyl Andruska, another Facebook volunteer, is delighted when adoption and foster applications flood in once she posts a dog's photograph or video on her Facebook page.

Being the fur-baby mom of two rescued dogs, I've experienced the frightened looks and yearning for affection when a dog is adopted. Then, a transformation occurs. When they know they have a human to lick and cuddle with the rest of their life, you'll see it in their eyes and their doggy smile.

You have just made a best friend of the four-legged kind. It's hard to imagine a more loving, worthy companion.

Linda Berry is the owner, consultant, trainer and reader for the Spiritual Discovery Center in Southern California. She's a spiritual and metaphysical books author, international astrologer and radio show host. More at www.MeetOurAuthors.com.

May 21
A Lifetime of Gratitude
Sharon G. Teed

"If you concentrate on finding whatever is good in every situation, you will discover that your life will suddenly be filled with gratitude, a feeling that nurtures the soul." ~ Rabbi Harold Kushner

Born May 21, 1945, to a woman who had become infatuated with a uniformed sailor in port during World War II, I was the by-product of that encounter.

Since Margaret was already married, she could not keep me. Out of the hospital at 6 days old and straight into an orphanage was my exit from her world. The orphanage was full of 400 wartime babies.

A marvellous thing happened there. A childless couple, Marjorie and Stanley, adopted me at 6 weeks old and gave me a life that was full of tender, loving care. I felt very special when I learnt, at 5, that I had been chosen.

Privilege is not always the material things one purchases. The kindness and compassion taught by one's loving parents cannot be bought. To care for all human beings was my greatest gift from them.

My gratitude has no boundaries. My mother and my dad were very special people. I wish I had told them when they were alive. Now, at 75, as a grandmother of three beautiful grandchildren, my cup of gratitude runneth over. My parents gave me the strength to walk on this path of life.

Sharon G. Teed, an inspiring writer since she was a little girl, now lives in a country-style area near Ottawa, Ontario, Canada. More at www.MeetOurAuthors.com.

May 22

Pamela
Theresa Scandale

"A friend is someone who understands your past, believes in your future and accepts you just the way you are." ~ Bernard Meltzer

This quote perfectly describes my friend. I want to call her my best friend, but she is much more than that. So, I'll call her who she is to me—Pam. For 22 years, she's been like my sister. I cannot look back on my life without seeing her in it.

I'm thankful to Pam for her strength and optimism and the unwavering loyalty she shows toward her family. She puts others' needs before her own and pushes past hardships because she is faithful to what is on the other side. She supports me wherever I am in life without any judgements or criticism. Much of what I have accomplished has been due to her constant encouragement. Her courage helps me to be brave, and her friendship helps me to be strong. I am inspired by her every day.

I know that friends like Pam are to be cherished, and I am grateful not only to have cultivated such a strong friendship but to have been blessed with it throughout most of my life. Despite tragedies and setbacks that may come, I know I have someone in my corner, and I hope she knows that I'll always have her back.

Theresa Scandale is a writer, teacher of English as a foreign language (EFL), aspiring linguist and genealogy enthusiast. She travels with her dog, Topanga, and runs a blog and YouTube channel. Discover more about Theresa at www.MeetOurAuthors.com.

May 23

Love It or Leave It
Dr. Robyn MacKillop

"I want someone to ride the river with." ~ Charles Martin

Don and I didn't have a plan for getting engaged or married. We knew we were going to, but that was the extent of it. Our engagement occurred one Thursday evening on a blustery spring day. We had been arguing, and he needed to leave for a night class. With jacket and backpack on, he started to head for the door, then turned down the hall. He rushed back, sliding on his knees, and presented me with a ring.

I said, "What's this?"

"What do you think?"

"Want me to say yes?"

"Of course."

"Okay, yes."

He kissed me quickly and ran out the door.

Some people might find this engagement less than romantic, but it was ideal for us. Neither care for tradition. We thought about eloping, but I knew we'd never hear the end of it if my mother wasn't in attendance. We married in May, the weekend after I earned my MBA. My dad was in town for graduation, so we worked the wedding in before he left. Our parents and my brother witnessed the event.

Our partnership has always been about us, on our terms. For that and all we are together, I am grateful.

Dr. Robyn MacKillop, Ph.D., is an online course writer and savvy business owner; technologically advanced; fiercely independent; a lover of cats, dogs, skulls, husband; pro-education; fun; and unstoppable. More at www.MeetOurAuthors.com.

May 24

Mocha: Love at First Sight

Teresa A. Castleman

"Hear our humble prayer, O God, for our friends the animals, your creatures." ~ St. Francis of Assisi

In January 2018, not too long after our beloved 15-year-old Lucky Kitty crossed over the rainbow bridge, a friend sent me a text about a 1-year-old cat named Mocha Latte who needed rescuing or was going to a high-kill shelter. With some trepidation, I showed her beautiful picture to my husband, Brad, worried that he was not yet ready to add a new kitty to our world. However, his immediate response was, "When can we get her?"

We drove two hours the next day to Dana Point to pick her up. Mocha came out of the car carrier in the first five minutes of the return trip, sat on my husband's lap while he drove, and then moved over to my lap for a big selfie for Facebook. She then perched on me contentedly while we called her Mocha, Mochalicious, Mocha Sweetheart, Mocha Baby, and Mocha Fabulous the whole way home telling her how much we adored and loved her. Mocha chattered back telling us how much she loved us already.

I always thank my father, Walter Kozik, who has been gone from earth for 28 years and who sends us the perfect kitty at the perfect time.

Teresa Castleman is a certified health coach and is changing lives helping people reach their optimal health. Find out more by connecting with Teresa at www.MeetOurAuthors.com.

May 25
The Last Love Lesson
Diana Bianchi

"Death is an endless night so awful to contemplate that it can make us love life and value it with such passion that it may be the ultimate cause of all joy and all art." ~ Paul Theroux

Sam looks up at me with joyful eyes and pointed ears, seemingly asking, "What do you wait for? Throw the light!"

My dog is a spiritual dog—he's always searching for the light! He learned to recognize when the perfect conditions are met to play his favorite gem: running after the sun's light that I'm gathering with my phone's screen and sending it over the shadowy wall of our daily walk path.

I am so relieved to see him jumping all around after the frightening illness he had.

Both my husband and I have had the same feeling about it: anything that reminds us of his mortality makes us shiver! He is 13 years old and he's slowly teaching us to let him go. Meanwhile, we are enjoying the smallest bits and pieces of time we spend with him, each minute of joyfulness and warm presence being a heavenly present for us.

His love for us taught us what really unconditional love means.

Diana Bianchi is an intuitive business coach helping entrepreneurs create their successful business as a playground of self-expression, using Akashic Records readings. Find out more at www.MeetOurAuthors.com.

May 26

What Do You Want?

Beth Munro

"Cats seem to go on the principle that it never does any harm to ask for what you want." ~ Joseph Wood Krutch

"Whisky-Whiskers needs a new friend, or she'll keep terrorizing your feet." At the shelter, "Hold each one upside down," sounded like a test for if we'd mistreat a kitten, but it's a test of their temperament. That the Tortoiseshell had no temper upside-down meant she'd balance out our beloved Tuxedo cat's propensity to swat. (One swatter's enough!)

Asking friends for names honoring my Italian heritage, (the Tuxie honored the Scottish side), kept yielding, "Vino." Perhaps we're who needed a new friend! Finally, came "Pesto-the-Pest." (Better than signing Christmas cards, "…Whisky & Vino.")

Pesto-the-Pest inspired me to be a stomach-sleeper—lower back and hollow of knees—their beds. Whisky-Whiskers swatted me if I then moved. That Tortie said, "Buongiorno," by gently licking our eyelashes. That Tuxie swatted us for falling back to sleep. Besides that daily helpfulness, Pesto-the-Pest-Heat-Seeker lobbied for a thermostat timer by balancing like a cornering race car on the baseboard heater. Whisky-Whiskers-the-Empress lobbied for good posture by swatting when I slouched, disturbing her perch. With her on my shoulder and the Heat-Seeker purring on my lap, I finally sat long enough to finish my thesis. Thanks, comfy good cop/bad-cop!

Ask for what you want? React to the opposite? Sometimes both.

Beth Munro, CPC, helps you keep what you want and make space to enjoy it. She offers information about coaching and organizing your life and home. You can find out more about her at www.MeetOurAuthors.com.

May 27
A Reason and Season for Everything
Holly Fitzpatrick

"Each experience will lead you to where you need to be when the time is right." ~ Holly Fitzpatrick

When we acknowledge something as a gift, we see the world differently. That different perspective can make the mundane seem like miracles and the tough situations become blessings.

I, like many people, am grateful for my children. See, I was a teen parent and before I was 20 years old, I had three healthy babies. While this is not something I recommend, it was not the end of the world for us. A couple years after my last child was born, I developed health problems that led to me not being able to have any more children. Had I waited till a more acceptable time to start my family, I would not have been able to.

Being grateful for the timing of everything, even if it might not be the timing you thought was right, will give you peace of mind that there really is a reason and season for everything. Take a moment and look at your past. Find the moments that didn't make sense or did not stand out so much at the time. But, in hindsight, and with the eyes of gratitude, you can see the many miracle moments in your life.

Holly Fitzpatrick is the founder of Authentic Self Revealed. As a transformational coach and hypnotherapist, Holly empowers women to release blocks and barriers while creating the lives they truly desire. Find out more: www.MeetOurAuthors.com.

May 28

Living Beyond My Potential
Katherine Cobb

"In our daily lives, we must see that it is not happiness that makes us grateful, but the gratefulness that makes us happy." ~ Albert Clarke

I always knew I was a girl with potential, a girl who was going places. But by the time I turned 25, I was an alcohol- and drug-addicted, jaded-about-love, often unemployable mess.

Luckily for me, 25 was my pivotal year.

I met a man and fell in love. Realizing he was worth fighting for, I saw my addiction for what it was and climbed out of the bottom of my pit and into recovery.

I am eternally grateful for both occurrences. That man became my husband and loved me until I could love myself. He showed me unconditional love and taught me how to give it in return. Conversely, recovery catapulted me into a new stratosphere, one that began a great physical, mental and spiritual metamorphosis that continues to this day.

I no longer have potential—I live it to the fullest every day. I dream, I achieve, I give, I inspire, I love.

Do I count my blessings? You betcha. I give thanks—out loud—to the universe, a higher power, mankind. I thank others. And I share with the world through words spoken and written. My connection to gratitude reminds me that anything is possible, and nothing impossible.

Author Katherine Cobb has published five books, written for several publications in the Mid-Atlantic and won Best Lifestyle Columnist by the WVPA. Find out more about her at www.MeetOurAuthors.com

May 29
You Suffered a Loss? Great!
Kiva Fecteau

"I never thought of losing, but now that it's happened, the only thing is to do it right." ~ Muhammad Ali

OK, OK, let's reframe things a little. There's no downplaying the fact that it's rough when someone we love passes on or when something we were really hoping for doesn't come through. Part of this is perspective, though, and THAT we can certainly change.

What if we were playing a game and didn't get the winning score? Did we lose? Well, we may have lost the game, but did we lose at the experience of playing the game? Not if we look at it another way. Maybe we were with family or friends whose company we really enjoy. Win! Maybe we found ourselves open to a new opportunity. Win! Maybe we learned something from the experience. Win!

So, take the time you need to process whatever sadness you may feel from losses in your life. And, when you're ready, be grateful for the best of what comes with it.

Kiva Fecteau is a catalyst who exponentially magnifies the efforts of those she works with. Find out how to connect with Kiva at www.MeetOurAuthors.com.

May 30

Gratitude Is a Choice

Irena Kay

"Gratitude is a powerful catalyst for happiness. It's the spark that lights a fire of joy in your soul." ~ Amy Collette

Gratitude lets you experience the joy of just being here now. Savor the moment. Let the heart swell with thankfulness for all your blessings.

Imagine your favorite place in nature with all of your senses. See the beauty; hear the sounds of birds or water; feel the sunshine on your skin; smell and even taste the sweet air. Ahhhh...

Instantly your brain will release feel-good hormones, triggered by pathways that were shaped by memories when you felt happy. Feeling grateful, even for little things, gets the same neurotransmitters flowing.

The good news about that? Feeling joyful and happy becomes a choice!

You have the power to control your thoughts and thus your feelings. You know that anything practiced long enough becomes a habit.

"Practice makes perfect," right? Well, not really. Practice only makes permanent; perfect practice makes perfect!

It stands to reason, therefore, to actively practice gratitude. It's such a simple tool; use it!

Pause when you are stressed, look around you, and think about what you can be grateful for right in this moment. Perhaps it's that perfect cup of coffee. Perhaps it's your faithful dog lying at your feet. Choose to be grateful and you choose happiness!

Dr. Irena Kay is a relationship coach, retired physician, and the creator of Married Love Success. She helps people revive the love in their committed relationships. Learn more at www.MeetOurAuthors.com.

May 31

Dance of Joy
Heather Aquilina

"Dancing alone is often easier and certainly less complicated than dancing with someone else, but there is nothing quite so satisfying as creating even one moment of real beauty moving gracefully with another." ~ Oriah

I wasn't looking for love when you danced into my life. Badly wounded, I'd decided I was better off alone. That night, music and a progressive dance brought us together for a time. Then, week by week, we danced a dance of laughter. You called me vivacious; I ticked off smart, funny, able to listen and change. You didn't attract me in my usual "Fatal Attraction" kind of way, giving hope you might break the mould of bad mistakes. You understood my cheeky humour: laughing not at people but with people at life with all its absurdities.

Two hurt souls, yet those hurts not colliding, we made space for each others' injuries to heal. Through the years, we've worked and lived and grown together. Some bumpy years as two strong souls, wanting the best but afraid to lose ourselves, struggle to learn new ways. When the days are hard, it is the loving, gentle you I bring to mind, the many years we've laboured on together, building, battling, bantering our way. Then, drawing a breath and opening my heart, I give thanks again for the joy you bring me and step again into your arms for the dance of life.

Heather Aquilina is a habitual learner working to balance running a management consultancy with communicating authentically through her writing and art in the hope of inspiring others. Discover more about Heather at www.MeetOurAuthors.com.

June

June 1

A Sister's Loyalty

Patricia Bumpass

"Life is a battlefield, and we remain loyal to those who fight for us, those who would die for us." ~ Crystal Woods

I came out of the doctor's office in tears. "Why are you crying?" asked my sister, who had been in the waiting room. "What did he say to you?" Through my sniffles, I managed to answer, "He said if I wasn't so fat, I wouldn't have any problems with my eyes." By the time I caught up with her, this 5'4" whirlwind had barged into that doctor's office and was giving him a piece of her mind. She and I laugh now whenever we think about the shocked look on that man's face, even though at the time I was horrified.

Whenever life knocks me down, I can always count on my sister to lift me up. With a smile, a "woo woo woo," or a good, old-fashioned belly laugh. I'm so grateful to have such a powerhouse in my corner. She's always been my biggest cheerleader and supporter. We have our squabbles and get on each other's nerves. In fact, I'm always telling her little sisters are a pain, but I can honestly say, "My sister has my back." When the chips are down, there's nobody better to have on your side than your sister.

Patricia Bumpass is a freelance content marketer and coach who encourages and empowers people to be true to their authentic selves. Learn more about Patricia at www.MeetOurAuthors.com.

June 2

The Power of Five Senses
Cory Stickley

"Life is not measured by the number of breaths you take but by the moments that take your breath away." ~ Maya Angelou

Each morning in spring, I hunt treasure in my garden. What's come up? Today, the peonies, roses and lavender are like vibrant jewels in the treasure chest, having bloomed for my pleasure alone.

Every aspect of the garden calls forth half-forgotten memories. The fragrance of the roses reminds me of gardens in France—manicured hedges, gnarled vines, ancient olive trees. Many of my favorite photographs were taken there.

Watching the bees, I marvel at how the flowers they visit change the taste of the honey. My mouth waters at the thought of lavender honey drizzled on yogurt, breakfast on Santorini. My mind creates a virtual taste test of foods discovered on my trips—paella, tapas, souvlaki.

At sunset, the sensation of walking barefoot on the warm stone path calls up another memory—the din of 150 trumpeting elephants at the watering hole in Hwange Game Preserve. I passed close to them in the dark of night as I dashed to the outhouse, praying they'd ignore me.

My garden, my senses, my travels, stories and photographs are all parts of the creative me. Without one, the others suffer. Used together, they express my gratitude for being alive.

Cory Stickley was born to travel, write, photograph and teach. Her book, *The F.I.X. Code*, shares how she overcame burnout and fear of writing. More at www.MeetOurAuthors.com.

June 3
Magical Beginnings
Katie De Souza

"And suddenly, you know: It's time to start something new and trust the magic of beginnings." ~ Meister Eckhart

I woke up excited. This was the day I started a new, wonderful chapter of my life, marrying my beautiful, Brazilian boyfriend and becoming his wife.

Fifteen months earlier, I went out with my friends to a small Latino nightclub, the only club that turned a blind eye to my friends who were underage. I was the eldest, aged 18, yet the smallest; they all looked older than me.

Happy, energetic club with lovely people from around the world. The security guard asked me to dance on behalf of Alex, as he couldn't speak English. We danced. Alex was working as a glass collector. We danced on his breaks; we danced when he was working.

Studying together, Alex learnt English fast. I learnt Portuguese. Fast-forward to June 1997 and getting married with a magical secret only others would know six months later.

A simple ceremony at our local registry office attended by close family and friends.

With little money, we appreciated each other more than material items. Our basic his 'n' hers ring set was £100. Alex's Debenhams silver suit, £99, and my long, flowy white dress with loose jacket, £100.

A beautiful, sunny day in Bournemouth, a great start to a beautiful life.

Katie De Souza is an author and entrepreneur who inspires couples to achieve their dreams and live a happy and fulfilling life together. More at www.MeetOurAuthors.com.

June 4

The Killdeer

Holly Pitas

"All the universe is full of the lives of perfect creatures."
~ Konstantin Tsiolkovsky

Her feathers and coloring act as natural camouflage for the killdeer nesting in our stone garden. Perched near the decorative lighthouse, she is nearly invisible. It's my good fortune to see her out the bedroom window each morning. Heat of the sun, cold of the night, wind, rain and hail, the little bird is steady on her nest. I admire her fortitude. Her mate keeps a watchful eye and acts as a distraction for any potential predators. He makes quite a ruckus when any of us need to walk through the yard. They have a devoted partnership with each taking turns on the nest.

This is the only life they can have. Seeing the killdeer obey their law of nature, I appreciate that I have choices. I get to live in a protected environment. Wherever I want. Safe and comfortable, no matter the weather.

A few weeks pass. Both birds are very noisy today. The little ones have hatched, and the parents are calling them away from the nest. I'm lucky to see the tiny ones run from the stone garden to hide in the tall grass. They will grow rapidly, then fly off to a life of single destiny.

Holly shares insights on caregiving with *Don't Get Caught Naked: Tips for the Adult Family Home Caregiver*. She works globally as a certified emotion code practitioner. Discover more about Holly at www.MeetOurAuthors.com.

June 5
Close Call With Nature's Fury
Diane Rasmussen Lovitt

"Security is mostly a superstition. It does not exist in nature."
~ Helen Keller

We could see for miles where we lived on our Kansas farm, and one sultry summer day, we saw a large tornado coming straight toward us. It was daylight, but luckily we were not scattered around the farm. We squeezed the five of us into a small area under the cement foundation away from where the house might explode or collapse on us. We hung onto each other in fear. The wind finally died down, and our house was still over us.

We climbed the stairs and stood on the back porch. We were glad to see the barn still standing and the animals huddled nearby. We sighed with relief until my dad exclaimed, "The grain bin is gone." It had been about 50 feet from the house. I glanced at my mother, who turned pale as she clutched my father's arm. There was our precious wheat grain sprayed into the mud, and our metal bin had vanished, but we were safe.

It hit us. We realized what a close call we had with nature's fury.

Diane Rasmussen Lovitt grew up on a Kansas farm and now lives in Pleasanton, California. She writes short stories and memoirs. Find out more at www.MeetOurAuthors.com.

June 6

Earthly Bonds in High Flight

Marguerite Senecal

"We each of us are angels with only one wing, and we can only fly by embracing one another." ~ Luciano De Crescenzo

Dad spoke so highly of "Butch," his navigator when he piloted torpedo bombers in the war.

"Butch was never lost."

Ross Burtch could navigate by the stars. A useful skill; equipment failures were routine.

When Dad died, I set out to find Butch. The RCAF sent the phone number of every Canadian with that name. I chose one at random and called. Butch knew immediately who I was. I told him that his pilot had taken his last flight. We became friends. He'd never spoken about the war before. Because I asked, he talked and wrote his stories.

From Dad, I heard of exhilarating adventures. From Butch, I heard of lethal dangers, always the fear of being hit, being set on fire. "I was always cold, and I was always afraid."

But he trusted his pilot. Courage is not the absence of fear. Both men felt that the only way they'd get out of the war alive was if they flew together.

At Butch's funeral, I read from his memoirs. I was there to close the circle. Through me, Dad felt present—to fly his navigator safely home one last time.

Marguerite Senecal empowers executives to communicate their vision powerfully, project authentic presence and to create, inspire and lead successful organizations. Find out more about Marguerite and her offerings at www.MeetOurAuthors.com.

June 7

Thanks for Having Us, Dad!
Lisa Khera

"Gratitude turns what we have into enough...denial into acceptance, chaos into order, confusion into clarity...It brings peace for today."
~ Melody Beattie

I didn't really believe the neurologist when he said that things would just "come back on like a dimmer switch," and as he remarked that my chapter wasn't over. I'm so thankful he was right. The doctor was referring to the pain and challenges associated with persistent post-concussion symptoms.

Things got worse before they got better, but by the end of June 2018, the neurologist was right—everything suddenly improved. I had been working on things like having a daily gratitude practice, positive mindset, and daily Pilates (I've enjoyed teaching it for 20 years).

After my mom died suddenly, I had an even deeper appreciation for being grateful for what we have in life as it can change in an instant. I'm so grateful for healing as it allowed me to travel, socialize, and live a life filled with gratitude.

My husband, children, and I have spent the last three summers at my dad's. The gratitude I have in my heart that I get to hug my dad goodnight each night is priceless. Spending these summers connecting and watching my children spend time with their poppa and grandparents is a priceless gift we've all shared together.

Cherish the time with your parents.

Lisa Khera is an author, Pilates instructor, owner of In Balance Pilates and creator of the online program Breathe Into Calm. Find out more about Lisa at www.MeetOurAuthors.com.

June 8

Today Is Her Birthday!

Anne Hunter Logue

"Any day spent with you is my favorite day. So, today is my favorite day." ~ A.A. Milne, *Winnie-the-Pooh*

Today is my best friend's birthday! Friendship is one of the greatest blessings we have in life. I have been so fortunate to have had a wonderful friendship with Diane Markert for over 35 years. We have shared many adventures.

One of my favorite memories is from a time when my kids were very small. It was a time before cell phones and GPS. My friend Diane and I had planned to get together for the afternoon with the kids. We were going to meet at a Friendly's for lunch and then go to Diane's favorite store. We both were traveling from different locations and were to meet at 11 a.m.

I arrived at Friendly's, but my friend wasn't there. I waited for a while, but my kids got restless, so we left. We had no way to call each other. When I got home, my friend called me. I found out we had each gone to Friendly's but in different towns. We are both so bad with directions that Diane's husband used to joke that half of the miles on her car were from going in the wrong direction! We still laugh at our misadventures!

Anne Hunter Logue is a healing practitioner and children's author of *The Story of the Sun* and *I Once Had a Tiger*. Learn more about Anne at www.MeetOurAuthors.com.

June 9

Living Libraries Require No Card
Norm Hull Jr.

"Never argue with a librarian; they know too much."
~ Carole Nelson Douglas

Is your library open and your librarian overdue for a visit?

When the responsibility to take care of my dad rotated to me, I was initially hesitant because of the time needed, the level of attention focused on his care versus my career responsibilities—common considerations before you accept the responsibility of taking care of another, especially the remaining family patriarch.

I was fearful it might feel like a chore until my family librarian started to share stories about life before I arrived in the world, and his name was replaced with "Dad." Access to our family library made me grateful, and I relished his storytelling of history I cannot Google.

When your librarian's age tries your patience, take a step back, and ask a question to hear a new story. It changes your mindset and provides insight into a previous part of life you will not have access to when your library is closed. I am grateful to have my family librarian who never tires of questions and delights in sharing family history.

Express your gratitude to your librarians, and appreciate the days your library is open.

Operating hours are limited. Visit your library while you still have access.

Norm Hull is a leadership alchemist who teaches clients how to enhance their leadership influence on peers and staff. Discover more about Norm at www.MeetOurAuthors.com.

June 10

Choosing Joy
Lisa Willis

"There is no better opportunity to receive more than to be thankful for what you already have." ~ Zig Ziglar

When life shows up, I choose joy. Even when challenges occur, I try to see the bright side and feel gratitude for whatever blessings I discover. As I sit quietly and look back over my life, I am grateful for the love, protection and guidance from God. He has given me more than I could ever ask for. I'm thankful for my parents, sisters, relatives and supportive friends who have always been there for me. I have an "attitude of gratitude" when I think about all the blessings around me. I experience joy when I am serving others and look for ways to do more. Additionally, I'm grateful for my clients who trusted me to help them establish a healthy work-life balance.

I believe gratitude is a state of mind that builds a sense of gratefulness toward others. As a gratitude challenge, I thanked one person each day for one week for something they had done for me. I genuinely want the people in my life to know that I appreciate them, and when they think of me, I hope that they are filled with joy. It is a satisfying feeling to give to others and not expect anything in return.

As a certified coach, Lisa Willis has worked with individuals to establish a balanced lifestyle. As a therapist, she has helped individuals recover from addiction and mental health issues. Find out more about Lisa and her offerings at www.MeetOurAuthors.com.

June 11

My New Power Over Stress

Clay Ryan

"If you have peace of mind, you don't need anything else.
If you don't have it, it doesn't matter much what else you do have."
~ Dalai Lama

Anxiety and stress are punishing us at an overwhelming and ever-increasing rate. Us is me. I never thought it would be me. But it is. How can I find gratitude and joy when anxiety has burrowed itself so deep that it often awakens me with a gnawing in my gut and that frazzled, energy-drained feeling. How can I?

When the student is ready, the teacher appears.

Now, I gratefully use two powerful tools: biofeedback programs and breathing control. Combined, they transform me back to the positive and productive force my friends and family always knew. In only five minutes, I turn energy drains into empowering thoughts such that a clear mind or restful sleep become my companions.

How good it feels infused deep in my core. I am grateful that simple "things" can unlock invisible emotional burdens inside me. Most importantly, instead of stress, I now carry calm strength to my family as we address life's hurdles.

It is now a lifestyle. I get joy showing others the freedom coming from this de-stressing routine. A need has become a gift. As the Dalai Lama knows, "We can never fully enjoy life if we are regularly stressed out just beneath our own surface."

Clay Ryan is a former engineer turned self-health advocate and biofeedback coach for optimal performance and stress resilience. More at www.MeetOurAuthors.com.

June 12

Gratitude and Prosperity

Afolake Janet Oyelami

"Gratitude is the fastest vehicle to your success." ~ Janet Oyelami

I had never deeply understood what gratitude really meant until 2017. This was the time I was desperate for a change, and I began to listen to many motivational speakers. Terri Savelle and most motivational speakers said gratitude is the best. So, I decided to try it out. I got a gratitude notebook and started writing seven things I am grateful for daily. I was grateful for my hair, my skin, the hot or cold weather, the water I drink and the food I eat. I was in debt, yet I was grateful for learning new ways to overcome my debt. I was grateful for my five family members living in a one-bedroom flat. Believe me, I was grateful with my whole heart.

By 2019, my afro hair began to grow longer, and we got a five-bedroom house at a very lower rate monthly. My skin began to glow to the extent people around me started saying I am looking younger and more beautiful. Now, I cannot stand negative comments, for gratitude has turned my life around for success.

Janet is a new author of the book titled *Your Mindset: Freedom and Dream Achievement Quotes Book* on Amazon. She is an entrepreneur. More at www.MeetOurAuthors.com.

June 13

Small-Scale Gratitude
Linda Luhman

"Through the eyes of gratitude, everything is a miracle." ~ Mary Davis

My former career as a public safety dispatcher required speedy resolutions to problems and then moving forward to the next one. Working with under-socialized dogs in the local shelter's behavior program challenged this goal-achieving mindset immediately.

Fearful dogs require patience and time. You cannot impose your agenda on them and expect good results. You need to build trust in an animal and let it set the pace. Sometimes, that meant merely sitting on the floor outside a kennel door with my back turned, throwing treats near the dog until it was ready to move closer. Once the dog consistently came to the kennel door, it was time to open the door and begin again.

The slower pace of working with fearful animals became an oasis in my typically frenetic world. I learned success could be as small as feeling a dog sniff you through a cage door or take a treat from your hand. I now recognize and revel in small victories that happen every day in my life. It took "broken" dogs to teach me to be grateful for seemingly little things I might have previously ignored. If I ever forget, there will surely be someone to remind me.

Linda Luhman is a freelance writer and editor who currently ghostwrites in product marketing. She is always game for new projects! More at www.MeetOurAuthors.com.

June 14

Three Powerful Ways to Leverage Gratitude

Shirley J. Noah

"Gratitude is a quality similar to electricity; it must be produced and discharged and used up in order to exist at all." ~ William Faulkner

Here are three characteristics I have learned about being grateful to be happier, more content and fulfilled in life:

What you give out, you get back. If I am prone to thinking negatively, my life will reflect those thoughts and give me negative experiences. But if I practice gratitude, I can begin to experience love, joy, contentment, serenity and even bliss.

Gratitude to strengthen my resilience muscle. The more I practice the art of appreciation, the more I can reinforce it. Soon, I will think in this new positive way, and I will experience a warm glow in my heart.

Stay in the now. Gratitude can help me focus on what is in the now. When I practice mindful eating, listen to the sound of birds singing or feel the wind in my hair, life is more enjoyable. When I focus on what is, I cannot worry about the future or obsess over the past.

Try it yourself and see. Practicing gratitude is like magic. By focusing on gratitude and staying in the present, I feel happier and become more resilient. When the difficult times come, if I have practiced the habit of gratitude, the negativity around me will diminish.

Author and entrepreneur Shirley Noah is passionate about health, wellness and stress management. Learn more about Shirley at www.MeetOurAuthors.com.

June 15

My Godmother, Skip

Cassandra Lee

"When you are aware of it, you can then work toward changing it."
~ Cassandra Lee

Have you ever had someone in your life who thought the world of you to help you change into your best self? Many of you can answer yes because you had that someone in your life as a family member. Others of you can say yes because that someone was outside of your family as your mentor, your coach or your friend.

For me, that someone was a woman God blessed me to meet who would later become my coach, my life advisor and my godmother, Skip. I met her at the start of my life's journey of changing and becoming the person, woman and professional God needed me to be.

My godmother, Skip was there—in the trenches— helping me through those important and sometimes challenging life changes. Occasionally, she would tell me, "Baby, you're so busy stressing out about the change that you're missing the blessings behind the change."

That valuable "kitchen table" lesson shaped me on forgiveness, professionalism, family, anger management, conflict resolution, relationships and thought power, just to name a few. Thanks to her unconditional love and selfless teachings, I am who I am today. I am grateful for— and will always love— my godmother, Skip.

Cassandra "D.I.V.A. of Dialog™" Lee uses Divine Inspiration Vocally Applied™ to educate and empower audiences toward personal growth and career success. Find out more about Cassandra at www.MeetOurAuthors.com.

June 16

The Dawn of Discovery

Ruth Polden

"What you truly learn best will appear to you later as your own discovery." ~ Moshe Feldenkrais.

Walking at daybreak has been my anchor during lockdown. Leaving a home enveloped in sleep to greet the rising sun. A space of possibility. Focus. Just me. A quiet stillness bathed in pinky rays. The promise of the approaching day. A precious time of reflection.

Often, I walk submerged. Wrapped in thought. Lulled by the hypnotic rhythm of the weighted shift of my steps.

It arrives. Dropped suddenly into my field of attention. A bud on the cusp of unfolding its colours to the world—that wasn't there the day before. The fresh sounds of a new bird's song. Unfamiliar to my ear. Musky, floral, fruity smells of the natural world that find their way along my nostrils. A new path that reveals itself as I tread my known route. The excitement and adventure of exploring where it leads and what I might find.

What was there unseen, unheard, unnoticed reveals itself. Treasures unburied. Sharp and crisp the present moment. The gift of discovery. The magic, the bringer of joy, awe and privilege. I sense my world afresh. Recalibrated, energized, fueled. Humbled by a bigger picture and a fresh perspective. I step into my day.

Ruth Polden is a movement specialist who helps people move with comfort, ease and efficiency and function better in what they do in life. Learn more about Ruth at www.MeetOurAuthors.com.

June 17

The Sun Will Rise

Rick Binder

"You must embrace the darkness before you can see the light."
~ Miyamoto Musashi

I am eternally grateful for the person I've become. After all, it's taken me my entire life to get to this point. Intermingled with the good have been a lot of very dark periods that I've had to overcome. I've survived a great deal of loss and disappointment—material possessions, relationships, financial ruin, career setbacks… The list goes on, but had I not taken the lessons I've learned and overcome, I would not be this version of myself.

I am compassionate. I help those in need. I get to walk my daughter down the aisle soon. I get to experience love once more. I place more value on the people in my life than the things in my life. I make the world a better place, and I strive to be an inspiration to others.

None of this would be possible without the setbacks I experienced during those dark days. I am who I am because of who I was, and that's a very good thing. So for those who still suffer, take heart. Tough times pass, and there's an ocean of good times yet to come. Embrace the darkness. Tomorrow the sun will rise.

Rick Binder, author of *The Four Pillars of Cellular Health*, helps others activate their bodies at the cellular level in order to eliminate pain and reduce oxidative stress. Find out more about him at www.MeetOurAuthors.com.

June 18

Transforming Grief into Gratitude
Patti Smith

"The soul would have no rainbow, had the eyes no tears." ~ John Vance Cheney

Was there a sound?

Did the world pause its spinning for just a moment when it happened?

In an instant, she was gone. The mother I had loved so dearly was part of a tangled mess of metal and concrete.

Overwhelming grief consumed me, and I took refuge in a tiny hermitage cottage in the country to come to terms with my loss.

No telephone, no computer, no television, no running water. Only an 8-by-12 foot cabin at the tree line, where the snow still clung to the branches of the evergreen forest, and a smallish spider traversing the ceiling to keep me company.

Over three days, I plunged into my grief headfirst and opened my wounded soul to God.

Sobbing subsided as I was shown the truth of what happened, and limiting beliefs I never even knew I had rose up and were released.

I was reborn in that trinity of days. Peace arrived, accompanied by acceptance and wisdom.

I was humbled by the incredible love that surrounded and protected me.

And, finally, the visit of a wolf just before I left. Our eyes locked and I received his blessing, then departed in grace and gratitude.

Patti Smith is a success coach who teaches women CEOs, entrepreneurs and leaders how to create "conscious businesses" for impact and profit. More at www.MeetOurAuthors.com.

June 19

Keeping Dad's Memories Alive
Susan Veach

"All he has to do is breathe on the plants and they will grow!"
~ Unknown

I got a call from one of my dad's caregivers. She requested information about his background to increase his memory skills. I supplied details about our family, Dad's likes and dislikes, and his work and social history.

Dad grew up during the Great Depression. During that time, his father died. His large family survived on what they could grow or raise themselves, including livestock. They had no electricity or running water.

Dad worked long hours in a hot, noisy factory as a machine operator.

In the summer, he tended his vegetable and flower gardens. He cultivated his own variety of tomato, with extra-solid flesh.

Digging potatoes was a huge event. The neighborhood kids gathered potatoes as Dad unearthed them. Cries of "There's one!" echoed. Each child was rewarded with a bag of potatoes to take home. Dad was pleased he didn't have to bend over to pick them up.

Dad had a fierce competition with his best friend over who grew the biggest potato or had the first red tomato of the season. No prize, only bragging rights.

He loved my mother and our family with all his heart.

I was grateful some of Dad's memories are being kept alive.

Susan Veach is a book designer living in the suburbs of Philadelphia, Pa. She is a bibliophile, wife and mother, gardener, traveler, and art lover. Find out more about Susan at www.MeetOurAuthors.com.

June 20
And Away We Go!
Kelly Fedge-DuBose

"How can I possibly be expected to handle school
on a day like this?" ~ Ferris Bueller

Contrary to popular belief, the longest day of the year is not the summer solstice. The longest day of the year is, in fact, the last day of school.

Waiting for the last bell to ring, tortured as each second lingers. Tick…tick…tick booms the official clock. We can barely contain ourselves as the long, thin, red second hand jerks its way closer to 12:05. The vibrating energy bounces through the classroom like a trapped Ping-Pong ball. Finally, the sound of freedom rings. We catapult off our chairs and rush through packed doors outside to sign yearbooks and exchange hugs.

Wahoo, it's summer!

Towels, skim- and surfboards, cooler, sunscreen and flip-flops are already packed in anticipation of our traditional road trip to Laguna Beach, California, immediately after school. After a decade of annual visits, we are practically locals.

Our eyes search for Mom. Suddenly, out of nowhere, armed with Super Soaker squirt guns, she ambushes us. Suspecting her likely attack, we are prepared. In true ninja style, midstride I toss my brother a loaded squirt gun, and we let loose on Mom. Soaked and squealing with joy, we all pile into the Jeep for our 1,107-mile trip to catch the perfect wave!

As a healer and strategy success coach, Kelly helps people live fearlessly. Together you will take systematic action and elevate your environment and inner game. Discover more about Kelly at www.MeetOurAuthors.com.

June 21

Healthy Mind, Healthy Body Journey

Connie Ragen Green

"Keep your vitality. A life without health is like a river without water."
~ Maxime Lagacé

When you walk past a mirror, do you acknowledge yourself? On June 21, the longest day of the year, I made the decision to focus on developing a healthy mind and body. Being in gratitude each day is part of my practice.

I took my health for granted when I was young. I ate foods that weren't nutritious, did not sleep nearly enough and refused to listen to my body. I was invincible and could always make up for it later.

Later arrived when I was 37 and was diagnosed with stage 3 breast cancer. I learned that a healthy body begins with a healthy mind. Meditation, whole foods and lots of naps helped me to save my life.

I slipped back into my old habits, and illness came knocking once again. This time I snapped back to health more quickly because the first lesson was still so fresh in my mind.

Now, I'm on a new journey and acknowledging myself each day. Getting older doesn't mean you are less than you were before; it means you now have a relationship with your body around putting yourself first. I live each day in gratitude for my healthy mind and body.

Connie Ragen Green works with new authors and entrepreneurs and mentors them on how to create massive passive income streams with a joyous online business. Find out more about Connie at www.MeetOurAuthors.com.

June 22
Dog Spelled Backward Is God
Kathi McKnight

"If you don't own a dog, there is not necessarily anything wrong with you, but there may be something wrong with your life."
~ Roger A. Caras

It was raining, and I was stuck in traffic when I looked up and saw them. The fateful words, "Who rescued who?" plastered to the rear end of the gray jeep in front of me—complete with an adorable set of paw prints.

A couple of weeks later, we found "the one" on a rescue farm in a beautiful town in Colorado named Loveland. Coincidence? I think not. The cutest thing I ever saw, a shih tzu-bichon, aka "teddy bear" puppy.

We changed his rescue name to one that fit him. Cody Beau. Cody: helper, giving, positive, energetic, super nice, rough and tumble, very family oriented, cheerful. Beau: handsome, fine, attractive.

Cody Beau gave my husband endless joy and energy those final eight months until the cancer took Sam. He gave me endless comfort after. Especially during COVID, refusing to let me cry. If he heard me whimper, he'd scamper across the room, jump on me and fill my face with kisses, making me burst into laughter.

When the holistic vet came to our home, pre-COVID, she said Cody saw my husband as the Alpha and me as his sister and playmate. Really? Naw, he's my little soulmate.

As seen on Dr. Oz, Kathi McKnight is a professional speaker, author and master certified handwriting analyst. Find out more about Kathi at www.MeetOurAuthors.com.

June 23

From One Pilgrim to Another
Lisa McGrath

"One can never pay in gratitude; one can only pay in kind somewhere else in life." ~ Anne Morrow Lindbergh

My feet were bruised, blistered and raw. My backpack hung low across my back. This wasn't my first Camino.

"It's after five," my walking partner shared, "and we have to find a room."

I couldn't take another step.

"I think we're in the wrong place." I looked at the address. "Let's go into the hotel and ask the concierge."

We entered the lobby. The concierge took one look at us and answered Linda in English, "No, this is not where you're supposed to be."

We explained our predicament. I found him staring at me. "I am a pilgrim too. I know your pain."

Yes, pain. Besides the pain in my body, I was tired, hungry and thirsty. I smiled back.

"Please, follow me. I will bring you something. Then, I will take you to a room across the way. It isn't much, but it has two clean beds and a washroom in the hall; it is a quiet place to rest."

He sat us away from the other diners. He brought us wine and a platter of cheese, chorizo and bread. Later, he grabbed my backpack, and we followed him. Tears filled my eyes, and I realized I would never forget his generosity.

Lisa McGrath is an international best-selling author, speaker, teacher and life coach offering inspirational, practical and spiritual guidance to women through her coaching programs. Discover more about Lisa at www.MeetOurAuthors.com.

June 24

Kenzie MacKillop, aka Dad

Dr. Robyn MacKillop

"My father gave me the greatest gift anyone could give another person—he believed in me." ~ Jim Valvano

My dad took his role seriously. He was liberal in his politics but raised his children conservatively. My friends often heard yes while I heard no. Kenzie MacKillop instilled self-reliance, responsibility and work ethic in us kids. We believed him when he said our purpose in life was to make the world more equal for those who had less.

He was mysterious in that he rarely talked about his childhood. On my first trip back to Nova Scotia with him, it was clear he had fond memories. I began to see him more as a person instead of just Dad. Every so often, he would purposely embarrass me, but for the most part, I was extremely proud he was my dad. He watched out for me like a hawk.

I'm a lot like him. We have the same crooked smile, droopy eyes and auburn in our hair. I have his hands. I mirror his stubbornness and generosity. He could be stern, and that enabled me to know where I couldn't cross the line. He was wicked smart, and his soul was gracious and kind. He left a lot of himself with me.

Dr. Robyn MacKillop, Ph.D., is an online course writer; savvy business owner; fiercely independent; a lover of cats, dogs, skulls, husband; pro-education; fun; and unstoppable. Find out more about Robyn at www.MeetOurAuthors.com.

June 25
The Words Before All Else
Linda Bittle

"Nature's beauty is a gift that cultivates appreciation and gratitude."
~ Louie Schwartzberg

I was sitting on a damp log next to a fire that had been started with a bow drill the first time I heard the Thanksgiving Address. At 47, I was the oldest "kid" in a class of 18. I'd traveled 1900 miles to an unfamiliar rain forest to learn about nature.

The Thanksgiving Address became a core routine that began each class, community gathering and even staff meetings at Wilderness Awareness School. Originating with the Iroquois people, it has been shared around the world with instructions to make it personal. It's also called "bringing our minds together."

It begins by giving thanks for people. Next, we express gratitude to the earth, waters, fish, birds and animals. Then trees and plants, the weather, the sun, moon and stars, then all the things we forgot to mention, and finally, to the Creator.

My faith requires that I give thanks to the Lord for everything. The Thanksgiving Address helps me remember what I am grateful for and gives structure to my prayers.

Adopting the daily practice of expressing gratitude has profoundly changed the way that I view the world. If everyone practiced gratitude, what a force for good we could become!

Linda Bittle lives in rural Idaho with two cats and a small dog. More information about Linda and her blog, This Is Not Where I Thought I Was Going, is found at www.MeetOurAuthors.com.

June 26

Start Your Day with Gratitude

Roberta Gold

"Gratitude doesn't have to be a serious matter!
If you want to thank someone, do it by putting a smile on their face
or even making them laugh." ~ Unknown

We have all heard the saying that we should live every day as if it is our last. I am not a fan of this kind of thinking. I suggest we should live every day. What I mean by this is we should spend time each day doing something that makes us smile and laugh; spend some time each day being grateful for what we have; spend some time each day doing something for someone else; spend some time each day being mindful of all the beauty around us; and spend some time each day just being silly.

Cultivating mindfulness, gratitude, forgiveness, and kindness has shown to increase our sense of well-being and strengthen our connections with the people who matter most in our lives. In my opinion, gratitude is one of the most moving emotions we have. It gets us out of ourselves and focused on someone or something else.

Studies confirm that people who nurture relationships with fun, laughter, and gratitude form tighter bonds, report being happier, and live longer. Try starting the day giving thanks for what we have; I believe this will make us happier and more content.

Live every day—with gratitude.

Roberta Gold created Laughter for the Health of It and Laughter Rocks! with a mission to empower everyone to have a more positive outlook. She's a speaker, author, and coach. Connect with her at www.MeetOurAuthors.com.

June 27

Living a Life of Gratitude
Bill McCarthy

"Gratitude is the inward feeling of kindness received. Thankfulness is the natural impulse to express that feeling. Thanksgiving is the following of that impulse." ~ Henry Van Dyke

Gratitude is one of the blessings of life.

The first blessing is life itself, the second is every breath we take, the third is the ability to appreciate our life experiences and the fourth and central blessing is the feeling of gratitude for all the other blessings.

Every morning, at the end of my meditation, I reflect on my experiences and express my gratitude for all the blessings in my life.

I usually find myself in tears as I experience the depth of my gratitude for these blessings.

Beginning each day in this manner sets a tone of appreciation and gratitude for all that I will experience throughout the day.

As the days go on, the depth of my gratitude grows deeper and deeper as my understanding of the preciousness of the gift of life expands.

The source of all life—God, Energy or whatever one chooses to call it—has shown great compassion by creating us and allowing us the blessing of being alive in this beautiful world.

The only way of expressing my appreciation for this amazing gift is to live in a state of gratitude every day of my life.

Bill McCarthy is a special event, television, and internet broadcast producer. He is also the founder and president of Unity Foundation. Find out more at www.MeetOurAuthors.com.

June 28

Like the Bear

Sarah-Jane Watson

"Whenever one person stands up and says, 'Wait a minute, this is wrong,' it helps other people do the same." ~ Gloria Steinem

On June 28, 1969, Stonewall Uprising began as a battle for LGBTQ rights and equality. That fight is still very much alive. Lately, our hearts have had their fill of fighting. Riots, rallies and uprisings, perhaps not enough about advocates and allies.

Allies are people who have your back, who stand up not to be right but for what is right. They accept you as you are. If you are a person that fits into a bowl of alphabet soup, like I am, these people are so much more.

An ally is a Winnie; yes, like the bear. This Winnie isn't cuddly like the bear, though. I met her 19 years ago during an interview for a potential place of employment. I replied to one of her questions with a "ma'am" and was quickly informed that she wasn't that old. Shortly after that, we became friends.

Although I fly a rainbow flag with pride, I never know if someone I care about will accept me when I come out to them. Winnie did unconditionally and as is. From day one, her voice has never been one of silence. She's an advocate. She's an ally. More importantly, she's my best friend.

Sarah-Jane Watson: creative professional in wild and wonderful West Virginia, with more than 16 years of experience in photography, design and marketing/advertising. Discover more about Sarah-Jane at www.MeetOurAuthors.com.

June 29

When the Saints Come Marching In

Linda Berry

"Saints were saints because they acted with loving kindness whether they felt like it or not." ~ Dan Millman

It all started at a second-hand store with a tattered book held together by aged masking tape staring at me from a shelf. It called out to me. The biography of a 16th century saint, Martin de Porres, started me on a journey of study that I call "saintology." A modern-day devotion similar to the belief of ancient deities.

Saints have rulership over certain areas of life and nature, becoming spiritual allies akin to that of angels. Hundreds of years of belief continue to this day for the saints' ability to intercede on behalf of humans who invoke their aid.

This day worldwide celebrates the first-century saint that intervenes for individuals in the writing professions. Authors, writers, publishers, publicists and journalists can all turn to Saint Paul, the patron saint of their trade. Today is his day.

This determined man with a delightful sense of humor spent his life communicating ideas he passionately believed in, spreading his message to those who needed his inspiration. He now oversees the messengers who continue this mission in their lives.

If you are experiencing a trying situation in your life and need some guidance, turn to the saints. Let them march in for you!

Linda Berry is an angel whisperer and the owner, consultant, coach, and reader for the Spiritual Discovery Center. She's also an international astrologer, podcast host, and spiritual and metaphysical book author. Learn more about Linda at www.MeetOurAuthors.com.

June 30

It's Never Too Late

Garry Trent

"The only person you are destined to become is the person you decide to be." ~ Ralph Waldo Emerson

Being grateful is something I'm very familiar with. I'm a recovering alcoholic and addict and well aware of how my life could have turned out. When I compare the person I am today to the person I was years ago, I can't help but reflect and feel gratitude. Through sobriety, I have earned my loving wife, a job that I enjoy, maintained my freedom and learned how to appreciate every day I have on this earth. I'd be remiss not to acknowledge that alone I wouldn't have achieved these things.

Through his patience, tough love and generosity for sharing his personal experience, I would never have been able to come to terms with my past and the trauma I endured as a child if it weren't for Herb Kay. I will always remember the words he spoke that changed my life: "You are not alone."

But, above all, without the help of God to not only grant me the willingness to change but also the strength to make the necessary changes, I would not be as blessed as I am. And, in paying it forward, it's my honor and privilege to help others as they have helped me.

Garry Trent has been in recovery for nearly 20 years and happily married with a dog. He is a mentor and speaker for others in recovery and healing from past traumas. Find out how to connect with Garry at www.MeetOurAuthors.com.

July

July 1

Different Together

Marguerite Senecal

"When the power of love overcomes the love of power, the world will know peace." ~ Jimi Hendrix

Dad was raised on the prairies of Saskatchewan; Mum, in the big city of London. War brought them together in England. She drove ambulances during the Blitz. He was an RCAF bomber pilot. She survived bombs on the ground; he survived attacks in the air.

He was born Catholic; she was born Protestant. His ancestors were French; hers were British. French, English, Catholic, Protestant— that's centuries of conflict right there. They brought two strong personalities and two hot tempers to that marriage. It wasn't always easy; at times, it was the vows that kept it together. But they had pledged for better or worse. Like the freedom they had both fought for, love demanded from them not just eternal vigilance but sacrifice, generosity and actions that speak far louder than words.

Canada exists because its two founding peoples ultimately allowed vision and possibility to bridge two solitudes and overcome entrenched justifiable animosity. The most multicultural country in the world, Canada makes its share of mistakes. We just keep on trying, as my parents did, to grow, understand and live together in peace. Sometimes, like them, we really get it right.

Whoever and wherever you are, Happy Canada Day.

Marguerite Senecal empowers executives to communicate their vision powerfully, project authentic presence and to create, inspire and lead successful organizations. Find out more about Marguerite and her offerings at www.MeetOurAuthors.com.

July 2

More Flow, Less Hustle

Kerri McManus

"The goal of life is to make your heartbeat match the beat of the universe, to match your nature with Nature." ~ Joseph Campbell

The grey finch perched on our living room window staring and cheeping at me from the outside as if to say, "Welcome!" He sat there as if he expected me to open the window and invite him in. And I'll be honest, I nearly did!

After many years of living in a crowded Los Angeles neighborhood and working in an intense office, my husband and I moved to a quiet hillside where we're surrounded by nature. Before we moved, I had tamped down my own nature to navigate the noise in my life. As a sensitive, creative soul, it's no surprise that it manifested in heart palpitations.

Something had to change.

Living and working in this new serene space, I feel as if I've returned to my own natural rhythm. I have a newfound appreciation for my own sensitivity. As I watch the sway of the palm trees in the afternoon wind and the butterflies flitting from one bush to the next, I am creating a natural flow in my own work and I'm able to access my empathic gifts more deeply to help others connect to themselves.

Kerri McManus is a certified life coach who helps artists, entertainment professionals, and creatives connect more deeply to their gifts and talents to consciously create their lives. Find out more at www.MeetOurAuthors.com.

July 3
A Powerful Motivator for Change
Veronica Hollingsworth

"Gratitude turns disappointment into lessons learned, discoveries made, alternatives explored, and new plans set in motion." ~ Auliq-Ice

Perched on the second floor of a shopping complex, a small family resource center is a hub of hope for a rural mountain community. A high school dropout saunters through the doors, ashamed of not finishing school yet determined to attain his GED and get a better job so he can marry his girl. A grandmother raising her grandchild gets help with an overdue bill, and for the first time in her life is taught to budget so she can better provide. A single mother battling addiction acquires a mentor to clean up her life and keep custody of her son.

These people have one thing in common: They came through the door at their lowest point, ready for change. Each one was heard and understood; all had strengths they weren't seeing. The young man had a knack for numbers and is now exploring engineering. The empowered grandmother is teaching her granddaughter smart consumerism. The single mother recognizes her worth and is setting and meeting goals. They acknowledged their strengths, tapped into gratitude, and used these to carry them forward through challenges.

That's the specialty of this family resource center—focusing on strengths and using gratitude as fuel for self-motivated change.

Veronica Hollingsworth is a certified health/relationship coach who uses gratitude practices to facilitate real change. Find out more about her at www.MeetOurAuthors.com.

July 4
Freedom To Choose
Sherri K. Coffelt

"What, then, is freedom? The power to live as one wishes."
~ Marcus Tullius Cicero

It's Independence Day here in the U.S., a day to celebrate and relish our freedom.

Back in 2017, I had one of those knock-upside-the-head moments. I'd always wanted to travel the world, taking my business with me. Yet, I'd built a successful business that required me to be there or my leads dried up. Not my idea of freedom.

That was the day I made the decision to design my business to give me the freedom and flexibility to live my bucket list now while I serve my clients from wherever in the world I'm living. Since 2018, I've traveled full time, taking my coaching business with me. That's freedom and independence for me, and I'm so grateful for my life today.

What does freedom mean to you? Only you know the spark that lights you up—that way of being that fills you with joy and that feeling that anything is possible. Give yourself permission to live that life now. To end the shoulds and the somedays and instead take powerful steps toward turning your vision into your reality. Today, be grateful for your freedom to choose.

Sherri Coffelt is the creator of the Freedom Finder Formula, your road map to design your business so you can work *when* you want, from *where* you want. Find out how to connect with Sherri at www.MeetOurAuthors.com.

July 5
Work Story and Multiple Twists
Marla Hall

"Change: walking a path not yet traveled, exploring the unknown and uncovering its hidden treasures." ~ Marla Hall

While five co-workers haven't received the All Hands Meeting email, we each ponder our employment future. Meeting day arrives. Woman's intuition enabled and on high alert. Two hundred people from our Information Technology Division gather. It's our final time together. One other person is present, our very own department head, who we haven't seen in two years. She is offering hellos, hugs and handshakes.

We sit. She stands. She announces we are being outsourced in one month. I guessed right. The transfer of knowledge process is explained. Because most in our 20-person department are vested, leaving isn't an option, or we sacrifice our well-deserved severance package.

We return to the office, somber and uncertain. We learn our five friends were terminated. Five months later, I am one of six assigned to work with our former clients. Appreciative, and 66, I decide to terminate, file for unemployment and regroup.

One facet of my job, I dearly love. I take an advanced training course. One day after earning certification, I received a call from my former employer offering me a consultant position using that very skill. Is that NOT a miracle, an unexpected surprise! Only God knew my plan!

Marla Hall believes you never retire, and as CEO of Your Life Inc., you're never unemployed. Let's ignite your passions and transform those old hours called "work." Find out how to connect with Marla at www.MeetOurAuthors.com.

July 6

Gracious Healing

Fiona-Louise

"Gracious words are a honeycomb, sweet to the soul and healing to the bones." ~ Proverbs 16:23-25

I never thought I would be grateful for becoming ill, but I am.

When I first got sick, I was bedridden for six months, exhausted, depleted, and with not much will to go on. My body had crashed and burned, my mind had shutdown, and my soul had ground to a halt.

Then, slowly but surely, my energy began to return. Step by step, day by day, I was able to accomplish small things, such as having a shower, making a meal, and taking a stroll outside. Things that, when I was healthy, I took for granted. Yet, here I was, appreciating every small milestone on the road back to health.

It was a long journey, with twists and turns, setbacks and relapses. I read every self-help book I could get my hands on, delved into counseling, meditation, yoga, reiki—you name it, I tried it!

But the one thing that helped me turn the corner was gratitude. Changing my mindset to thankfulness has given me an inner strength I didn't realize I had. I now see the illness as a blessing because it inspired me to stop and smell the roses.

Gratitude has revealed beauty, love, and kindness. Gratitude has facilitated forgiveness, mended a broken heart, created peace, reprioritized my life, and enabled healing.

Fiona-Louise is a nutritional therapist, educator, and author. Discover a link to her best-selling book collaborations and musings at www.MeetOurAuthors.com.

July 7
A Month of Heartfelt Reflection
Melody Juge

"Gratitude is not only the greatest of virtues but the parent of all others." ~ Cicero

Each year, I enter this uniquely personal month of celebration with delight and appreciation. July is my birthday month! I don't believe in celebrating solely for a day, but instead I choose to celebrate for this entire month. My approach is something I look forward to each year. I use this time to reflect and savor all the experiences of the past year with gratitude.

Stepping back and viewing the past year of my life with heartfelt appreciation, unexpected awe and often with some amusement. Looking at my year's experiences like pieces of a puzzle, I always feel a renewed joy from the contributions made by those that I have been blessed to share my time with.

As I reflect on all the nuances of my experiences, I begin to plan how I will express my sincere appreciation to those friends and family who have contributed their love and support and made the past year both interesting and pleasurable. Often, I will create notes of appreciation, reminiscing of our shared experiences and expressing thanks for how they have touched my heart. It's this act of expressing my gratitude in joyful appreciation that makes this time ever so meaningful each year.

Melody Juge is founder of Life Income Management™: Creating Income for Life and creator of RetirementSense™, a proprietary retirement planning process. She is an investment advisor registered with fiduciary status. Learn more about Melody at www.MeetOurAuthors.com.

July 8
A Full Circle of Gratitude
Nancy J. Haberstich

"Gratitude turns what we have into enough." ~ Unknown

It was Thanksgiving Day in Liberia. Doris, Jerry and I set out on a two-mile hike through the rubber forest to a leper colony. The residents are elderly, no longer infectious but still ostracized.

I visited a man who was blind with no hands and only a portion of a foot on his one skinny leg. He scooted across the concrete floor of his mud-brick dwelling to welcome me. With no hand to shake and no vision to see the smile I brought him, he still thanked me repeatedly for coming.

Doris says that worse than the physical impairments is the pain of feeling forgotten. We learned that their water pump was broken and the closest water source was nearly a mile away. Jerry was able to fix the pump with the wrench he always carried in his back pocket. The water began flowing along with the gratitude.

As we walked back home, I was overwhelmed with gratitude for my shoes, the feet I had to fill them and good health that enabled me to hike four miles in an afternoon. That day we experienced a full circle of gratitude. For that precious memory, I will always be grateful.

Nancy J. Haberstich, RN MS, creates STEAM resources featuring the nanobugs to help people of all ages understand microbiology and infection prevention. Learn more about Nancy at www.MeetOurAuthors.com.

July 9
The Butterfly Effect
Cory Stickley

"Each of us has cause to think with deep gratitude of those who have lighted the flame within us." ~ Albert Schweitzer

High on a mountainside in Zimbabwe, I momentarily sensed my life's purpose. I felt alive—cloaked in the velvety darkness of the starlit night, moved to tears by this exquisite view of the universe.

Going forward, I longed to recapture that awe-inspiring moment. Why couldn't I feel it?

I protected my true inner self while exploring many paths, searching for connection until the moment that life finally intervened.

Trusting my instincts and hopeful for answers, I booked time to explore my internal conflict using a new technique unlike anything I knew. A unique visualization eliminated deeply hidden fears and anxiety that blocked true self-expression. With them gone, I changed. Life changed.

Can you imagine my joy at feeling connected and alive every day?

With confidence and appreciation, I began to pursue long forgotten dreams. I learned that gratitude must be heartfelt and can be as subtle as the whisper of a butterfly's wings.

After years of suppressing any desire to write creatively, I am now inspired to begin. For that, my gratitude is endless.

My deepest gratitude is reserved for Stacey K. Nye, whose work lit "the flame within" through a simple, elegant transformational technique called The F.I.X. Code. Thank you.

Cory Stickley was born to travel, write, photograph and teach. Her book, *The F.I.X. Code*, shares how she overcame burnout and fear of writing. More at www.MeetOurAuthors.com.

July 10

Grateful for Exercise

Tara Alexandra Kachaturoff

"Take care of your body. It's the only place you have to live."
~ Jim Rohn

Exercise. I love it. I've always loved it—even as a child. I grew up in a sports-oriented community in Southern California. Whether it was swimming at the Olympic-sized pool, riding my bike for miles, or playing tennis, I enjoyed being outside, moving my body and enjoying the beautiful weather year round. That early imprint created a lifelong love for physical exercise.

Over the years my tastes in physical activities modified, and I found myself engaging in martial arts, tai chi, yoga, and my all-time favorite—walking.

As an adult my love of exercise continues. I exercise daily—rain, shine, or snow! Nowadays, my routine includes yoga, assorted stretching exercises, light weights, and a lot of walking. The day isn't complete unless I exercise. While I try to get it done first thing in the morning, I sometimes split it up and do some in the afternoon.

Exercise invigorates my body, infuses it with endorphins and strengthens the connection between mind and body. It fuels me with the best energy to navigate my day—and my life! I'm grateful for the gift of exercise which has not only brought me health and wellness but also happiness.

Tara Alexandra Kachaturoff is a business coach and the creator, producer, and host of *Michigan Entrepreneur*, a weekly television talk show featuring businesses from startup to stellar. Find out more at www.MeetOurAuthors.com.

July 11

The Wedding Day I Became a Mom
Linda Lilyquist

"I did not give you the gift of life; life gave me the gift of you."
~ Unknown

There they are, the three of them. Standing at the end of the red-carpeted aisle is my groom in a perfectly fitted tux with his two little grinning kids. They're waiting for me to join them, not just at the altar but in life. Saying wedding vows, I'm aware of the new life the four of us are beginning. Today, I'm not only a bride, I become a mom.

From the first day I met Jessica and Andrew, they melted my heart and let it flow into theirs. They gave me all the joys any mom could hope for—catching snakes and pollywogs, learning to drive, proms, volleyball camps and basic training, watching each of them walk down their wedding aisles and giving me five amazing grandsons. It's been a full mom experience.

The gift they gave me that wedding day, not only to call me mom but to BE their mom, is the best present I received. The hugs, calls, sharing of life and loving words have remained consistent over these 40 years. God truly did give me the gift of my daughter and son, and I'm grateful for the heart to love them as my very own.

Linda Lilyquist is a speaker, minister and marriage and family therapist in San Diego. She loves family, friends and helping people experience life-changing transformation. Find out how to connect with Linda at www.MeetOurAuthors.com.

July 12

Precious Loaves of Bread

Grace Kusta Nasralla

"Now and then it's good to pause in our pursuit of happiness and just be happy." ~ Guillaume Apollinaire

It was during the time of the war in Lebanon when one day Mom hollered at me to go and get a pack of bread.

There was a bakery beside us and we had to line up to get it, as flour was scarce. I ran down the stairs from our first floor condominium, out the door and down the street where the bakery was to find the line of people extended to the other street block.

In the distance I could hear the sounds of shelling and sniper fire, but we were a family of five and we needed bread for dinner, so I had to stay.

As I waited in line I prayed for safety and provision when suddenly I saw a militia car stop and gunmen come out, go into the bakery and start giving out bread randomly in a rushed manner. They wanted to empty the streets to start a new round of combat. I quickly took my share of bread and fled back home with a grateful heart. Many lives were spared that day.

Gratitude is an attitude that brings joy to the soul even in the middle of strife.

Grace Nasralla is a business instructor and founder of Ontario Small Business Network. More at www.MeetOurAuthors.com.

July 13
The Best Gift
Carol Trant Dean

"Every good gift and every perfect gift comes from above."
~James 1:17

Nine years ago, right before Christmas, I was driving home from my office when I received a call from my daughter. At that time she and her husband lived about eight hours away. Initially, we discussed our day's activities, but I could tell she was rather excited by the tone of her voice.

She then revealed the purpose of her call: She had been to the doctor that day and discovered that she was pregnant with our first grandchild! I was so excited I wanted to shout, but because I was retrieving the mail, I decided against it. We ended our call all too soon with her promising to let me know how she was feeling, when her doctor's appointments were scheduled, the gender of the baby, what colors she wanted to use in the nursery, prospective names for the baby—in summary, everything.

After all, this was to be our very first grandchild and I was over the moon in love already. We have five beautiful grandchildren now that we love dearly, but I'll never forget how thankful we were for our first.

Carol Trant Dean resides in Alabama with her husband and old rescue dog, where she enjoys missions, foreign travel, and especially spending time with her grandchildren. Find out more about Carol at www.MeetOurAuthors.com.

July 14
The Silver Lining
Pam Murphy

"It is only with gratitude that life becomes rich." ~ Dietrich Bonhoeffer

Can you imagine how hard it is to write about gratefulness when you are losing your hearing? This is the project I was given. Actually, it turned out to be a wonderful challenge, which I am grateful to have had. It helped me adjust my mindset.

Mindset is so important. Consider, if you will, losing weight isn't just about what you eat. Growing your wealth isn't just about saving money. Being successful in anything isn't just about being good at it. Mindset is a thread which runs through everything in life and determines your level of success and happiness.

Feeling grateful while losing your hearing is, like most things in life, about mindset. I may not always be able to hear the sounds I treasure. But not being able to hear well has made me appreciate the beauty around me better. Whatever challenge you have in life, the silver lining is that there is still a lot for which to appreciate and be grateful, no matter the left turn your life has taken.

Pam Murphy, MSHN, RRT, is on a mission to help you achieve optimal health. More about Pam at www.MeetOurAuthors.com.

July 15

Let's Create Peace in Our World
Marcelle della Faille

"Gratitude can transform common days into thanksgivings, turn routine jobs into joy, and change ordinary opportunities into blessings." ~ William Arthur Ward

When I feel down and a bit depressed—yes, it happens, even to an expert in universal laws—I focus even more on the tasks that bring me joy: writing, sharing, playing with the Universal Magic in practical situations.

I cannot spend a day without doing this and being in that frequency. And because I chose to teach this concept as my business, and as I decided recently to attune my desires to new values, I feel so blessed by my lifestyle: a great family, a magnificent business community, a beautiful environment, new opportunities and new beginnings.

What I love the most in my work is creating new games with the Universe, expressing gratitude being the primary one.

Each day, I intend to express gratefulness from the minute I'm awake to the minute I fall asleep. And having a community of people listening to my teachings and reading my books helps me to feel grateful for the contribution I'm making to the world. This helps me feel at one with each of my fellow people and at peace with the world.

Let's create peace in our own world today: just be grateful for what is—for you and all of us.

Marcelle della Faille is a writer and trainer of financial abundance coaches, helping them develop their love and passion into a profitable and fulfilling business. Find out more at www.MeetOurAuthors.com.

July 16

Glitter with Gratitude

Carol Stockall

"Sprinkle the world with gratitude, and it sparkles with happiness."
~ Carol Stockall, MD

Like the glitter of fairy dust, gratitude has powerful magic more precious than gold. Gratitude makes eyes twinkle with appreciation and hearts glow with happiness. A simple thank you can take a frown and turn it upside down.

When you show appreciation you can see it smiling right back at you. It's like a hug because when you give one, you get one right back. Who isn't grateful for a thank-you?

The magic of gratitude is a gift that must be opened and shared to be experienced and enjoyed. Tossing out thanks like confetti creates contagious feelings of celebration. Never miss an opportunity to give thanks. Never take a thank-you for granted. Public and private displays of gratitude bring intimacy and intensity to your relationships.

Gratitude is also a gift you give yourself. Counting your blessings is a healing salve for a weary soul. An attitude of gratitude creates a paradigm shift that can turn your burdens into blessings and your sadness into gladness.

Let gratitude spark your joy. Make counting your blessings and sharing your gratitude with others a daily habit. Begin and end each day sprinkling "thank-yous" and watch your world sparkle with happiness.

Carol Stockall, MD, is a physician, coach and counselor who inspires people to build resilience and flourish. Find out more at www.MeetOurAuthors.com.

July 17
Another Day with Charlie and Eli
Dale Troy

"No one appreciates the very special genius of your conversation as the dog does." ~ Christopher Morley

My daily routine wouldn't be the same without them. Every morning, I hear Charlie and Eli scratching at my bedroom door while I'm still enveloped in my weighted blanket. My husband opens the door a crack, and they bound in, headed straight for my side of the bed.

I reach my hand down to feel their silky, brown coats, and I open my eyes. When I see their fluffy tails wagging with excitement, I smile. They encourage me to get out of my cozy bed to start the day. Without them by my side, it would be so easy to turn over and go back to sleep.

Once I'm up, Charlie and Eli become my trusted companions. They won't leave my side. Whether I'm going down the stairs to eat breakfast or down the hall to put in a load of laundry, they accompany me.

When the doorbell rings, they protect me with their barks. While I'm working at my desk, they sleep close by, never wanting to lose sight of me. At night, I rub their tummies and tuck them into their dog beds with a soft blanket.

I'm grateful to have Charlie and Eli in my life.

Dale Troy, college success coach, teaches students the skills and habits needed to thrive in college. Dale and her three daughters graduated from Yale. More at www.MeetOurAuthors.com.

July 18

I Am So Grateful!

Michelle Francik

"We often take for granted the very things that most deserve our gratitude." ~ Cynthia Ozick

I'm grateful for the multitude of scars across my belly because they show that I am a survivor. They show that my life has not been easy. They show that I know how to heal.

I'm grateful for my two sons. Each of them is a joy, a source of pride and a pain in the butt, just like their mama. One is friendly, talkative, anxious and wants to be the center of attention. One is quiet, reflective, laid back and serious. But they are both good men, and they know how to love and to be respectful. Even If I have done nothing else right in my life, I have raised two fine men.

I'm grateful for my son's cat, Oreo. Even though he likes to jump onto my bed and roll into my face, waking me up and making me sneeze, he loves me even when I'm cranky. Even when I'm sick.

I'm grateful for being alive. The pain is incredible; the fear is immobilizing. But every morning the sun comes up. Every morning I have another opportunity to make today the very best day of my life. And I'm grateful that I'm being given that opportunity.

Michelle Francik is a writer and a ghostwriter. You can find out how to connect with her at www.MeetOurAuthors.com.

July 19

Health Is Wealth

Michelle Barrial

"The greatest wealth is health." ~ Virgil

I am most grateful for my health and my life since I have had my share of health crises. I almost didn't make it to being alive at birth since I had the umbilical cord wrapped around my body. My mother said the doctors called for emergency backup as a code blue.

When I was less than a year I almost died from pneumonia and had to be hospitalized for a week in intensive care. Many years later, I noticed I was dropping weight due to hemorrhaging during my menstrual cycle, which was increasingly painful, and I had severe anemia.

My doctor told me I had to have a hysterectomy to remove two large fibroids from my uterus. I was worried and scared since I hadn't had surgery before.

But, after I recovered from the surgery, I felt like I received quality of life back since I had no pain, no more shortness of breath, and I could run and walk again. I feel blessed and have transformed my life through yoga and dietary changes.

I know that having good health is wealth!

Michelle Barrial is a life transformation coach who specializes in helping people through difficult life changes to get clarity and feel peace of mind. More at www.MeetOurAuthors.com.

July 20
Legacy Adventures with Dad
Marla Hall

"At birth, Dad held me close to his heart.
Today, he lives in my heart forever." ~ Marla Hall

It's Saturday. My girlfriend and I sit at the soda fountain at the Rexall Drug Store, corner of Hollywood & Vine. My father is the store manager. One, two, three, smile. Camera clicks. Photoshoot over. And it's ice cream sundae time with Lawrence Welk.

Dad's surprises continue. He tells me to tune into Dick Whittinghill's radio program when I wake up—that's 4 a.m. The DJ calls out my name and informs the listeners I'm up studying! What!

Ten years older and workday Saturday with Dad. He sets me up in his office with assigned tasks. Completed and paid. Next mission: Shop at The Broadway department store.

When I return, two handsome young men approach, inquiring the location of the Jewish New Year's cards. We talk and walk. They are engineering students from Iran. I give one my phone number. My father laughs at my being "picked up" right in front of him.

Friday night tradition includes watching boxing matches. TV trays in place. Mom serves lamb chops and veggies, followed by ice cream. I scream, cover my eyes and share a special evening as Dad's best bud.

He's gone now. Remembering cherished moments brings endless smiles. I love my dad.

Marla Hall believes you never retire, and as CEO of Your Life Inc., you're never unemployed. Let's blaze a new pathway for those old hours called "work." Learn more about Marla at www.MeetOurAuthors.com.

July 21

A Daily Gift in "Thank You"

Mary Anne Strange

"A heartfelt 'thank you' are two of the most powerful words we can say." ~ Mary Anne Strange

In my family, opening presents has always been a special ceremony. Presents are wrapped and opened with care, appreciation and gratitude. I love giving presents, and to this day it is a way of making someone feel both special and valued. Yet I benefit too, as there is pleasure in the giving.

Physical gifts work well when spaced over time or for special occasions. The gift of gratitude can be present daily through the spoken word. Many of us were trained as children to say "thank you." It was, though, as an adult that I discovered the power of those words.

In today's busy world, people appreciate it when you pause to acknowledge their efforts. A sincere "thank you" is simple and efficient. Expand the thank-you with some detail to increase the direct appreciation and impact.

A few years ago, my husband was driving me to the station. We were in a rush. Stress was in the air. I paused and said, "Thank you for going to such trouble to help me catch the train." My husband beamed and we both felt calmer.

And that is the secret of gratitude and the words thank you. The recipient feels valued and acknowledged. But gratitude also makes the speaker feel happier, more present and connected.

Mary Anne Strange helps entrepreneurs master the art of sharing their message and becoming more visible through live and virtual public speaking. More at www.MeetOurAuthors.com.

July 22
The Joy of Doing Nothing
Shari-Jayne Boda

"A happy life must be to a great extent a quiet life, for it is only in an atmosphere of quiet that true joy dare live." ~ Bertrand Russell

I've never been a morning person. For years I've secretly craved the superpower that belongs to those who bounce out of bed at 5 a.m. bursting with energy and eager to tackle a to-do list that would make Superman feel inadequate.

I've dreamed of watching the sunrise while stretching into all manner of yoga contortions, lifting my own bodyweight at the gym or discovering the meaning of life in a dawn meditation. After all, getting more done is the whole point of adding extra hours to your day, right?

For months I tried. My heart and even my head were willing, but I still wasn't "feeling it." Eventually, I conceded that my body preferred sleep to self-improvement and the overwhelming pressure to be a 5 a.m. multitasker was finally lifted.

For posterity I vowed that, for one last time, I would rise early but I would do simply nothing. Sipping coffee in the garden, I basked in the sun's warm embrace while two visiting ducks frolicked in the pond beside me. Enchanted by the stillness, I realized that the joy of being an early riser comes purely from being in the moment and doing nothing at all.

Shari-Jayne Boda is an international spiritual life and prosperity coach, hypnotherapist and counselor who guides people to live authentically and in tune with their higher self. Connect with her at www.MeetOurAuthors.com.

July 23
Favorite Photographs
Rich Liotta

"Taking an image, freezing a moment, reveals how rich reality truly is." ~ Unknown

I fondly remember family as I look at a black-and-white picture of my sister in her bell-bottoms, jean jacket and peasant blouse, smiling at me with her head tilted inquisitively.

Beautiful landscapes taken from the top of the Adirondack Mountains take me back to glorious hikes with my dog. The gestalt of the moment resurfaces—the vista, the breeze, the feeling of that day.

My heart smiles at my wife and I dressed as a witch and wizard one Halloween. So many captured moments of laughter with friends and loved ones reflect a life well lived.

Reviewing newer photographs keeps fun fresh. I feel joy looking at pictures of our cute and curious springer-doodle puppy growing every day.

I celebrate my life by looking at photographs through a lens of gratitude! Old photographs refresh blurry memories and make them vivid again. Though some photographs are bittersweet, such as those of people I have lost, I do not censor the feelings that arise. Instead, I focus on the positive in the memory, the good that was, keeping the negative in perspective. Reminiscing inspires gratitude with awareness of how life continues to unfold and evolve.

Gratitude for my favorite photographs enriches my soul!

Rich Liotta, Ph.D., is a psychologist, coach, writer and photographer. Find more information and inspiration on his blog or Facebook page, Enrichments for Mind & Spirit. Find out more about Rich at www.MeetOurAuthors.com.

July 24
Be Grateful for Every Day
Linda Faulk

"Embrace every new day with gratitude, hope, and love." ~ Lailah Gifty Akita

You are not the same person that you were yesterday. Whatever happened yesterday is finished. You may have been wronged, you may have been hurt or you may have hurt someone else. But today you have a fresh start. Even on good days, I am grateful for another fresh start. I learned this lesson of daily gratitude long ago but still practice it today.

When my husband died many years ago, I thought it was the end of my life as well. I could not see past my own pain. Then I got a health scare myself. I prayed for another day and vowed that I would embrace each day I was granted. I gave thanks for the next day, and every day since. Just a simple step of being grateful brought me from depression and gave me the courage to begin again. Thirty years later, I am still grateful.

All life's blessings begin with gratitude. Spend a few minutes each morning to jot down all the things you are grateful for and your day will improve. Use a few minutes each night to do the same and you will sleep better. And with each new day, give thanks.

Linda Faulk is a high school math teacher, writer, and entrepreneur. More at www.MeetOurAuthors.com.

July 25

Sweet Moments

Tammy Atchley

"Life is not measured by the number of breaths we take but by the moments that take our breath away." ~ Maya Angelou

The first moment I saw those tiny hands and feet. The beautiful sound of a delicate cry filling the room. Holding my firstborn son in my arms and kissing those soft, chubby cheeks.

These are the sweet memories that take my breath away.

That tiny, sweet baby of mine is now a man, a husband and a daddy. He has a tiny, sweet baby of his own. What a thrill it is as a mother to watch your son as he holds his newborn daughter. To see him snuggle her in his arms while caressing her soft, chubby cheeks and giving the gentlest kiss on her forehead.

All those years of teaching him what it means to be a man, a good man. Teaching him right from wrong and how to treat his family, then witnessing it firsthand. How exciting to see my baby boy first become a man, then a father. Life could not get any better than this.

Until he puts his newborn daughter in her crib, sits me down and, with tears in his eyes, thanks me for being a good mom.

These are the sweet memories that take my breath away.

Tammy Atchley is a parenting coach that helps moms learn how to have those difficult conversations with their children. Find out how to connect with Tammy at www.MeetOurAuthors.com.

July 26
The Path I Walk
Julie Roy

"One tree makes thousands of matches; one careless match incinerates thousands of trees." ~ The author at 13 years old

I look to the north. Vibrant hues like an emerald forest saturate my senses. I'm captivated by the sensation of symmetry—perfectly balanced, lush, leafy green branches adorning straight trunks thrive in harmony with a healthy forest.

I look to the south. Shades of black, grey, dusty, khaki green resembling an abandoned, sooty scrap heap tear at my heart. I cringe and look away from the twisted, broken, burnt trees. With a deep breath, I walk south into the burn scar, into the unknown.

Skeleton-like, leafless oaks subsist with distorted, blackened, barren pine branches. Such devastation! Such sadness! I see rocky hillsides exposed like Mother Earth's bare bosom. Charred relics of magnificent giants reduced to rubble. The recent rain carried ashes into pools of sullied sludge that often block my path. Yet, the burn scar beckons. Acres of ghostlike, scorched woodland lay ahead. The firefighter's defense line now becomes evident.

As I turn right, I catch a glimpse of green. Wide-eyed, I look closer. There, at the base of several delicate ribbonwood trees, sprouts a few inches of renewed life, a few inches of hope, a few inches of beauty. Filled with gratitude now, I continue on the path.

Julie Roy, author, business coach and former alpaca owner, helps alpaca owners with their sales and marketing strategies to increase their income dramatically. Find out how to connect with Julie at www.MeetOurAuthors.com.

July 27
Of Wrinkles and Doc
Karole Hough

"Age should not have its face lifted, but it should rather teach the world to admire wrinkles as the etchings of experience and the firm line of character." ~ Ralph B. Perry

2017: This day, July 27, was our anniversary. Doc, my husband William, had been diagnosed with multiple myeloma cancer the month before, and it had progressed rapidly. Now, on our 48th anniversary, he was admitted to the ICU. Two weeks later, he went into hospice care and died four days later.

I look back on our 48 years as a blessing. We had our ups and downs. We didn't always agree. His profession as a family practice physician often took him away on our date nights and special family occasions.

But together we laughed often. We grew as a couple and as individuals. He encouraged me to become whoever and whatever I needed to be, including a counselor and a life coach. Together we raised three children and were then blessed with 16 grandchildren.

Without Doc, I wouldn't be the person I am today. I hope any wrinkles I have can testify that I have weathered some life storms, overcome challenges, and dealt with sorrows. But even better, I have laugh lines and love lines to prove that my life with Doc was a life of joy.

And for that, I am truly grateful.

Karole Hough (pronounced "huff") is a life coach who encourages former family caregivers to find purpose beyond the loss of their loved one. Find out how to connect with Karole at www.MeetOurAuthors.com.

July 28

Ritualize a Life of Gratitude

Leasha West

"Gratitude is one of life's remarkable shortcuts to happiness."
~ Unknown

Remember when you were a kid and adults always taught you to say thank you? Somehow, when we grow up, saying thank you tends to subside and, with some, is eliminated altogether. I believe this is not due to a shortage of things to be thankful for but rather a lack of mindfulness.

To cultivate a mindfulness of gratitude, I have two surefire rituals to bring appreciation to the forefront of your life.

First, start a gratitude journal. Every night before bed, record 10 things you are thankful for. Coming up with 10 things daily forces you to give thought and closely evaluate your life. Keep the journal by your bed and habitually do this every night. As you incorporate this ritual, each day you will become aware of more things you are grateful for.

Next, send a minimum of two handwritten thank-you or congratulatory notes each week. This ritual will cause you to look for opportunities to write your sentiments of gratitude and celebrate another person's win. Receiving a handwritten note in this digital age is special and memorable.

These two powerful rituals will improve satisfaction with your life.

And don't forget to say thank you.

Leasha West is the CEO of West Financial Group, decorated Marine Corps veteran, member of Million Dollar Round Table and Forbes Finance Council. More at www.MeetOurAuthors.com.

July 29

Sam

Diana Bianchi

"Dogs have a way of finding the people who need them, and filling an emptiness we didn't ever know we had." ~ Thom Jones

One, two, three, four... I slowly inhale and then count again until four while keeping the air in my lungs and then exhale counting to eight. I do it two more times, eyes closed.

Next stage: I'm setting my focus on my heart area, and I'm calling the image of my cute, small, furry ball of love, Sam. As soon as I picture him, sleeping all curled up or joyfully playing around me, my heart has widely opened and sent waves of energy for miles around. I'm ready now to connect to the Akashic record field.

I was using heart-opening techniques from the moment I was taught reiki years before, but it never felt so easy to be in the state of gratitude as it is now, picturing my dog, or, I might say, becoming aware of the waves of love he's always sending me.

I'm literally melting each and every time this is happening, and this state of pure love he's bringing me into is the best gift I could ever receive. I'll be forever grateful to him for this.

Diana Bianchi is an intuitive business coach helping entrepreneurs create their successful business as a playground of self-expression, using Akashic records readings. Find out more at www.MeetOurAuthors.com.

July 30

Gratitude Works!

Carol Caffey

"In everything, give thanks." ~ St. Paul the Apostle

What? Give thanks in absolutely everything? It turns out that is excellent advice. Scientific studies show being grateful is a way to increase happiness and satisfaction with your life. Studies also indicate gratitude benefits your physical health in dozens of ways.

Expressing your gratitude to the people around you in tangible ways even increases the rewards. One of them is that your relationships will be more fulfilling. Loving ties will be strengthened. People will want to be around this genuinely positive energy.

It is also especially rewarding to list things you are grateful for every day. It doesn't even have to be on paper. Reminding yourself often during the day of whatever you are grateful for is a powerfully good habit to cultivate.

It seems to be a truism that whatever we focus on increases. It helps in the going to sleep process to think about things that happened during the day that you are grateful for. It is an effective tool for getting to sleep and a way to program yourself for good things to happen tomorrow.

Thankfulness reaps a bountiful harvest, and the fields are always ready to be harvested.

Carol Caffey is a forever student of how to live better on the planet. Find out more at www.MeetOurAuthors.com.

July 31
The Best Worst Thing
Rachel A. Kowalski

*"Life is a series of thousands of tiny miracles.
Notice them." ~ Unknown*

Neil Young was softly singing in the background, "There's a full moon rising; let's go dancing in the light…I want to see you dance again…on this Harvest Moon," as my mom and I lightly two-stepped around her hospital room.

She had recently undergone surgery to remove a brain tumor, which thankfully turned out to be nonmalignant. Her doctors encouraged our dance sessions, as they not only lifted her spirits but also aided in the reconnection of her brain synapses.

Thinking back to those days of her recovery, I can still envision her smiling face, her head wrapped in bandages, and hear her sweet, contagious giggle-laugh as we twirled around the room.

Prior to my mom's brain tumor, I was moodier and had a sharper temper. After spending five-plus months in the hospital and during recovery with my mom, I now have a different lens on life. Are those who I love and care about alive and kicking? Yes? Then anything else is manageable. I've learned to take life in stride and enjoy every moment.

This is why my mom's brain tumor was the best worst thing that ever happened to me, and I am forever grateful for the experience.

Rachel A. Kowalski is an attorney, ghostwriter and creative force behind Free Wave Productions Inc. Find out more at www.MeetOurAuthors.com.

August

August 1
The Gift of Gratitude
Dr. Helen Holton

"When you have an attitude of gratitude you wake up saying thank you." ~ Maya Angelou

Gratitude is an attitude that elevates your altitude. Most people have heard some version of this statement at least once. What does it mean to you? When you awaken to a new day does it begin with a grateful heart? Where's your gratitude in times of trouble?

One of the darkest periods of my life taught me the resilient power of gratitude. Going inward to find your strength and resolve to get through combined with a gratitude mindset will change your life.

Shifting your attitude plays a major role in getting you beyond what seems impossible. How do I know? I did it, lived through it, and have witnessed the transformation of others.

What's the secret?

Consistency. Building a system of daily habits and practices works. It will increase your capacity for joy, peace, love, and contentment. It's doable if you do it. Unlock your potential to be more, do more, and have more than you ever thought possible. Distress, disruption, and "dis-ease" can rob you of your life. Gratitude helps you reclaim it. Your attitude about any situation in your life is directly connected to your reservoir of gratitude.

How deep is the well that stores your gratitude?

Dr. Helen Holton is a Gallup-certified strengths coach and thought leader in diversity, equity, and inclusion. She's a resilience guru who works with leaders to achieve more success and less stress. More at www.MeetOurAuthors.com.

August 2
Sisters Day
Carole MacLean

"Chance made us sisters; our hearts made us friends." ~ Unknown

Sisters Day? Who knew the first Sunday of August is dedicated to that person who, if you are lucky enough to have a good one, means so much?

I've not just one but two good ones, who, for over 60 years, have been my cohorts, confidants and co-conspirators.

Sandy is two years older. Growing up, we would play with our tiny troll dolls, braiding their wild, neon-colored hair and making troll houses out of cardboard coat boxes from Macy's. Our joyful giggles filled the bedroom we shared.

Chris is five years older. I called her Tee-tee because when I was little I couldn't pronounce Christine. She was there for me when my heart was broken in college and when I needed money to buy my first car.

Our lives weave in and out with varying degrees of closeness based on geography, careers, family challenges, but we continue to nurture our relationships and make each other a priority.

It's not by chance that my sisters are forever connected to me. It's our hearts that have made us available for support, a shoulder to cry on or just a good belly laugh—and that's worth celebrating at least once a year.

Carole MacLean is retired and volunteers for local hospices by singing with the Threshold Choir. She conducts women's retreats, enjoys yoga, hiking, scrapbooking and blogs about self care. Learn more about Carole at www.MeetOurAuthors.com.

August 3

A Paper-Route Wedding

Linda Lilyquist

"Nothing fancy, just love." ~ Unknown

Howard and Lula Belle were on their paper route that morning of August 1940, traveling through the rutted back roads of Tennessee. My dad's car was a luxury item even with its wheels that would sometimes need my mom to get out and aim to make the next curve. They were in it headed to the home of the justice of the peace. Their plan was to deliver his paper as well as have him perform their marriage ceremony.

The excited couple had planned ahead that Sunday and picked up their cousin Effie to be a witness of the grand event. They pulled up in the car under the giant oak tree in the judge's front yard. He was eating breakfast. Could they wait? Of course! What else did they have to do besides finish their paper route? As the judge came toward them, they were snuggled up close in the front seat. He began the vows, which they faithfully recited to one another.

The best part is they honored that car and didn't even get out. As my mom would quip 67 years later, "Why get out? It took, didn't it?" Yes, Mom and Dad. I'm grateful it did.

Linda Lilyquist is a speaker, retreat leader, minister and marriage family therapist residing in San Diego. She loves family, friends and helping people experience life-changing transformation. Find out how to connect with Linda at www.MeetOurAuthors.com.

August 4

Second Chance at Family

Luisa Falsetto

"If you find it in your heart to care for somebody else, you will have succeeded." ~ Maya Angelou

We were estranged for a very long time all because I listened to peoples' stories, for I thought you didn't care or love me. If only I didn't listen to others. I am so very grateful we reconciled seven years ago today.

I am grateful to my sister Sandra for facilitating our reconciliation. Since that day, my soul has been singing happy tunes. Although we were apart, you were always in my thoughts and in my heart.

I remember you always made certain we had an abundance of food so we would not go without. I remember you told me, "Daddy loves you." I remember growing up as a child times when my siblings and I would argue. You always told us to do our best to get along, for we are sisters and brother, and we should love one another. Because of you, my siblings will always have a special place in my heart.

I am grateful that we are in each other's lives, for we are now creating new, beautiful memories together. Today you have taught me self-forgiveness; for that, I am so ever grateful. I know now you always loved me, even when we were apart.

Luisa is a conceptual thinker, author, writer, facilitator and believes in lifelong learning. She is a natural leader, and her ability to help others is her ultimate desire. Find out how to connect with Luisa at www.MeetOurAuthors.com.

August 5

Thankful for a Stitch

Joel Bloom

"Enjoy the little things, for one day you may look back and realize they were the big things." ~ Robert Brault

Don't you just LOVE to laugh? It can be so wonderfully contagious, ease away tension, and even exercise your abs!

I am so grateful for the role of laughter in my life. Some of my favorite memories of my departed brother and parents have everything to do with being brought closer together and laughing at a joke or a TV show. Now, older with my own family, laughter is just as present.

My wife has been known to literally laugh so hard she gets a stitch in her side, and my daughter will often laugh so hard she cries! I am so thankful we are all actively overcoming our "negativity bias," something scientists say we humans have evolved with, where we are predisposed to more prominently feel negative emotions like stress and fear. Doesn't calm and positive sound so much better?

Kids don't have to make a conscious effort to laugh like adults; they laugh naturally and far more often than adults, according to studies. Thankfully Siri and Alexa can now tell us jokes, so there is truly no excuse not to help yourself and others laugh all the way to feeling happier and healthier every day!

Joel Bloom is a loving father and husband whose lifelong goals include helping others to move in a positive direction in their lives. Find out more at www.MeetOurAuthors.com.

August 6

My Happy Place
Roberta Gold

"For whatever we lose (like a you or a me) / it's always ourselves we find in the sea." ~ e.e. cummings

I am in my happy place as I bury my toes into the wet sand and let the cool, refreshing Pacific Ocean waves break on my ankles. The sun has begun its majestic descent, and I have the perfect spot to watch the sky burst into brilliant hues of rose and purple.

I have always had a special relationship with the ocean, and it has never failed me whether I am floating on top of the rolling waves, swimming out, hoping to be with the dolphins or diving to explore the incredible underwater wonders. I am in awe of the powerful pull the sea has on my heart. I feel a freedom unlike any other. A freedom from all the weight I have put upon myself. I am free to fill up my soul with the beauty I never tire to breathe in.

I capture this feeling so I can conjure it up when I need a respite from the daily hustle and bustle I get caught up in. A feeling so pure and pleasurable, it puts me at peace. I feel blessed to be able to be a part of this glorious earth. I am in my happy place

Roberta Gold, RTC, CHP, created Laughter for the Health of it and Laughter Rocks! She's an inspiring speaker, author and an attitude adjustment coach. Find out more about Roberta and her offerings at www.MeetOurAuthors.com.

August 7
A Parent's Love
Heather Aquilina

"To understand your parents' love,
you must raise children yourself." ~ Chinese Proverb

This special day would bring us all together. You said, "I do," and the story of your entwined life began and the stories of five small lives that you created. It's been a tale of adventure round the world. A tale of work. A mundane story of everyday life, everyday laughs and struggles, tasks and pastimes, the everyday humdrum that makes up time on Earth.

Mum: You gave me attention, teaching, guidance. I know it hurts that I rejected your most precious beliefs for my life. These differences lie starkly between us, dividing us. Be sure that there are myriad other things you taught that I keep with me—a love of learning, teaching, walking, singing, guiding.

Dad: You took me with you to explore your many wondrous worlds—car maintenance, carpentry, sound effects for amateur theatre, soldering, TV crime series…Being by your side was a special gift to share.

Together, you gave me four mates to play and fight and be with. Most of all, you gave, and give me still, the both of you to love me and support me when I need it most. I say thank you for this day you said, "I do."

Heather Aquilina is a habitual learner working to balance running a management consultancy with communicating authentically through her writing and art in the hope of inspiring others. More about Heather at www.MeetOurAuthors.com.

August 8

The Wonderful Lure of Mushrooms
Carla Parvin

"Everybody needs beauty...places to play in and pray in where nature may heal and cheer and give strength to the body and soul alike." ~ John Muir

For me, that place has always been the woods. I am grateful for every chance to be in the woods because that is where I find mushrooms—tasty, healthy, soul-saving mushrooms.

Mushrooms are tasty (think chanterelles in cream sauce) and a great source of healthy nonmeat protein. My husband shares my love of mushrooms—they lure us out of the house and into the woods, and I am grateful for that.

We grew up playing in the woods, spending every possible moment outside. But as we became adults, the woods became an ever-smaller part of life as raising a family consumed our time. In our 60s, arthritis came calling and the woods retreated even further from our lives.

Then I discovered mushrooms. I learned how to find and identify them, how to cook them, how to grow them—I was hooked. My husband started going with me. We explored acres of woods on an ATV, and we were in heaven. The ATV gave us legs—four-wheel drive legs, no less!

After a few productive trips where chanterelles, lion's mane and black trumpets were found (resulting in delightful feasts), he, too, was hooked.

Our mantra has become: "Mushrooms are calling, and we must go."

Carla Parvin (wife and mother of three with two grandchildren) is a writer and operations manager of WNC Woman magazine. She muses on mushrooms and other topics at her website. Find out more at www.MeetOurAuthors.com.

August 9
Four Powerful Paws
Steve Sponseller

"Such short little lives our pets have to spend with us, and they spend most of it waiting for us to come home each day." ~John Grogan

Four paws left a permanent impression on my heart! I'm grateful that I had an opportunity to spend almost 16 years with Harley, a yellow labrador retriever who was an important part of our family.

Harley had a unique personality and always seemed to know what I was thinking. On many occasions when I was deep in thought, I would notice him sitting quietly and looking at me. As soon as he saw me look up, he came over to visit me—always wagging his tail.

He knew I was busy but also understood it was time to say "hi" when my critical thinking was done.

Harley was a master at communicating through his body language—wagging his tail, turning his head sideways, or running in circles. He knew what I was feeling and just wanted to help me by being nearby. If I was sad, he would jump around and act silly. If I was stressed, he would just stand next to me until I started petting him—a fantastic stress reliever!

I'm grateful for the years I spent with Harley and appreciate the many lessons he taught me about communicating and interacting with others.

Steve Sponseller is an intellectual property attorney who helps entrepreneurs and business leaders identify and protect their innovative ideas. Find out more at www.MeetOurAuthors.com.

August 10

The Moon and the Sun
Holly Pitas

"It's not what you look at that matters, it's what you see."
~ Henry David Thoreau

Each night as I'm headed to bed I walk down the hallway and look out the window to see a perfect view of the moon. Some nights it's only a sliver, on other nights clouds create a mysterious frame. It may be the way the window glass refracts the light, but most nights I see the light beams of the moon stretch out into the arms of the cross.

I say a prayer of thanks for all of the wonderful gifts in my life—my husband, my family, which is ever expanding into the next generation, my loving dogs, fulfilling work, my good friends and the new opportunities that will come my way. I am aware that I am blessed to live in a safe place filled with love and abundance. My life is full.

I feel like this sight of an illuminated cross is a reminder that this life is a gift, and we are to be a gift for those around us. Was I a gift to someone today? For any of my infractions, I hope to have another chance tomorrow when the day will begin with the new light of the sun.

Holly Pitas has decades of experience as both a family and a professional caregiver. She's the author of *Don't Get Caught Naked: Tips for the Adult Family Home Caregiver*, and you can learn more at www.MeetOurAuthors.com.

August 11

Giving Thanks for the Brains
Heather Aquilina

"Intelligence is like underwear. It's important that you have it but not necessary that you show it off." ~ Unknown

I'm grateful to be me. Some days are hard. Frustration, disappointment, discouragement can visit me. When I pine for a different present filled with all my dreams come true—more life, more fun, more things, more love, more meaning. Those days are hard, and they may linger for a time.

But I'm grateful to be me. Grateful to be born with intelligence to spare, which feeds a curiosity and burning need to analyze and understand all that I encounter. Intelligence that has brought me work to sustain me, and the means to take care of myself.

And, while I might from time to time take a dip into the misty depths of sadness, jealousy, regret, it does not last long. Soon I'm distracted by a darting flash of life—a bird, the glinting sun casting shadowed patterns, the sound of laughter, the softness of a cat against my leg. Tiny moments call me back awake to life around me and remind me I have everything I really need. I am endlessly lucky and grateful to be me.

Heather Aquilina is a habitual learner working to balance running a management consultancy with communicating authentically through her writing and art in the hope of inspiring others. More at www.MeetOurAuthors.com.

August 12

A Heart of Thanksgiving

Letitia Hicks

"I am grateful for what I am and have. My thanksgiving is perpetual."
~ Henry David Thoreau

Thanksgiving means the act of giving thanks. The Bible says we should give thanks to God, the one who created the heavens and the earth. I give thanks to God in anticipation of answering my prayers, knowing that His answers will always be in accordance with His perfect will for my life. First Thessalonians 5:18 states, "In everything give thanks, for this is the will of God in Christ Jesus for you." I thank God for His mercy and love for me each day.

Thanksgiving is inseparable from prayer. When I pray, I give thanks and praise God for all things. As I make my request known, I do not exclude thanksgiving. Every situation I face in life, good or bad, is a subject of gratitude and thankfulness. I always give God thanks for my daily provisions.

I give God thanks for my body, mind and spirit. I am always grateful to God for his blessings. Giving thanks to God is as natural as breathing. I have a heart of thanksgiving each day, thanking God for my family, friends, health and career. Do you have a heart of thanksgiving?

Letitia Hicks is a women empowerment strategist, entrepreneur, minister and author. She helps to transform the lives of women with a renewed sense of power, passion and purpose. Find her at www.MeetOurAuthors.com.

August 13
The Gift of Three Words
Kamin Samuel

"Being deeply loved by someone gives you strength, while loving someone deeply gives you courage." ~ Lao Tzu

I was older when I got married on this day 10 years ago. I had a lot of time to think about what I wanted to create in a relationship and a partnership.

I chose three key characteristics to be the hallmark of my marriage: kindness, love and respect. Those three words have guided me to come from a higher consciousness in every interaction with my husband. What I didn't know was that, by choosing those three words, I would experience more joy, more laughter and more gratitude each and every day.

When we started our journey together, we wrote love notes to each other—a tradition that continues to this day. Here's one that I read often: "Kamin, you are my joy, my love, my true believer. I am so grateful you chose me, and I am blessed every day to hear your laughter and be loved by you!"

Here's one of mine: "Mark, I love you beyond words! You light up my life in so many extraordinary ways. Thank you for loving me so completely. I love you more every day."

I am eternally grateful to know this kind of love, which started with three simple words.

Kamin Samuel is an international rapid transformation business coach specializing in helping people reinvent themselves and transform stuck beliefs and behaviors to accelerate growth, performance and wealth. Learn more about Kamin at www.MeetOurAuthors.com.

August 14

My Dirty Little Secret

Nancy J. Haberstich

"If you don't own a dog, there is not necessarily anything wrong with you, but there may be something wrong with your life." ~ Roger A. Caras

It was just a week ago that I was banished from the big house to the dog house. The offense? After a long, soaking rain, the backyard was deliciously muddy. I came into the big house expecting dinner and instead got the wrath of HumanMom. She obviously didn't appreciate my muddy footprints on the kitchen floor and the wonderful fragrance I had collected outside.

I ended up in the doghouse for one long, uncomfortable night. But Alex says I was "saved by science" when he showed his A+ research paper on the human microbiome to HumanMom as Exhibit A in my defense. (I'm sure glad I didn't eat that homework assignment!) Apparently, scientific research now shows that canines serve as a natural conduit for healthy species of bacteria found in soil to enter the indoor environment and ultimately make it to the human gut. Now, that makes me a hero because a healthy, diverse microbiome improves immunity in humans, reduces the development of allergies and asthma in children, and improves mood and emotions.

This redeeming quality of dogs is not found in cats (indoor cats don't go outside, and outdoor cats don't come inside). Don't get me started on that.

Nancy J. Haberstich, RN MS, creates STEAM resources featuring the nanobugs to help people of all ages understand microbiology and infection prevention. Learn more about Nancy at www.MeetOurAuthors.com.

August 15
A Grateful Day
LaVerne M. Byrd

"If you haven't any charity in your heart, you have the worst kind of heart trouble." ~ Bob Hope

Lulu has always expressed concern for the homeless. Even as a young child her heart would break whenever the commercial about hungry children came on the television. So it became natural for her to give money or clothing to charitable organizations. She also volunteered to prepare meals that would be distributed to senior citizens.

Over the years Lulu's employer noticed her efforts to help people in need. The employer decided to set aside a day of "giving back to the community" and appointed her as the leader of the event.

Lulu decided she would adopt a neighborhood school as a charitable outlet. After much planning, the big day arrived for distributing the items. Lulu called a meeting to thank everyone for participating. Because of their compassion, the company was able to supply each student with every item needed to succeed in the classroom.

The overwhelming joy and excitement from the children could not be contained. It became a ripple effect. Everyone was laughing and shedding tears at the same time. That day will no doubt change many lives. It was a lesson for both the receiver and the giver. It was indeed a grateful day!

LaVerne M. Byrd is the author of *Heal My Pain, A Journal for Grieving Mothers.* She has recently started a blog, "The Journey of Grief." More at www.MeetOurAuthors.com.

August 16

The Transformative Power of Love
Carol Brusegar

"This I know for sure: it is not judgment or isolation that changes us. It is love. Love can transform our negative experiences into new realities. I am so grateful." ~ Carol Brusegar

I had never anticipated standing before groups of inmates in multiple correctional institutions to talk about the power of love. There I was, a silver-haired woman over 70 years of age, disarming them by asking if I reminded them of a grandmother, mother or aunt—or a do-gooder church lady. We all agreed that we make immediate assumptions about people. Then I proceeded to tell my story.

I spoke of years being on "the other side" of the picture as a crime victim multiple times, having friends shot and even killed, and working for the police department. I described how my very first time participating in prison visits with Timothy's Gift Prison Ministry shifted my perspective profoundly. My negative experiences were transformed into a deep passion for this outreach.

The message that people's attitudes can change gives hope to inmates. They express gratitude for that, and for our core messages: "You are Loved," "You Have Great Worth," "You are Not Forgotten." I am profoundly grateful for the transformative power of love available to all of us and for the opportunity to communicate that to people who need it so desperately.

Carol Brusegar is the author of *Create Your Third Age, Steps to Making Your Years Past Fifty Fulfilling and Joyful* and related books. Find out more at www.MeetOurAuthors.com.

August 17

The Healing Power of Crochet

Gwyn Goodrow

"Crochet is an accessible art that comes with a license to be prolific." ~ Francine Toukou

A crochet hook and a few colorful scraps of yarn were only the beginning when my mother taught me how to crochet. As a child, I played with crochet patterns and stitches. Yarn transformed into complicated knots of woven fabric. My mother and grandmothers encouraged crafting and lovingly shared technical crochet knowledge.

Our world is often stressful, filled with chaos and uncertainty. That uncertainty manifested after a tumble in my home resulted in bruises, skin abrasions, and a swollen knot on my forehead.

Final diagnosis? Traumatic brain injury—and my world exploded.

My mental filing cabinet had dumped its contents. Item by item, I had to relearn physical movement and speech. My brain's dictionary was an untidy clutter of mismatched words and phrases. Crochet skills, deeply ingrained in my memory, however, were graciously available as I fumbled through rehabilitation and regained physical and emotional strength.

With silky soft yarns and familiar stitch patterns, I escaped the rigors of these anxiety-filled circumstances. Skeins of yarn became afghans, scarves, and hats. Inner peace appeared as gradual healing intertwined with crochet. My gratitude for crochet weaves a colorful tale that began with a mother's love, a crochet hook, and some bits of yarn.

Gwyn Goodrow blogs about hospitality destinations and personal transformation benefits of journaling. Gwyn enjoys travel, photography, creative arts, and laughter with family and friends. Find out more at www.MeetOurAuthors.com.

August 18
Grateful for Every Day
Connie Ragen Green

"Whatever our individual troubles and challenges may be, it's important to pause every now and then to appreciate all that we have, on every level." ~ Shakti Gawain

Every morning when I awake and my feet touch the floor I express my gratitude for being alive. I thank God for everything I am and all that I have and for everything that is possible during this magnificent day.

But I didn't always feel this way.

I was a complainer for most of my life, living an existence of mediocrity, going through the motions, blaming others for what I did not have and could not do. I played the victim, unable to achieve even the smallest goals because of so many issues I refused to call my own.

Then one day I decided to take full responsibility for everything, big and small, that occurred in my life. For the first time since childhood, I exhaled. Breathing out the sadness, the loneliness, and the goals not achieved.

And when I had let it all out, I took a long, steady, focused breath in. In with the new, the possible, and the dreams. My gratitude grows with each new day. I have the power to create the life I choose. It's up to me as to what I will manifest. Sometimes I even surprise myself with what I come up with.

Connie Ragen Green works with new authors and entrepreneurs and mentors them on how to create massive, passive income streams with a joyous online business. Find out more at www.MeetOurAuthors.com.

August 19
Gratitude for Life
Metka Lebar

"Appreciation is a wonderful thing. It makes what is excellent in others belong to us as well." ~ Voltaire

Gratitude is an acknowledgement of the perfection of life as it is in the moment. It is also the priming of the pump for even more blessings to manifest in your life. By being grateful you acknowledge your readiness to receive them. It is like saying, "Thank you, life, I accept your gifts."

Try giving thanks for the things that are not yet in your life, and watch the miracles unfold in front of your eyes. The universe is abundant and overflowing. Gratitude opens your heart so you are able to receive what the universe has to offer.

You can be grateful even when things are not looking so good. Be willing to find blessings in most unexpected places. If you find yourself in a challenging situation, do not resist it. Instead welcome it into your life by asking it to reveal miracles it has in store for you. Carefully unwrap the gifts hidden within adversity. By acknowledging the good in even the most challenging circumstances you can turn any situation into a blessing.

Gratitude reminds you that you are whole and complete. There is nothing that you could be missing when you embrace life with a grateful heart.

Metka Lebar is a best-selling author, visionary and consciousness facilitator who helps people activate their true potential. Read more at www.MeetOurAuthors.com.

August 20

'Tat You!'

Rocky Henriques

"To be grateful is to recognize the love of God in everything He has given us—and He has given us everything." ~ Thomas Merton

Gratitude is not just about what has happened in the past; it also can be expressed in future tense.

When my daughter Jennifer was just a toddler and barely talking, she taught me a lot about gratitude. She had one of those little cups with a lid, so very little would spill out if she knocked it over. I was teaching her to say please and thank you. She would come to me, drop her empty cup into my lap and say, "Thank you" (though it came out as "tat you").

She fully expected me to fill her cup, and so she said thank you in advance. I can close my eyes all these years later and still see her doing that, even brushing her little palms together as she said it, as if she were washing her hands of the matter, leaving it all to me. That cute little habit of hers was as close to a fleshed-out example of real gratitude in future tense as I've ever seen. She had the utmost confidence that I would provide for her and take care of her need.

So will our Heavenly Father. Let us thank Him in advance.

This essay is an excerpt from *What Shape Is Your Pumpkin?: The Size and Shape of Faith*. You can find out more about Rocky Henriques at www.MeetOurAuthors.com.

August 21
My Personal Primary Caregiver
Dr. Donna Mogan

"If there are no dogs in heaven, then when I die
I want to go where they went." ~ Will Rogers

When I think of my pet dog, Mystique, my heart swells with a deep gratitude for all that she taught me about unconditional loving. During several years of severe medical conditions, her loving presence could really brighten my day, especially when I was experiencing pain and depression. I know it aided me in my recovery.

After a couple of long hospital stays, Mystique would jump with happiness when I returned home. Heck, there was no one else doing that.

Her antics would get me laughing and releasing all the healthy endorphins for healing. I'm convinced that the dog spit that came with all of her wet, sloppy kisses added a magic elixir that pharmacies do not provide.

When a family crisis came about, some major life changes were involved. There was a necessary move to another state, new home, community and way of life. Through them all, Mystique adapted and served as my constant personal caregiver. Many tears were buried in her fur. Yet, as usual, dog spit elixir saved the day.

Gratitude and appreciation were instilled in me by this sweet animal over our 17 years together. When I exercise them on a daily basis my life is, indeed, richer.

Dr. Donna Mogan is a life legacy, retirement and wealth coach. Her clients blend leadership, practicality and spirituality with their core values to experience new successes right now. Find out more at www.MeetOurAuthors.com.

August 22

Look Up!

Amy Elizabeth Kelsall

"Clouds come floating into my life, no longer to carry rain or usher storms but to add color to my sunset sky." ~ Rabindranath Tagore

I was introduced to clouds at the age of 2 by my grandfather and was forever changed. The appearance, variations in type and colorations, throughout the day and seasons keep us aware of weather, emotions and imaginative play. Clouds are the source of life for plants and animals on all continents.

Without clouds as the source of fresh water, there would be little life on land. The continents would be barren. All water on land comes from clouds. Clouds are progenitors of mighty glaciers, seas and lakes, of water in rivers, reservoirs and wells, of mist in the air and dew on flowers.

Clouds descend as snow, sleet, hail, rain, mist and dew. Clouds are water, lifted from oceans, suspended in air, transported by wind, falling on Earth, carried by rivers and reentering the ocean to become salty again. Clouds are an inspirational bonus for those who look upward.

The beauty of clouds is a reward for not being downcast. The necessity of clouds for life increases appreciation of their beauty and power. The form and manner of water falling from clouds is determined by temperature and wind.

Let's not forget to look up for inspiration, creativity, hope and beauty.

Amy E. Kelsall, M.A., MFT, Ph.D., coaches/counsels local and national clients on personal, professional, relational and communication issues. Find out how to connect with Amy at www.MeetOurAuthors.com.

August 23

Gratitude in the Tough Times

Bonita Bandaries

"Give thanks in all circumstances; for this is God's will for you in Christ Jesus." ~ 1 Thessalonians 5:18 NIV

This verse had particular meaning for me during the years I was my mother's full-time caregiver. In her 80s she came to live with me after having fallen while getting into her wheelchair. Nerves were damaged in her back making it impossible for her to stand or walk again.

During the years of caring for her there were many challenges to face. So, you might ask, "How can you be thankful in circumstances of disabilities and chronic illness?"

Encouraging words and deeds from family, friends, and the medical community became very important to me. Keeping a positive attitude wasn't always easy as a caregiver, but taking time each day to reflect on something I was grateful for made it easier to focus on the blessings in my life. Being grateful made me more optimistic and happier as I cared for Mother. I am especially thankful for strength and guidance found in the scriptures.

I now write books and host events to encourage other family caregivers.

Bonita Bandaries is the author of inspirational books for family caregivers. Find out more at www.MeetOurAuthors.com.

August 24

Gratitude to My Heavenly Father

Tracey Doctor

"If I am not good to myself, how can I expect anyone else to be good to me?" ~ Maya Angelou

I thank God for all that has been given to me. After surviving a stroke six years ago, I realized how very precious life is. I began prioritizing things I had put off before. I know that God saved me for a reason. I am very grateful. I no longer procrastinate, waiting for things to be perfect in order to move forward toward my goals and dreams.

Now is the time to share my message, and this is the moment to start. I began practicing self-care by being more focused on self-love and enjoying every precious moment. I make a conscious effort to enjoy quality time with my family. I use every opportunity to improve the way I take care of myself. The most important self-care was eliminating overwhelming situations that were contributing stress to my life.

I realize that learning to really love myself is essential to thriving and is a sure way to reflect and explore the many facets of my life. I let go of the things that no longer served me. I surround myself with positive people who have mutual respect for each other. These decisions empower me to focus on maintaining a genuine appreciation for my life.

Tracey Doctor is a holistic lifestyle coach and radio host. Her passion and purpose is to inspire women to find their joy. Find out how to connect with Tracey at www.MeetOurAuthors.com.

August 25

Gratitude and Mental Illness

Kathryn Jingling

"Every challenge, every adversity contains within it the seeds of opportunity and growth." ~ Roy Bennett

If we played word association with mental illnesses, the last word that would probably come to mind is "gratitude." You might instead think of words like "burden," "suffer," or "struggle."

Being diagnosed with anxiety and depression has been both a blessing and a curse. Anxiety has given me days where I couldn't eat, sleep or leave the house. Depression has given me days where I couldn't leave my bed, and my head ached from crying so much.

But perspective is everything. I had a choice: Be a victim or turn things around and look for the positive side of mental illness. The challenge became shifting my perspective to find the seeds of opportunity and growth in the experiences. I'm now thankful for the difficult days; they made me more grateful for the good days. The days where I see glimpses of who I really am, the days where I can function and the days I feel loved.

The good news is that cultivating gratitude and finding optimism during difficult times can make them easier to manage and reduce anxiety and depression. So, developing an attitude of gratitude is one of the simplest ways to improve your mental health.

Kathryn Jingling is a wellness coach who empowers female entrepreneurs to manage their mental health and create a guaranteed six-figure income. Learn more about Kathryn and her offerings at www.MeetOurAuthors.com.

August 26

Must Love Dogs—A Nod to National Dog Day!

Linda Berry

"A dog is the only thing on Earth that loves you more than you love yourself." ~ Josh Billings

Do you feel you're always being watched? If yes, then you must love dogs. At all times, I have 12 eyes staring at me from my terrier-and-chihuahua-mix family.

It all started while walking Bailey when a precocious dog followed us home and decided to hang out. She couldn't stay away from him, and they fell in love through the fence. Forced to move him inside after he parked on the window shelf, I named him Cognac.

Bailey would flip her nose to male dogs until Cognac. Soon, she was pregnant, and three puppies were born on my bed. Kalua-ha, the oldest, looks like Mom, with signature white front legs. Champagne, with white paws, is my "Dennis the Menace." His little sister, Tequila, is named for her hot temper, which scares her brothers and dad.

Immediately hooked on these wagging-tailed, wet-nosed bundles of fur, I wouldn't let them leave my home. My last addition was a lost dog on the road desperately looking for a new home who found it with me. I instantly named him Whiskey, and, surprisingly, Tequila fell in love with him.

So, do you think I'm crazy? Maybe, but I do love dogs!

Linda Berry is an angel whisperer and the owner, consultant, coach, and reader for the Spiritual Discovery Center. She's also an international astrologer, podcast host, and spiritual and metaphysical book author. Learn more about Linda at www.MeetOurAuthors.com.

August 27

The Birthing of King Richard

Richard LoveJoy

"Be yourself; everyone else is already taken." ~ Oscar Wilde

August 27 is my birthday! I am 77 years old and just reaching a wonderful and fantastic time in my life. I was extremely fortunate to be born into a loving and caring middle-class family. I am grateful for the divine guidance I have been given in my life. I believe that I am the divine living, loving, joyful, healthy and playful essence of the Lord!

I have learned over the years that it is really about who I am becoming instead of what I am accumulating. I am learning deeply every day to be loving and joyful for the thriving life I live. I take responsibility for the opportunity to decide in every moment who I want to be and what I want to do.

I love roller coasters, and my life has been like a magical roller-coaster ride! For me, magic is "Manifesting Awesome God Into Consciousness"! I love using acronyms in my life to create the energy that I want to be in each moment. I now finally understand that I have sovereignty over my life and my life only! I am profoundly grateful to be King Richard, king of the kingdom within me!

Richard LoveJoy is a highly experienced executive consultant, certified professional success coach and mentor who inspires and empowers clients to find magical and simple solutions. Find out how to connect with Richard at www.MeetOurAuthors.com.

August 28

Gratitude to Grace

Maria E. Davis

"Gratitude can transform common days into thanksgivings, turn routine jobs into joy, and change ordinary opportunities into blessings." ~ William Arthur Ward

It is easier to be grateful when things are going good. How can we be grateful in the midst of pain, sorrow, illness, family or relationship drama?

Gratitude is a quality of the heart—a soothing balm to all that is out of alignment with gratitude. It promotes peace. It fuels courage to face everything that is uncomfortable.

Find something to be grateful for to prime the pump. Build on it daily. Give sincere appreciation. Think of ways to share gratitude with others. Especially to those who ruffle your feathers. Instead of complaining about what you don't like, find something you do like.

Choosing an attitude of gratitude in the face of discouragement and grief promotes healing. It opens the door to grace and endless possibilities. Knowing we cannot control others—certainly we've tried, for their own good of course!—we can choose to control ourselves and how we feel, resolve, and transcend our circumstances. What we do sets an example for others.

Gratitude is truly a gift worth giving and receiving. It lightens our load and gives opportunity to lighten others when accepted. Building a momentum on gratitude can only return blessings—an amazing grace.

Hear, O Universe, I am grateful!

Maria Davis shares lifelong experiences in *Keys to Overcoming Life's Irritations from the Common Cold to Crises*. Take back control of your life for more energy and less dis-ease. More at www.MeetOurAuthors.com.

August 29
Love for One Another
Gregory Hoffmaster

"If we cannot now end our differences, at least we can help make the world safe for diversity." ~ John F. Kennedy

Gratitude is a wonderful and simple thing. Life can be much happier when I remember to remain in gratitude.

For instance, I like to remind myself to be grateful for those who came before me—those who paved the way, stood up for their rights and the rights of others. I constantly remind myself how fortunate I am to live in a place where humans of all sorts have equal rights and are safe to be their true selves. It may be just one small corner of the world, but it's a great step toward a more peaceful and tolerant planet.

I am grateful for the people who banded together, fought long and hard for equality, and faced punishments with bravery and strong hearts. Because of them, I am not only allowed to walk down the street hand-in-hand with someone I love, but I can do so safely. Though there may be some differences among us, we are all human.

We're all people who want to live life and love.

Gregory Hoffmaster is currently working (coached by Donna Kozik) on a book about social anxiety and other mood disorders. Gregory is a contributing author to *Community Book Projects Success Is Yours!* and *Everyday Joy*. Discover more at www.MeetOurAuthors.com.

August 30

Our Wedding Day

Richard and Trisha LoveJoy

"This is the day that the Lord hath made; let us rejoice and be glad in it." ~ Psalm 118:24.

It was a day such as this, August 30,1997, that Richard and I rejoiced in joining in marriage. We chose the quote above to be front and center on our wedding program.

And that day was, indeed, a beautiful, warm and sunny day for a wedding! Guests were gathered to bear witness in the sanctuary at Unity Church in Palo Alto, California. This was an incredibly special and sacred space for us, serving as chaplains and attending services on Sundays.

Rays of sunlight glinted through the stained-glass windows as the sacred sounds of the organ, played by my sister, echoed throughout. As I walked down the aisle on my son's arm, my eyes filled with joyful tears seeing our family and close friends in attendance.

My husband-to-be, Richard, and his daughter, Jill, were waiting in front of a magnificent stone wall with the inscription "With God, all things are possible" (Matthew 19:26). The ceremony was intimate and touching. And, as we both said, "I do," we felt that truth deeply.

As the organ music rose to a crowning crescendo, together as one, we walked down the aisle entering our greatest adventure this lifetime in love and joy.

Richard and Trisha LoveJoy are consultants, certified professional success coaches and mentors who inspire principled and practical solutions for clients to live in love and joy. Find out how to connect with Richard and Trisha at www.MeetOurAuthors.com.

August 31
Smile and Change Your World
LaWanna G. Parker

"One of the most rewarding things in life is to always put a smile on your face." ~ Dr. T. P. Chia

At one point in my life, I didn't know how to smile or speak to anyone if they did not speak to me first. I was also afraid to write about my feelings or stand before a group to speak, because it meant opening myself up for others to see my weaknesses.

I am so glad I made the decision to smile and say hello to everyone I met even if they did not return the greeting. It has gained me many friends I have come to love.

I have published a book sharing one of the dark times in my life. Writing *Courage to Live My Dream*, has provided me many speaking opportunities, and I now share my story.

I have been blessed to make a difference in the lives of others seeking my help, and it gives me great joy to see the growth in them. I am so grateful and much happier with the person I am becoming. My world changed with a simple smile and a hello. What would it take to change your world?

Thank you, God, for giving me the chance to make a difference in someone else's life.

LaWanna Parker is an author, blogger, motivational speaker, radio show host, creator of the Emerging Personal Development Program, senior citizen companion, and assistant with Project P.I.N. blog. Find out more at www.MeetOurAuthors.com.

September

September 1

In Grateful Memory of Vernon Dawson

Marge Dawson

"Be grateful for all of life's blessings, no matter how small."
~ Unknown

On September 1, 2007, we lost a wonderful husband, father and grandfather, Vernon Theo Dawson, who was born February 6, 1932. Though we miss him dearly, there is so much we are grateful for and have fond memories of him.

As a loving husband of 52 years, we had many wonderful times together and had so much to be grateful for. I am grateful for having a loving, caring, fun-loving, generous and all-round super husband. He was a very good handyman and didn't hesitate to help others too. I am grateful for our four beautiful children, who adored him, and for the happy memories we made together.

As a father he was always there and loved unconditionally. He taught our children many life skills, most of all kindness, patience and love.

He was a grandfather to seven grandchildren and loved them all dearly. He loved to play with them, and they all loved him and still speak fondly of happy memories with him.

Vernon may not be with us anymore, but he is forever in our hearts and minds, and we are most grateful for the blessing that he was to all.

Marge Dawson is the award-winning author of Pearls of Creation A-Z of Pearls. More at www.MeetOurAuthors.com.

September 2
Receiving in Giving
Danielle F. Romer

"The best way to find yourself is to lose yourself in the service of others." ~ Gandhi

"Would you like to volunteer?" It was my first year on the night shift at my new job. I'd decided to do something during the day but something I really wanted to do. I started to look in the newspapers. It was a pretty normal thing to do in the '90s, at least for me (the internet was not it). A request caught my eye: "Be the voice of a foster child in court as a guardian ad litem. Would you like to volunteer?"

This sounded like what I would want to do. By signing up, I entered a world where those innocent creatures came to have me as the only consistent contact in their foster-to-foster-home journey. I had the privilege to watch sad eyes turn into exciting looks. I witnessed kids that were mature beyond their years because of abusive homes. I did it for almost 10 years. But nowadays, I still stay in touch with my "kids." Some send thank-you texts, surprise gifts, grateful calls or birthday cards even today.

But when they thank me for helping, the most grateful one of all is me, receiving such personal gratification from my time with them. In addition to what I've learned and the love I've received, which was priceless, I have the utmost gratitude for the experience.

Danielle F. Romer is an experienced life coach helping survivors of abuse regain peace of mind and emotional wellness. Find out how to connect with Danielle at www.MeetOurAuthors.com.

September 3
Quiet Gifts
Jane Glendinning

"For the eternal tendencies of all toward happiness make the only point of sane philosophy." ~ Walt Whitman

It has been said that the happiest people are women between the ages of 60 and 80. Several months after my 60th birthday, I noticed a change in my daily outlook, and it has led me to reflect on reasons for this happiness.

As a child, a typical night at home consisted of lying on the sofa watching television. Mom lounged nearby in her usual chair, a book in her hands. She was setting a lasting example that I would absorb—her love of creativity.

This morning, as I slipped my red-and-gold pen into its sleeve, I realized I was mentally saying, "Wow." I do this frequently. It is an exclamation in appreciation for having something beautiful and for being able to put that pen to paper to write out a thought or idea that is meaningful to me. Gratitude over these moments when I feel joy for simple things in my life is a gift. I do not have to look hard for these occurrences. This feeling is so much like the "wow" I knew as a child, having fresh experiences and getting a feel for the vast life that I am a part of.

Jane Glendinning lives in Oakland, California. Find out how to connect with Jane at www.MeetOurAuthors.com.

September 4

Intention, Interruptions, Unexpected Manifestation

Carol Brusegar

"Life is all about timing...the unreachable becomes reachable, the unavailable becomes available. Have the patience; wait it out."
~ Stacy Charter

Intention to interruptions to unexpected manifestation in nine months! In January of 2020, "move to California" was on my vision board. I would finally rejoin my family—daughter, son-in-law and two grandchildren. Four years ago, they moved from Nashville after living there six years. From that day on, my goal was always to join them. But my ties, commitments and financial limitations delayed the process. Quarterly visits with them were wonderful but not enough.

It was time. My intention was strong—and then the pandemic halted me in my tracks. I actually didn't think about moving as I hunkered down in my home, barely leaving it for months.

Unexpectedly in August, my daughter emailed information about an available small home 15 minutes from them. She made sure I was ready to move and pursued it.

Less than 60 days after first hearing of this possibility, I arrived at their home in California to wait for my car and belongings to arrive and the house to be ready. Now settled in, I am incredibly grateful for all my daughter did, for a smooth move, for my lovely new home and especially for being back with my precious family.

Carol Brusegar is the author of *Create Your Third Age: Steps to Making Your Years Past Fifty Fulfilling and Joyful* along with related books. More at www.MeetOurAuthors.com.

September 5
Dreams Really Do Come True
Natasha E. Williams

"All dreams can come true, so don't allow anyone to convince you otherwise because small minds can't dream big dreams."
~ Natasha Williams

I grew up poor in Louisiana. However, I always dreamt of living a better life. My biggest dream was to travel the world. Most people told me I couldn't do it. I often felt I didn't have anyone to share my dreams with; however, my grandmother was my biggest cheer-leader.

My grandmother worked all her life as a housekeeper for wealthy families. One particular day, I was introduced to one of the ladies. She asked me, "Are you going to clean my house, too, when you grow up?" Somewhere from the depths of my soul, I replied, "No, ma'am. I'm going to college. I'm going to be somebody one day!"

Even at a young age, I desired more in life than to simply "get by." My grandmother encouraged me to follow my dreams no matter what anybody said and to live the life she never had the courage or the opportunity to live.

As of today, I've traveled to 60 countries, living the life of my dreams while doing work that I love. Every time another dream comes true, I look to heaven and say, "Thank you, Grandma, for giving me the courage to pursue the life of my dreams."

Natasha Williams is an international speaker, an author, a coach who served on the development team for two Chicken Soup for the Soul books and the founder of Think Rich Society. Discover more about Natasha at www.MeetOurAuthors.com.

September 6
Aging Gratefully
Dr. Lynne Mitchell-Pedersen

"You are never too old to set another goal or to dream a new dream." ~ C.S. Lewis

Gratitude floods as I count my blessings. I am healthy, fit and welcoming 80 years this autumn. To celebrate this transition, I challenged my adult children, their spouses and my four grandchildren to bike 80 km with me. My challenge was well received but quickly modified by my clever 14-year-old granddaughter to, "Well, why can't we each ride our own age?" Each person then chose what would be an individual challenge, and plans were set.

On a beautiful August day, my son, son-in-law and I set off through attractive city paths, heading gradually out into the country. At km 52, my daughter picked us up and drove us to their cottage near Lac du Bonnet, Manitoba, where the rest of our family waited. Some had done an initial ride as part of completing their personal challenge. We set off jubilantly together for the final 28-km section of the trip. Oh, the pleasure of riding along the dike beside the Winnipeg River, surrounded by my beloved family.

As the day culminated in a celebratory dinner with champagne toasts, each person honoured his or her own accomplishment. Come on, 80! I am ready and grateful!

Dr. Lynne Mitchell-Pedersen is a retired psychotherapist with a background in geriatric nursing. She loves to be outdoors walking, biking or cross-country skiing. Her first novel, With One Stroke, is soon to be published. Learn more about Lynne at www.MeetOurAuthors.com.

September 7

An Antidote to Conflict: Gratitude

Dawn Rafferty

"Some people grumble that roses have thorns; I am grateful that thorns have roses." ~ Alphonse Karr

I see people who are angry. I am a mediator and a conflict management coach; in my work, emotions run high. I strive to provide a space that is calm and compassionate for potential resolutions.

Gratitude during these times is so powerful. To shine a light on things that people are grateful for in one another is often hard work but so rewarding. Sometimes this requires reaching back in memory to when times were good or digging deep into the bag of common denominators to find the appreciation. But for those who are weary of the fight, gratitude offers a graceful, healing balm.

It is scientifically proven that focusing on thoughts of appreciation, gratitude, and love brings the frequencies of our hearts and minds into coherence. We think better; we make more rational decisions; we operate from the more evolved places within ourselves.

When frustration, anger, irritation or any of the not-so-productive paths loom large, enumerating the things we are grateful for is a quick way home to a peaceful heart.

Dawn Rafferty is a conflict management coach, mediator, and facilitator. She supports and guides people to better conflict outcomes. You can find her at www.MeetOurAuthors.com.

September 8

Count Your Lucky Stars

Margy Lang

"Showing gratitude is one of the simplest yet most powerful things humans can do for each other." ~ Randy Pausch

Not long ago I was overweight, undernourished and battling an incurable autoimmune disorder. It was depressing and frustrating and led me to shun even the smallest of life's gifts.

Eventually a medical practitioner recommended I "rewire" or "train my brain" to choose healthier foods over highly processed and sugar-laden ones. Choosing healthier foods and beverages resulted in permanent weight loss and eliminated a variety of pesky food cravings.

As a bonus, I stopped the progress of the autoimmune disorder.

To support changes in my behavior I recorded my progress and setbacks. I logged the number of calories saved, hours of sleep, and minutes of exercise. Also, I jotted down what I was grateful for and how I could show gratefulness. Soon I saw the powerful connection between being grateful and healing a broken body. I titled my journal, "Count Your Lucky Stars."

At about the same time, I joined my local astronomy club and attended their observational star parties. I used my journal to record star and meteor sightings. Now when people ask me the secret sauce to losing weight and keeping it off, I tell them, "Start by counting your lucky stars."

Margy Lang is a sports marketer, author, and certified youth sports nutritionist who is completing her latest book, *500 Ways to Save 100 Calories a Day.* Find out more at www.MeetOurAuthors.com.

September 9
The Gift of Family
Melanie G. Robinson

"Families are like branches on a tree; we all grow in different directions, yet all our roots remain as one." ~ Unknown

In my front garden, there is a Japanese cherry tree, which flowers every year. It has the most beautiful blooms, and the scent from the flowers is beautiful.

During these difficult times, staying at home hasn't been easy with all the fear and grief gripping us during this pandemic. My family and I have also had our own crisis we've been going through, which has been very painful.

I've also come to realise and be acutely aware that being connected to our family is what matters above all else. We may not have it all, but together we have it all. That's a gift of insight and gratitude it has given me. After all, everyone needs a house to live in, but it's a supportive family that makes it a home.

Melanie G. Robinson lives with her family in the United Kingdom. She loves to encourage and motivate everyone to live the life they love. Find out how to connect with Melanie at www.MeetOurAuthors.com.

September 10
Reach Your Goals Through Gratitude
Moira Shepard

"Gratitude is riches. Complaint is poverty." ~ Doris Day

If you are struggling to reach a goal and haven't gotten very far, consider using this manifestation method. It goes like this:

Close your eyes and envision your desired outcome, like a movie in your mind.

Let your heart fill with gratitude for the fulfillment of your dream.

Watch how things unfold in your vision as your sense of gratitude and wonder intensifies.

Notice how you feel. Store that feeling in your heart.

Then, get on with your day.

Why it works: When you express gratitude before the outcome happens, you release your attachment to how it should come about and when it should happen. This is a good thing for two reasons. First, trying to micromanage the Universe can drive you crazy. Has it ever worked for you? Second, when you surrender your attachment to how the desired event happens, you free the Universe to work its magic in wonderful ways. You can trust the Universe to figure out how to turn your dream into a reality. It's smarter than you think. See what happens when you practice this manifestation method once a week for four weeks. Prepare to be amazed. Let me know what happens, okay?

It has been Moira Shepard's privilege to help thousands of creative entrepreneurs to develop the confidence to do what they came here to do. Discover more about Moira and her offerings at www.MeetOurAuthors.com.

September 11
Be Grateful for the Imperfection
Caroline Ravelo

"No one who achieves success does so without the help of others. The wise and confident acknowledge this help with gratitude."
~ Alfred North Whitehead

Can we feel grateful when things don't go our way?

Years ago, I was excited about a new job. I had the business, technical, and leadership experience to do well, and I was asked to write a major document for a new project.

The paper covered business process and system changes on a topic I knew well. It was initially released to a few of the senior leaders. And it was a flop!

I felt so embarrassed, disappointed, and lost.

Someone approached me and noted that I was writing for different audiences—senior leaders, middle managers, and the people doing the work. Each person would read from their perspective, and my challenge was to keep them in mind when I wrote.

She offered some technical tips, yet the most important comment came when she asked me to overwrite. Something clicked and I reworked the entire document, which was then well received.

I am very grateful for that experience. I've shared this story with people I have mentored, managed, and led who are tasked to produce something similar. I believe we learn from others, so we can pass it on.

The gift: Be grateful for the imperfections.

Caroline Ravelo is a business architect, consultant, and coach. She works with ambitious business leaders who want to implement major changes to grow their business. Discover more at www.MeetOurAuthors.com.

September 12
Best Birthday Gift Ever
Kit Rosato

"Of all God's gifts both great and small, children are the best of all."
~ Unknown

The day you were born was magical. Steady, early contractions were keeping me from sleeping. Needing a distraction, I decided to polish my beautiful silver platters that were badly tarnished from neglect. I hate polishing silver, but it seemed like a good idea at the time. Your dad happily went to sleep while I slaved away.

Hours later we were in the hospital walking the halls to encourage progression in my labor. You were coming a week early, and I was so grateful to be having you naturally without drugs. Your precocious brother had been born by C-section 18 months earlier. It was also the day before your dad's birthday.

My labor was long and I was so exhausted from polishing the silver that I struggled to push you out. The clock struck midnight and your dad whispered to me that I didn't need to wait any longer. You were going to be his best birthday gift ever! Hysterical at the crazy idea I had been waiting to deliver on his special day, his words renewed my strength.

With grateful hearts and God's perfect timing we welcomed you, our beautiful daughter, on your dad's birthday.

Kit Rosato is an online entrepreneur who loves helping others, writing, selling on Amazon, and taking the mystery out of online marketing. Connect with her at www.MeetOurAuthors.com.

September 13
Becoming a Grandmother
Katherine Wiens

"There's nothing like a grandchild to put a smile on your face, a lump in your throat and a warm feeling in your heart." ~ Unknown

September 13. On this day, I will become a grandmother for the first time. I have thought about this day for some time, not knowing how or when it will come about. At present, adorable pets fill my life with joy and laughter. They are in my heart to stay. However, a grandchild, a little human, is an entirely different situation.

I can't help but think of my mother and her excitement with each new grandchild. The day after I announced the arrival of a grandchild, she packed her bags and spent a week with us, selflessly cooking for us and playing with her grandchildren. Her presence also provided me with much-needed rest. My parents never missed a birthday. It meant a day of visiting, eating, catching up and, best of all, a delicious, homemade cake.

I envision this new day, September 13, with sincere gratitude and a growing sense of joy as the day approaches. My son and daughter-in-law will embark on their journey as first-time parents. I am thankful that they live nearby and I see them often. We will share this journey with them. I hope to be the best grandmother I can be.

Katherine Wiens is an online reading teacher helping elementary students achieve reading success. Find out how to connect with Katherine at www.MeetOurAuthors.com.

September 14

Because of Her

Adrienne Dupree

"All I am or ever hope to be, I owe to my angel mother."
~ Abraham Lincoln

A young 16-year-old girl in love with her high school sweetheart learns that she is pregnant and must suddenly make adult decisions. This is the 1960s, so continuing to attend high school is not an option and she drops out. She decides to not only have the baby but to keep it.

This is not some drama from a Lifetime movie but a story about my life. I am the daughter that my teenage mother decided to have and keep. I can only imagine how scared she was. I know when I was 16, I wasn't ready to face adult responsibilities.

My parents ultimately got married and raised me and my three siblings. I am so grateful that she decided to keep me, raise me and love me unconditionally. Growing up I didn't really realize the sacrifices she made for me. She sacrificed her education and teenage years for me. The significance of this selfless act didn't hit me fully until I became a parent myself.

Even though my mother is no longer here, it's my mission to show my gratitude to her every day by being the best person I can be.

Adrienne Dupree is an entrepreneur that teaches people how to get out of the rat race. More at www.MeetOurAuthors.com.

September 15

Life in the Breath

Bethany Perry

"She loved the world, and it loved her right back." ~ Unknown

Today is my birthday! It's always been a magical day. In my 63 years, I can count on one hand how many times it has rained. Not that I mind rain; it waters our earth, creating the lush greens. But the sky in Michigan turns the most breathtaking blue every single September!

What makes me happiest on my birthday, though, are the people that celebrate it with me. My family, who reaches out with love, my friends, who always make it so special.

Some people don't enjoy celebrating their birthday. Perhaps it's a difficult year where you find yourself especially alone, or you've recently lost someone and celebrating isn't on your to-do list!

I invite you just for a moment to close your eyes and see your uniqueness—never before and never again will there be another you! As you inhale, bring in joy, and on the wave of your exhale, breathe out gratitude.

The truth is there is always a reason to celebrate. There are many qualities and characteristics within you that only you can offer the world. As you discover them, give. As you do, watch and see the beauty the world gives back.

Bethany is a transformational health and life coach. An emerging thought leader on combining the power of neuroscience and intuition, Bethany guides you to create your desired life. More about Bethany at www.MeetOurAuthors.com.

September 16

'Tis Better to Give...

Martin Salama

"Two kinds of gratitude: The sudden kind we feel for what we take; the larger kind we feel for what we give."
~ Edwin Arlington Robinson

I thought I've always understood and appreciated giving gratitude for what I receive. But, until recently, I don't think I understood gratitude for what I am able to give.

In 2006 there was a bone marrow registry drive for a young girl with leukemia who needed a match. I immediately registered. Unfortunately, no match was found, and she passed away. As the years went by, and life with all of its ups and downs continued, I forgot that I even registered.

Until I got a call from Gift of Life Marrow Registry. I was a potential match for someone with leukemia. After extensive tests, it was confirmed I was indeed a match to donate stem cells. And I happily did.

Now I realize how lucky and grateful I am to be able to possibly save someone's life. So many things could have gone wrong to make it impossible, but they didn't. I was able to donate. It gives me a new understanding of the phrase 'Tis better to give than to receive.

Martin Salama is a life coach and author. In 2013, he published his first book *Recovering from Divorce: 7 Steps to Recover Without Drama to Create a New Life.* You can learn more at www.MeetOurAuthors.com.

September 17
Gratitude Knows No Bounds
Martin Salama

"I would maintain that thanks are the highest form of thought; and that gratitude is happiness doubled by wonder." ~ G.K. Chesterton

On this day, September 17, in 2018, through The Gift of Life Organization, I was given an opportunity to donate stem cells to a man I never met who had leukemia. Over time, I received limited information about his health status.

On the two-year anniversary, I was told he had my contact information if he wanted to reach out. Some emotions came to the surface for me—happy that he was alive, curious about his condition as well as trepidation that this episode might not have closure.

About a month later, I got an email from him. He detailed his journey from before his diagnosis until the present. I'm thrilled and grateful to report he has recovered from his illness and is doing well. He shared his many health hurdles along the way. The focus of the correspondence was to express his gratitude to me for my donation that ultimately saved his life.

Interestingly, our ancestral backgrounds were completely different. Our family lines were nowhere near each other on the globe. Yet, our stem cell profiles were perfect matches, which led to his recovery. It shows how the smallest act of kindness can make life altering effects.

My gratitude overflows with joy.

Martin Salama is a life coach and author. In 2013, he published his first book *Recovering from Divorce: 7 Steps to Recover Without Drama to Create a New Life*. For more information, check out www.MeetOurAuthors.com.

September 18

Appreciation Is a Wonderful Gift

Charles L. Harmon Jr.

"When someone shows you who they are, believe them the first time." ~ Maya Angelou

As fall of 2018 was starting, I was thanking my lucky stars the young lady in the Philippines I'd hired about two months before was working out much better than I expected. When I hired her, Jessica J. Dabu, I had several ideas for online projects I might pursue. I knew I needed help since I had little free time to do everything myself.

I definitely didn't expect it but really appreciated Jessica's excellent suggestions and work. She is the proverbial jack-of-all-trades. Good at everything she does. Under her guidance, we were able to update several websites, build new websites, create a presence on social media and hire part-time writers. We also hired her brother, John Dabu, a talented high school junior at the time, who creates YouTube videos for some of our articles.

With Jessica's help, now a full-time manager, we finally settled on one major site we're working on. That's TravelESP.com, a website we think will ultimately be our signature site. Jessica's a hard-working manager, someone I can delegate any task or project to and know with confidence she will do an excellent job. My thanks and gratitude go out to you, Jessica Dabu.

Charles, a California resident and senior citizen, enjoys creating websites. He often publishes articles from new writers on his sites. Find out more about Charles at www.MeetOurAuthors.com.

September 19

Proud To Be Me

Katie De Souza

"Enjoy life; earn a living doing something you love."
~ Katie De Souza

I started my life with Mutley. He's always been by my side. He would go everywhere with me. He was cuddled so much that I had to sew him together. He was my confidant, whom I'd create stories around.

I have always loved to write and draw. Little stories or poems. Painted pictures on walls. Doodles in notebooks. English was my favourite subject.

I remember deciding, when I was 16, I would earn money doing what I love. I didn't have to work somewhere I didn't like. Even knowing that, it took me until age 36 to start pursuing my dream. I always knew I would have my own business; I just wasn't sure what.

I met my husband when I was 18, got married at 19, had my daughter at age 20 and my son at 21. I turned my husband's passion for jiu-jitsu into a successful business, which we run together. Now, I'm helping other people start their businesses so they can live a life they enjoy, earning money doing something they love.

I am proud of who I have become and hope I'm a good influence and inspiration to my children. Mutley is still around, albeit in retirement sat in my wardrobe.

Katie De Souza is an author and entrepreneur who inspires couples to achieve their dreams and live a happy and fulfilling life together. More about Katie at www.MeetOurAuthors.com.

September 20

Call Me Grandma

Tammy Atchley

"A grandchild is someone who reaches for your hand but touches your heart." ~ Unknown

I awoke to the sound of my phone ringing. As I picked it up, I glanced at the clock: 3:30 a.m. My first thought was, I hope this is it. My daughter-in-law spoke first, "Mom, we are on our way to the hospital. Today's the day." I thought my heart would explode with excitement. I immediately started to cry remembering when my first child was born.

Every few hours we received a text giving us updates as to the arrival of our first granddaughter. With a full calendar of things to keep me busy, I accomplished absolutely nothing. I stayed by my phone so I wouldn't miss the call.

After nearly 12 hours of pacing the floor and praying, the call came. Our son said, "Hey, Grandma, baby Qyra is here." Those words were music to my ears. I heard the baby crying in the distance, and I started crying right along with her. I thought to myself, "That is my granddaughter. I am a grandma."

A friend once told me, and I agree completely, that once you become a grandparent, you'll never own your heart again, and that is fine with me. Welcome to my world, little Qyra.

Tammy Atchley is a parenting coach that helps moms learn how to have those difficult conversations with their children. Learn more about Tammy at www.MeetOurAuthors.com.

September 21
Celebrating World Gratitude Day
Peggy Lee Hanson

"At times, our own light goes out and is rekindled by a spark from another person." ~ Albert Schweitzer

Sometimes it's a word. Sometimes it's a phrase. But mostly, it's a feeling.

Everything seemed to go haywire at once, yet spanned years. I started a new job when all three kids came down with chicken pox. A co-worker began to harass me. My mother-in-law died. The co-worker continued to harass me. I moved to a new department within the company. Another co-worker began to harass me.

I don't remember the exact person who set me on the path to healing from the inside out, but Dr. Wayne Dyer was at the forefront. Learning that I cannot change others, only myself, proved to be the best life lesson. Like a sponge, I gravitated toward additional thought leaders—Angelou, Maxwell, Tolle, Chopra, etc.

Once implementing the teachings, the harassment stopped. The haywire way of life turned into one of abundance, blessings and compassion—especially for those who tried to block me from greatness, as I give thanks to them for being my teachers too.

God, the Universe, Source, angels and guides have all met me along my journey, responding in kindness, love and growth. My body quivers with acknowledgment. Gratitude has exponentially changed my life.

Thank you. Thank you. Thank you.

Peggy Lee Hanson is creating the most significant worldwide online resource for aspiring writers to share their wisdom, expertise and strategies in book form. Learn more about Peggy and her offerings at www.MeetOurAuthors.com.

September 22
The Gift: My Daughter's Daughter
Kathi C. Laughman

"I've been given this blessing, which is my granddaughter. You're no longer just you. You suddenly fit into the chest drawers of life."
~ Joanna Lumley

September 22 will always be one of my favorite days of the year because it is my granddaughter Skylar's birthday! From the moment we knew she was joining us, our lives changed for the better. My daughter was just 17 and had faced many challenges already in her young life. Many said she was too young to be a mother, but provenance knew better.

Skylar's arrival didn't just mark the beginning of her life. In many ways, it also saved my daughter's life. Having a purpose beyond ourselves gives us a strength we can't find any other way.

Over the years, Skylar has brought the requisite joys and tears of children and grandchildren with her unique style and view of the world. Watching her life unfold has been one of my life's most treasured rewards.

She is in the Navy now, serving our country. Like many of us (including her Nana), she's uncertain what the future will bring, but one thing I know to be true is that, on this day, I cannot feel anything except wonder and delight for the gift of this life, my daughter's daughter.

Kathi Laughman is an author, business/legacy coach and mastermind leader. More at www.MeetOurAuthors.com.

September 23

My Mother's Unconditional Love
Julia D. Shaw

"People will help you when you're trying to help yourself."
~ Letha Shaw

My strength, passion and ambition are built on the foundation of my mother's unconditional love. As a teenager, I didn't listen to the wisdom and experience of this amazing woman. I had to make my own choices, and most of them she didn't agree with. I thought I had all the answers.

So, I left home at 16 thinking I was grown. Due to my lack of life experience, over the years, I had no choice but to return home several times. Each time, my mom's arms and doors were always open. The most painful return was when my marriage ended. With two children in tow, I moved back into my childhood room. I cried and wallowed over my unforeseen broken heart for months. My mom's faith gave me the strength to heal and create a new life for me and my family.

I am so grateful for my mother's unconditional love, patience, support and kindness. She shaped me into a positive and productive woman full of love and encouragement for my daughters and other young women in need of a mother's love. Every day, I thank God for my Mom, Letha Shaw.

Julia D. Shaw is a business consultant and life coach with over 20 years of experience, who lives in New York City. Find out how to connect with Julia at www.MeetOurAuthors.com.

September 24
Becoming a Grandmother
Sharon G. Teed

"Children are the hands by which we take hold
of heaven." ~ Henry Ward Beecher

On Friday, September 24, 2008, I was up early and off to work. I was retired and into my second adventure as a security guard. I also was waiting anxiously for the birth of my first grandchild.

What a marvelous day.

Lo and behold, at 11 a.m., I got a call from my son. I had a grand-daughter born at 7 a.m. I begged my boss for time off, saying that I would make it up later. He said yes, and the hospital was only 15 minutes away by bus (east on Sheppard Avenue in Toronto). I was so excited.

At the hospital, Gerry, my son, escorted me into the special room where my granddaughter lay in an incubator. He looked so proud. Gerry put his finger through the opening, and she instantly grabbed it.

Dominique was beautiful, and I wished she'd open her eyes. I swear she heard my wish, as she opened her eyes and looked at me. I was overwhelmed with a feeling like no other I had experienced. Her beautiful, big blue eyes gave me so much hope for the future. I couldn't have wished for anything more perfect.

Sharon G. Teed loves writing and editing. She's been in several editions of *The Community Book Project.* Discover more about Sharon at www.MeetOurAuthors.com.

September 25

57 Years of Gratitude

Donovan Wall

"Your children need your presence more than your presents."
~ Jesse Jackson

It has been a few months since my parents, Jim and Helen Wall, died. I still think about them daily. I'm grateful for all they provided me, both through nature and nurture. My parents taught me about making money, the value of hard work and integrity. They taught me about being honest and honorable. They taught me self-control and good eating habits. They let me be me.

My parents never outright bought me anything big, like a bicycle or minibike, but they taught me the value of working and earning money by agreeing to pay for half. I was too young for a real job, so I collected newspapers and sold them to a local factory for $20 per ton. My dad facilitated by driving me in the pickup truck with my load of newspapers. That gave me incentive to work and earn. I could see it was possible to make money, save and purchase things that were important.

Mom and Dad showed me acceptance and open-mindedness. They weren't perfect, but they never showed me intolerance or bigotry. They gave me good genes and good bones. They provided a healthy, happy home. And, maybe most importantly, they demonstrated what a healthy, loving marriage looks like.

Donovan Wall loves two-wheeled vehicles, his wife, Robyn, and his dog, Mika. He is an expert IT contracts manager, and he helps men lead a healthy lifestyle. Find out more about Donovan at www.MeetOurAuthors.com.

September 26
Motherhood—The Circle of Life
Joan Powell

"The natural state of motherhood is unselfishness." ~ Jessica Lange

On this day, a very special person was born—someone I also have to thank for my own existence. My mom.

My mom's occupation as a registered nurse was very fitting for her. She is a big-hearted, patient, very caring person, always thinking of and taking care of others.

One of my favorite childhood memories is of my mom, after working a long shift, picking me up from my babysitter and handing me a chocolate Nestle Crunch bar. That small gesture put such a big smile on my face. Even now, if I see that candy bar at the store, I become the little girl who was thrilled to see her mom at the end of the day.

Because of her job, my mom would miss important school functions like volleyball games or band performances. I resented it a little at the time, but I appreciate now that she worked to make sure we had what we needed.

And now, as a mom myself, I can appreciate even more the love, dedication and selflessness that comes with this ever-rewarding "job." I have a great teacher to thank for that. Thanks for all you do, Mom!

Joan Powell is a freelance writer, digital marketing specialist and Pinterest manager, helping entrepreneurs and small businesses grow their online presence. Find out how to connect with Joan at www.MeetOurAuthors.com.

September 27

Magical Movie Nights

Allyson O'Hara-Cribdon

"When you look at life through the eyes of gratitude, the world becomes a magical and amazing place." ~ Jennifer Gayle

Pop-pop-pop. "Almost ready," chime Robert and Mary in unison.

Shortly thereafter, my son and daughter slide beside me on the sofa, dropping a bowl of butter-laden popcorn on my lap, and the evening begins.

When the children were young, and my husband Jonathan traveled on fishing trips, we always held special movie nights. Mary and Robert would each select a movie, and the evening usually concluded with *The Last Mimzy* and *Last Holiday*. We'd snuggle under blankets, giggle, and grow closer.

Discussions about the films we were watching often led to conversations about the children's school experiences—joyful and challenging. More importantly, though, the children would share their precious dreams; their universe was filled with infinite possibilities, magic and wonder.

I've gratefully treasured these moments as they grew older, the social media monster seducing their world into triteness. Still, I've trusted that their belief in boundless uniqueness would return.

Jonathan is fishing this weekend. Interestingly, Mary suggests movie night to which Robert agrees. Pop-pop-pop.

We laugh and discuss the films. My teens' eyes sparkle as their current dreams enter the conversation; their universe is filled with confidence, imagination and passion. My heart smiles, and we begin the next movie.

Allyson O'Hara-Cribdon is a creative imagination and empowerment mentor, guiding and inspiring all generations toward living and expressing their passions using ancient wisdom and intuitive magic. Find out how to connect with Allyson at www.MeetOurAuthors.com.

September 28

Dad's Glory

Lynne Turbie Menon

"A father is neither an anchor to hold us back nor a sail to take us there but a guiding light whose love shows us the way." ~ Unknown

I am grateful that when I became an adult, my dad became a true father. Thank you, Dad, for shedding the darkness of your childhood and giving me the time to soak in your lightness. Thank you for your poetry. Thank you for your music. Thank you for resurrecting and becoming a model for what a husband and father should be. I am forever grateful that you connected with me in all of your glory and supported my growth. Thank you for sharing in my joy at graduation and for allowing me to glow in our after-dance. Thank you for being here to meet my beloved and behold him as I do.

Now, I see the day you passed, September 28, 1996, not as a dark day but as a day of transition. It was a challenge, but I summoned the strength you instilled and the fortitude to grow in love. I found a new normal with your light, August Norman Turbie, and that light shines through me.

Lynne Menon, MFA, is a freelance writer and blogger. She is a wife and mom, editor of the California Writers Club, Tri-Valley Branch website, and is working on her memoir. Discover more about Lynne at www.MeetOurAuthors.com.

September 29

Evan's Canyon at First Light

Anne Domagala

"When you rise in the morning, give thanks for the morning light."
~ Tecumseh

There is a trail called Evan's Canyon at the north end of Reno, the start of many miles of the Nevada landscape owned by the Bureau of Land Management. A trail runner could get lost up there, and for this I'm grateful.

There is no light like the pale salmon pink that takes the horizon at dawn. The bowl of Reno dotted with buildings and trees stretches toward the base of the Sierras, adopting the new hue of daylight. The temperature is cool, the air tinged with the scent of earth and sage. I am grateful for the morning light, for the muscles and breath that carry me up the winding narrow clay trail of Evan's Canyon, first along the creek and past the owl that turns his slow gaze toward me, then up past boulders and scrub to the vista overlooking the city.

I'm grateful for the dog that has accompanied me for years along the top of the canyon, the constancy of earth, the surprise of California quail alighting from behind a stone. I am reminded that I am a breathing human running along a tiny bit of land mined for precious metal, and that this is precious earth.

Anne Domagala is a writer, illustrator, and international finance professional living in Oakland, Calif. Find out more at www.MeetOurAuthors.com.

September 30

Light Up a Life

Suzanne Cousins

"Gratitude is a currency that we can mint for ourselves and spend without fear of bankruptcy." ~ Fred De Witt Van Amburgh

I had a wonderful childhood with lots of laughs, fun and happiness. Later in life I married and had two wonderful daughters and grandchildren—a life that would be envied by many. I will be forever grateful to my parents, brothers, husband, children and grandchildren for the happiness in my life.

After 40 years of marriage my husband decided he wanted someone other than me in his life, and I was absolutely devastated. It was one of the lowest points of my life, and I found it very difficult to cope. But life is full of ups and downs, and we have to find ways of traveling through the downs to come up the other side again.

My coping mechanism was my wonderful Spaniel dog Millie. She was there for me when I needed her, a friend and companion. The love and loyalty of a dog is endless, and I can't express the gratitude I felt for my little friend. She saw me through the devastation and traveled with me to the up side again. Gratitude works both ways, and she knew happiness from her gratitude to me. Thank you, my friend, for being there and bringing me happiness again.

Suzanne Cousins has created the group Sparkle After Divorce on Facebook to help people realize there is a life after divorce. Find out more at www.MeetOurAuthors.com.

October

October 1

Growing in Gratitude

Katrina Oko-Odoi

"There's a party inside of me that's celebrating everything I do."
~ Clifford Oko-Odoi

I've learned most of what I know about gratitude from my husband, Cliff. When we met in our 20s, we had tons of fun but shared a cynical outlook on life. Gratitude as a practice wasn't on our radar.

Two years later, I was in graduate school and Cliff was working full-time in sales while finishing his degree. Then he got fired. This single event paved the way for a new chapter in our lives. While unemployed, Cliff dedicated himself wholeheartedly to self-reflection and improvement. He read countless books, developed daily affirmations, and over time profoundly changed his outlook on life to one of positivity and gratitude. I was skeptical. But as I watched him grow into a more fulfilled and optimistic person, I started believing in a positive mindset too.

As Cliff has taught me, it all comes down to gratitude: being grateful for where you are right now and for what is to come. I began my own journey of gratitude thanks to his example, and our children and business emerged from this shared mindset. I am incredibly grateful for Cliff, our sons, and the life that we've built. I look forward to continuing to grow in gratitude.

Katrina Oko-Odoi is a published author, Ph.D., and founder and chief editor of ContentWorm, a company dedicated to content marketing, writing, and editing for businesses and entrepreneurs. Learn more: www.MeetOurAuthors.com.

October 2
Swimming Without Touching the Bottom
Jane Maliszewski

"Life does not have to be perfect to be wonderful." ~ Unknown

A shot of good bourbon. A roaring fire on a cold October night. The moon hanging full and low. Honoring the anniversary of their passing, days apart. "Here's to Mom and Dad dancing in the moonlight, together again." A swirl, a sniff, a deep swallow. My dad would have enjoyed this.

I emulated my dad. He had an outsize presence, infectious energy and curiosity, an insatiable zest for life. I spent my entire adult life trying not to become my mom. Our approach to life was like oil and water.

When she passed, I suddenly realized I had lost my springboard, the resistance that had propelled me to action. Like when you wade into the roaring ocean and are lifted with the waves, and then frantically scramble to feel the touch of the sandy bottom before you push off again into the swell.

I spent a year after Mom left flailing around trying to find my footing. Finally, feeling sand beneath my feet. Ready now to push into the swell and swim on my own, no longer touching the bottom.

Every day, a prayer of gratitude for who I have become because of them.

Jane Maliszewski is a leader and life coach using neuro-transformation and embodiment to help her clients learn new ways to take action toward what they really want in life. Discover more about Jane at www.MeetOurAuthors.com.

October 3

Ode to Bacon

Terri Stovall

"Cherish your precious memories from childhood; they will fulfill you for a lifetime." ~ Terri Stovall

My longest and most precious love affair has always been with bacon. I love bacon. When I was a young girl, maybe 6 or 7 years old, I used to get off of the school bus at my grandmother's house. Every day, that smoky, salty aroma would be wafting down the driveway as I skipped my way to the house. Heaven in a skillet. I loved my grandmother so much. She understood that bacon was always the answer.

Move ahead nearly half a century and tastes inevitably change. My bacon now has to be nitrate and nitrite free. Uncured, but smoked, of course, and I start my mornings with this delectable treat, too, rather than just daydreaming about my fix at the end of the workday. Bacon brings me the purest of joy.

Now that the Keto diet has been all the rage, the "good bacon" has become a little more scarce. When I find it, I bring it all home. Like a thief in the night, hugging my salty treasure until it makes it to my freezer. Some may think bacon is just a food, but it is my guilty, or not-so-guilty, pleasure.

Terri Stovall is an artist and travel blogger. She can be found at the site Sisterhood of the Traveling Brush and www.MeetOurAuthors.com.

October 4
The Celebration of Our Unity
Apelu Poe

"The deepest level of communication is not communication but communion. It is wordless...beyond speech...beyond concept."
~ Thomas Merton

They say that, in this Christian life, there are certain days that sort of stand out from our normal routine. Today is such a day. Today marks the end of the creation season, a time that we are called to acknowledge that God is the creator and the ruler of all created

beings. But today also sets the stage for the beginning of the providence season, a time for us to proclaim that God provides for our needs. And it marks it with the celebration of our World Communion Sunday.

What is World Communion Sunday? It is a Sunday on which we are joined with all our brothers and sisters in celebrating our sense of unity. Why bother to do that in a time characterized by racial divisions? Because, despite the differences in the colors of our skin, our national origin or our religious background, we are all part of God's global family. The Bible says, "God made, of one blood, all nations of men and women so that we should seek the Lord," (Acts 17:26). What, then, should be our response? Oh, let's give thanks to the Lord, for He is good, for His steadfast love endures forever.

Originally from Samoa, Apelu Poe, Ph.D., is the author of a forthcoming book series, *How to Live with God's Time: Hidden Secrets of the Master's Mind.* Find out how to connect with Apelu at www.MeetOurAuthors.com.

October 5
Gratitude: Most Effective When Least Expected
Lindy Schneider

"A grateful mind is a great mind which eventually attracts to itself great things." ~ Plato

I had been at my job for only two months when I felt the tap on my shoulder. "Please follow me to my office immediately," my manager said quietly.

He told me my company was laying off 20 percent of its employees. I was one of those employees. My mind whirled with worries of the future and how much I did not want to leave this job. I also realized I would not get another chance to express my gratitude to this man who had made the initial decision to hire me. I held out my hand and said, "Thank you for the opportunity to work here. I have loved it."

My manager was stunned. He said, "Of all the things I expected to hear today, thank you was not one of them!"

That evening when I plugged in my phone I noticed a voicemail from a number I did not recognize. It was from a recruiter. The message said that my manager had been so impressed by my graciousness he had forwarded my resume onto another company with his recommendation. If I wanted it, I had a new job on Monday. This day of loss ended in joy.

Lindy Schneider is the creator of the College Superhero Secrets online program. It helps students build great relationships and launch their careers before they graduate. Learn more at www.MeetOurAuthors.com.

October 6

Now, I Am the Voice

Monique McDonald

"When our hearts turn to our ancestors, something changes within us." ~ Russell M. Nelson

As I breathe in and out, I listen to the voices representing the echoes of time that live within me. I know that I am here because of the ones who have come before. If I get really still, I can hear them whisper words of encouragement and gratitude.

Gratitude? But what are you thanking me for? I am so grateful to YOU. For your courage and the legacy of life experience you have left for me to build on. For the sweet messages still left in my DNA that guide me through the dark. For all of the energetic code that flows through my body, encouraging me to grow past anything I could imagine.

I haven't done enough yet. I haven't made the mark I want to make on the world yet. I haven't helped enough people yet. Yes, they say. You are right. You still have more to do. You still have more souls to guide back to their magnificence. Yet, dearest one, you are living for us now. You are the passion and power that is still left unexpressed. Now, you are our voice.

Monique McDonald is a vocal specialist who helps leaders, speakers and coaches connect their voice to their power and passion. More at www.MeetOurAuthors.com.

October 7

The Joy of Journaling

Paula S. Webb

"Focus on the journey, not the destination. Joy is found not in finishing an activity but in doing it." ~ Greg Anderson

I awake every morning excited to start the day. I sit quietly with a cup of coffee and my journal. Here I write down ideas and possibilities. I record, explore, dream and create.

My journal holds my history. I write down something that happened yesterday or recall an event from the past. I note something I heard on the news or record a quote from a book I'm reading. I look back in the pages and see how far I've come.

While journaling, I often think about the day ahead and create a plan to easily navigate through it. My journal also holds lists. It may be a list of grocery items, vacation spots and books I want to read.

If I have a decision or choice to make I record the options. I take each possibility to its natural conclusion. I eventually create a picture and know how to proceed forward.

Journals today include bullet journals, digital, one-liners, prompts and more. I still find there's nothing like a cup of coffee and a blank sheet of paper. My journal serves as a map to get me to my destination and allows me to enjoy the journey.

Paula lives in east Texas, and loves writing, nature, and trying new things. You can learn more about Paula and journaling at www.MeetOurAuthors.com.

October 8

Morning Waking Ritual

Megan Saint-Marie

"Coffee is a language in itself." ~Jackie Chan

My hand reaches out and spreads along the smooth, soft, pale sheet, and I feel like I'm on vacation at a resort. I bought these pale blue cotton sheets after taking such a trip to Mexico. Once I was home in Oregon, I remember thinking that a small thing like quality sheets really can feel luxurious and make the morning that much nicer.

I look out my sliding glass door past the black European-inspired cafe table and cast-iron chairs with blue velvet cushions. I stare at the huge cedar tree across the lane that is so large, it houses several varieties of birds.

These trees are one of my favorite things about living here. They are dark green with a bark that almost turns orange at sunset when the sun's rays are at that magical angle. I often gaze at them letting my mind go blank, almost in a state of meditation. More often than not, I jump back into bed to stare some more after making a pot of dark roasted French press coffee. The pungent aroma fills my room, smelling like a cafe, as I slowly awaken to the day again savoring the bitter sips and sweet view.

Megan Saint-Marie helps women overcome fear and shame to embrace their creative, sensual souls. Find out more at www.MeetOurAuthors.com.

October 9

Naked Truth About Joy

Dr. Nicki Steinberger

"I choose to make the rest of my life the best of my life." ~ Louise Hay

Joy is a practice.

Unlike the instant pleasure one might receive from eating chocolate cake, drinking wine, or winning a lottery, deep, sustainable joy is cultivated through practice.

I learned to nurture this life lesson for the pure sake of survival. You see, I have an addiction to flour and sugar. What's the big deal? Well, besides feeling controlled by a substance, compelled to participate in self-defeating eating behaviors, and becoming wiped-out after indulging, it's dangerous for me to partake due to type 2 diabetes.

Our mindset is a life compass, so I learned to use mine wisely. I decided (an aha intuition) that deep joy (cellular, long-term, and readily-available) was what I desired. Here is where the practice began. Affirmations are powerful. This is because retraining our mind loops is necessary to living in the present moment, where joy resides. Dedicating too much time to the past or future pulls us away from real life.

"Deep joy is what I'm going for," is my daily mantra. It comes to me through nature, creativity, and connection. And guess what? Deep joy happens to be addictive. That's one addiction I can live with.

Dr. Nicki Steinberger is a holistic health educator, writer, and creator of the Holistic Lifestyle Practices (HLP) approach to preventing and reversing type 2 diabetes. Find out more at www.MeetOurAuthors.com.

October 10

Happiness Is All Around Us

Suzanne Alba

"There are so many beautiful reasons to be happy." ~ Unknown

I am a positive person. Always have been and always will be. I don't get upset when something small doesn't go right or flustered when I am running behind. It is my secret superpower. I know how to turn any bad situation into a great one.

There was a time, however, when I wasn't a joyful, smiley girl. When I was a freshman in college I was diagnosed with an auto-immune disorder. Like anyone else in this situation I was upset, but then I decided I wasn't going to waste my time being depressed over something I couldn't change.

People tend to be astonished by how I handled this life-altering situation. I am now on medication for the rest of my life, attend physical therapy, and have frequent visits to the doctor. They want to know how I remain so calm and cheerful. I simply tell them to look around. Look at the magnificent mountain ranges, the beautiful flower gardens, and the wonderful sunsets. Look at your family, your friends, and your partner. Look at your home, your job, and the food in your fridge. No matter what, there is always something to be happy about.

Suzanne Alba is a lifestyle, pregnancy, parenting, teaching, and finance blogger and the founder of Reveal and Revel. Find out more at www.MeetOurAuthors.com.

October 11

Atlas Holds My Celestial Heavens

Warren L. Henderson Jr.

"Each day of our lives, we make deposits in the memory banks of our children." ~ Charles R. Swindoll

Today's gratitude is for the growing life of this young grandson. Atlas is our littlest star. I am so grateful God gave us you. At 12 months old, your vocabulary is your tremendous smile. It welcomes others immediately. With it, you pronounce words of joy, gratitude and love. To be sure, your energetic laugh makes yours and the world around you a better place. Watching you ingeniously explore the world fills me with excitement and anticipation. Walking the long path of life with us is but one treasured thing we will share. As life experiences begin to evolve, you will learn stories that anticipate being heard. I can only begin to imagine the adventures, challenges, discoveries and dreams that await you.

I am grateful as well for your parents. Their life examples show that honesty is the only policy and that doing a good day's work will always make you feel better. With guidance and loving care, we will keep you safe as you grow and learn. My advice: Be a loyal person that others can count on and trust.

Atlas and I will be close always. Pray every day that God continues His blessings.

Warren L. Henderson Jr. is a college professor and the author of *Make-It-New Journal: Transform Your Outlook; Rekindle Your Life*. More at www.MeetOurAuthors.com.

October 12

A Daily Dose of Kindness

Leasha West

"No act of kindness, no matter how small, is ever wasted." ~ Aesop

When was the last time you unexpectedly surprised someone "just because" or spontaneously showed kindness to a stranger? My everyday joy is partially derived from my commitment to deliberately showing kindness to others and scattering sunshine on a daily basis. While some of this is rooted in my well-mannered southern upbringing, I've found that doing good deeds brings happiness and great joy. Watching someone's face light up or seeing that sigh of relief is the most heartwarming moment. What's even better is remaining anonymous and seeing the recipient's surprise.

Being mindful of ways to spread the warmth is a good way to start each day. Every thoughtful gesture no matter how big or small is an easy way to make a positive difference. And the best part? Kindness is contagious! Once you see people smile and witness their inspiration, you'll be committed to a life of altruism. Scientifically, being kind softens the arteries and lowers blood pressure—it's like a muscle that grows when developed and atrophies when unused. The more you practice it, the better you get at it. One act of kindness may not change the world, but it can change someone's world. Make every day count.

Leasha West is the CEO of West Financial Group Inc., a decorated Marine Corps veteran and member of the Forbes Finance Council. Connect with her at www.MeetOurAuthors.com.

October 13
Finding Joy
Angie Mangino

"The root of joy is gratefulness. It is not joy that makes us grateful; it is gratitude that makes us joyful." ~ David Steindl-Rast

When my husband died, family and friends surrounded me in love, a blessing that helped me discover joy again. My close friends since childhood invited me to brunch a few weeks later. As we hugged goodbye, one of them whispered in my ear.

"You've been a great caregiver. Now promise to take care of yourself."

I promised. The learning part, however, took much longer. It just felt so selfish to focus on myself!

Eventually I realized self-care isn't at the expense of others, so how can it be selfish? I practiced caring for myself by starting each day on my porch with a cup of coffee. While there, I began to reflect on the good in my life: family, friends, times enjoyed, all I have, what I want, accomplishments, and goals. With quiet time set aside just for me, I feel at peace. I rediscover joy. Joy increases, not lessens, my capacity to value others. Caring for myself, gratefulness propels me to accomplish more. I have a clear focus on the day ahead where problems are less overwhelming, and my choices are conscious ones.

The day runs more smoothly when I begin it in gratitude. Joy then sustains me in each moment of every day.

Angie Mangino is a freelance journalist, book reviewer, editor, and Tottenville History researcher. Learn more about her at www.MeetOurAuthors.com.

October 14
Music Helped Heal My Brain!
Kaye Suchmann

"Music can restore some of the cognitive functions, sensory and motor functions of the brain after a traumatic injury."
~ Sandhya Raghavan

I've always been grateful for my family, friends, rewarding career and health. But gratitude now has a different depth for me. October 14, 2018, I fell down a railroad platform staircase, shattering my skull. I am grateful for the witness that called 911 and waited for the ambulance arrival, and I'm grateful for renowned brain surgeon Dr. Jonathan Brisman being present at the hospital and agreeing to do my surgery at midnight.

The prognosis offered to my family was very grim. Survival was questionable, and if I did survive, I would likely suffer many deficits—worst of all being a vegetative state. I underwent two surgeries and was in a drug-induced coma for two weeks. As I regained consciousness and ability to communicate, I was gently given details as to what happened.

My overall reaction was questioning why I was so lucky to be on a course of optimistic recovery. Every doctor, nurse and therapist was surprised by my progress, and I'm grateful that my recovery is close to 100%.

My special thanks to Pete, Helen, Mike, Dave, Sophia, Robin, Angela, Vicki, Peter and Shiloh —our Beagle—who all stayed close by my side during my recovery.

Kaye is co-owner of an online scrapbooking business and spent 32 years as an orchestra teacher, which, she says, may explain her amazing recovery. More at www.MeetOurAuthors.com.

October 15

White Cane Safety Day

Darian Slayton Fleming

"The only thing worse than being blind is having sight but no vision."
~ Helen Keller

As a person who is blind with multiple disabilities, I am thankful for the white cane and the guide dog. I have utilized one or the other throughout my life to enjoy the benefits and privileges of community living.

On October 6, 1964, a joint resolution of the U.S. Congress, H.R. 753, was signed proclaiming October 15 as White Cane Safety Day. In 1964, President Lyndon B. Johnson proclaimed October 15 as the day every year when people who are blind celebrate the freedom and independence the white cane symbolizes. In 2011, White Cane Safety Day was also named Blind Americans Equality Day by President Barack Obama.

I am thankful to be living in an age when strong advocates continue to work hard for my rights to be included in all aspects of the community. The White Cane Safety Law means that drivers and cyclists who see a blind person, identified by a white cane or a guide dog, must stop and remain stopped until he/she has completely vacated the roadway. Thank you for being a responsible, safe driver.

Please make every day a white cane safety day!

Darian Slayton Fleming is a passionate disability rights advocate. She brings her own life experiences to supporting her clients as a clinical social worker and rehabilitation counselor in Portland, Oregon. Learn more about Darian at www.MeetOurAuthors.com.

October 16
My Brother JoeJoe
LaVerne M. Byrd

"When we give cheerfully and receive gratefully, everyone is blessed." ~ Maya Angelou

My brother JoeJoe, despite his disability, enjoyed life. JoeJoe always wore his watch to keep track of time and his radio to listen to his favorite DJ. He had limited mobility, but he would groove to the music of the '70s and '80s while holding on to his walker.

JoeJoe loved the television show *Sanford and Son*. He knew the punch lines by heart and laughed right on cue. Listening to my brother crack jokes just like Fred Sanford was a real treat. It was his way of cheering you up.

Recently, JoeJoe wanted me to call him "Kojak." I was told that one day after he got a haircut, he went to the community room, where the residents gather for coffee and conversation. Someone there called him Kojak because he had a bald head. So, he adopted that name for himself. It became his alter ego. He thought he was a ladies' man!

JoeJoe is no longer with us. He is one of the many Americans who did not survive COVID-19. I am grateful that I was able to assist in caring for my brother in his latter days. I am grateful for the memories I hold in my heart forever.

LaVerne M. Byrd is the author of *Heal My Pain, A Journal for Grieving Mothers*. She has recently started a blog, The Journey of Grief. More at www.MeetOurAuthors.com

October 17
Hopeless Run-Away Kid
Dr. Marilyn Joyce

"Joy can be real only if people look upon their lives as a service and have a definite object in life outside themselves and their personal happiness." ~ Leo Tolstoy

Have you ever had the experience of being "in the zone"? You know, that place where you can't say or do anything wrong, and everything you're saying and doing is guided by something far beyond you. Not outside of you but flowing through you. Well, that happened to me! As I stood there in the midst of a standing ovation from a roomful of students, I realized my passion and joy: being a messenger of hope.

I had experienced joy while trekking Machu Picchu, the Great Wall of China, the Himalayas, and the Galapagos Islands. But nothing compares to the natural wonder of standing in front of university and college students who are full of deep, soul-searching questions.

There I found myself sharing the journey that took me from a homeless and hopeless 14-year-old runaway living on the streets of Toronto to achieving several advanced degrees and professional success. That journey led me to now inspire hope, a sense of purpose, belief in oneself, and the knowing that whatever can be dreamed can be achieved.

I volunteered to speak at these business classes because I was looking for ideas from innovative young minds. I left with so much more. I was the one enriched and inspired.

Dr. Marilyn Joyce is an award-winning speaker and mentor, No. 1 best-selling author, and stress release expert. Find out more about her at www.MeetOurAuthors.com.

October 18
Everyday Joy in My Business
Michell Pulliam

"Knowing your worth and living your truth are the key ingredients to loving your life." ~ Michell Pulliam

I've spent the majority of my life motivating people. As a pastor's wife, encouraging others is second nature to me. Although ministry work was gratifying, I felt there was more God wanted me to do.

After going through what I like to call my "midlife enlightenment," I came out finally discovering my assignment in life. My season of study, self-reflection, and working on myself was intense, but the transformation I experienced was well worth it. The payoff? I had the tools needed to create a business and life that aligned with everything I desired.

I took the lessons I used to reinvent my own life and created personal and professional development coaching programs for women. My mission is to empower women to dream again, so they can fully walk in their God-given purpose—and start sharing it with the world.

My business is everything I could dream of. I wake up every morning excited to see how I can help women conquer their obstacles. I have the honor of showing women how to uncover their desires and live a life on purpose. I do this while building a business that brings me gratification, joy, and financial security.

Michell Pulliam is an author, speaker, blogger, women's mindset coach and the creator of The Cultured Life Signature System™. Find out more at www.MeetOurAuthors.com.

October 19

Age Is Just a Number

Sandy Anchondo

"I don't believe in aging. I believe in forever altering one's aspect to the sun." ~ Virginia Woolf

Memories flood through my mind's eye like tiny vignettes stitching my past experiences together. The years slip by, and yet I feel immune to the effects of Father Time. Today marks my 60th rotation around the sun on this glorious blue orb, and I'm feeling blessed and grateful to be here!

My excitement for life and love of family sustains me. But I wonder if it's my eagerness and curiosity to discover new places that inspires me the most.

Boating down the Amazon River was unbelievable. Traveling through Australia and snorkeling at the Great Barrier Reef were amazing, Fiji was like paradise, and exploring the Mayan ruins of Mexico was fascinating. Europe enveloped all my senses, Banff National Forest was breathtaking and, ah, the soft, white sand beaches of the Bahamas. All magnificent destinations but no comparison to the awesomeness of road tripping through America.

Sometimes I get introspective about what actual value I've contributed to humanity. Is life measured solely by the goals we achieve, or is it a mixture of our experiences and relationships that count most? I believe our life story is a wonderful combination of all these events, and I'm grateful to God for being here.

Sandy Anchondo is the founder and owner of Re-Style Interiors, a full-service design firm creating inspiring interiors you love to live in. Find out more about Sandy at www.MeetOurAuthors.com.

October 20

Early Morning Blessings

Gwyn Goodrow

"An early-morning walk is a blessing for the whole day." ~ Henry David Thoreau

Chaos begins. A sharp, chastising alarm clock buzz and the house shakes to life—ready or not. The rings, hums, and vibrations of technology jolt me awake.

Enough.

Imagine a day of joy, serenity, and calm. I've discovered that a small change in my routine pivots my perspective. My morning begins with a quick escape from the high-tech house and intentional entry into a nearby forest with my trusted camera in tow.

Golden sunbeams break through the towering pine and oak trees to rest softly on the forest trails. Ground fog dissipates around me. Birds share their morning songs and chatter amongst themselves in sweet harmonies. Animals scurry into the underbrush; even turtles, frogs, lizards, and ants provide entertainment as they begin their day's activities.

In the beginning, these walks were as rushed as the chaos I left behind me. My steps were continually trying to outpace my brain's stormy tempo.

Now, however, these quiet moments connect me to nature's nuances as each season unfolds. My photos capture my life's season of rural living with vivid colors and layered textures. I cherish my photography time with nature, and these short walks bless my entire day.

Gwyn Goodrow pursues opportunities to share travel stories through words and photographs. Gwyn contributes to online and print publications and holds memberships with ITWPA and TravMedia. Find out more at www.MeetOurAuthors.com.

October 21

Every Stage Is a Lesson

Bina Kozuch

"If I am not for myself, who will be for me? But if I am for myself, what am I?" ~ Rabbi Hillel

What is in store for us?

Yes, I read about the "fancy" life in America; the wonder word was uttered from everyone's lips. The dream world many spoke about when one left the movie theater.

We just left my birth country. I was in the prime of my teenage years. A life when one connects with peers and even falls in love. Was it difficult? As the saying goes, "You bet!"

The boat approached the pier. The waves were hitting lightly against the shore. The sun's rays were penetrating through the gray, soft, fluffy clouds. Thousands crowded the pavements waiting for their loved ones to descend the ship's steps.

Pangs of hesitation and fear hit the depth of my heart. Would my life be filled with waves of turbulence or would I ride the smooth wave of success?

As I reflect back on my rich life of experiences in this wonderful land of opportunity, the land of freedom, the USA, I am filled with gratefulness for every step I was able to take, whether it was filled with pain, despair, or jubilation.

For the past few years I have reached the epic of my life, which I never thought I could accomplish. I self-published " Triumph After All" and completed my second book. I am an author, and I am grateful!

Bina Kozuch is the author of *Triumph After All*. As an educator, she integrates into her lessons the philosophy of courage, tenacity, and the belief in God in the face of desolation. More at www.MeetOurAuthors.com.

October 22

Finding Joy in the Journey

Daphne Bach Greer

"She found joy and wonder in every little thing. And joy and wonder always found her." ~ Katrina Mayer

How much would our lives improve if we acknowledged and appreciated the little things in life? Everyday joy is hearing the deep giggles of a baby, embracing chaos, being mesmerized by the colors of the vibrant summer blooms and captivating sunsets. It brews happiness from within.

A friendly smile, silly antics from a pet, a kind gesture from a co-worker all bring that emotional fulfillment many of us crave. But life isn't always sunshine and rainbows. To make it through life's struggles, we must uncover the joy buried within, allowing us to transform our struggles into blessings. We must focus, choosing to keep our eyes on the prize. Seeking everyday joy drives us to be authentic with ourselves, letting seeds of hope and joy reign over our hearts.

It means finding beauty in the moment. Joy replenishes your soul and revives your spirit, igniting your faith and allowing you to rest in His peace. Intentionally choosing to recognize the simple gifts in everyday life grants us an eternal perspective which shall not be shaken. It just may be what you've been searching for all along.

"Those who sow in tears will reap with shouts of joy." (Psalm 126:5)

Daphne Bach Greer is the co-author of *Grief-Diaries: Will We Survive*. Focusing on inspiration, she writes about grief, faith and finding hope after loss. More at www.MeetOurAuthors.com.

October 23
Always the Same & Always Different
Cheryl Major

"The garden suggests there might be a place where we can meet nature halfway." ~ Michael Pollan

Confusing title? Yes and no.

Everyday joy is found in nature. Nature is always there, and it's always different. For example, the garden for me is a source of wonder. I never know in the morning what will be beginning to show off with a colorful bloom or what will be saying goodbye until next year.

I have mostly perennials and roses in the garden; it's been a journey of trial and error over the years. While I've done the initial planting, nature has done the deciding. It seems nature and the gardens decide which plants thrive and survive to revisit year after year bringing color and joy, and which are a soft, disappointing memory. A wonder as to what went wrong: Why didn't they like it here?

Sometimes it's the rabbits and the deer making the decisions. Healthy robust plants, like my cherished baptisia and many hostas, were gorgeous one evening and little stumps the next. Lesson learned: Always ask if a plant is going to be a favorite of my much-loved little yard critters.

Is it the color, the shape, or the fragrance? I don't know, but it is everyday joy!

Cheryl Major is a certified nutrition and wellness consultant who offers timely information and coaching to help you lose weight and depression and be healthier. Find out more at www.MeetOurAuthors.com.

October 24

T&T

Bettina "Sparkles" Obernuefemann

"I will give thanks to the Lord with my whole heart." ~ Psalm 9:1

Today, and every morning when able, I read one page from my favorite devotional booklet titled *Jesus Calling*. The daily articles invite me to turn to Christ with trust and thanks (T&T).

Today, I again thank my sister-in-law who gifted me nine years ago with this wonderful booklet that supplemented my spiritual growth. This call is for all of humankind.

Daily readings prepare me for another sacred day. Memory joggers awaken me to turn all my struggles over to Him, ask for His guidance and keep me focused on my purpose of life. In the silence, I feel His loving presence.

Every day, the experience of the COVID-19 pandemic points out the safety of living in a bubble. This metaphor gives clarity to the concept of God as being the higher self, oneness and love. I imagine all the universes, all of creation immersed in a bubble of this love, and therefore it must live inside of me eternally.

Today, I invite the reader to celebrate my 80th birthday with me, and I celebrate your life, seeing it empowered with praises, T&T. Today, I am full of gratitude for my life in the infinite bubble of love.

Bettina "Sparkles" found her self-worth and spiritual path with PTSD recovery. She conversed with her inner child, a continuous process that nurtures a closer relationship with the higher self. Find out more about Bettina at www.MeetOurAuthors.com.

October 25

Choose Joy Every Day

Shona Battersby

"Joy does not simply happen to us. We have to choose joy and keep choosing it every day." ~ Henri JM Nouwen

It is important to start the day by allowing yourself to recognize just how good things are. Spend time every morning reflecting on the small blessings in your life. This will move you from a negative mindset into a more positive and proactive one.

There are so many ways that you can bring joy into your life daily, but you have to make a choice to do so. Whenever you remember during the day, take the time to really look around you and appreciate the small things. Take some really deep breaths to relax and become aware of all that is around you and become present in the moment. You have five senses—sight, sound, taste, touch and smell—so use them to fully experience the moment. The more senses you use the greater and more memorable the experience.

What is it that brings a smile to your face? Music? Children playing and laughing? Just watching what others are doing or wearing? Funny movies? Remember, "Laughter is the best medicine."

Shona Battersby does spiritual healing and transformational guidance using reiki, massage, crystals and other tools. Discover more about her at www.MeetOurAuthors.com.

October 26

One Step at a Time

Cody Wooten

"You can do anything once you stop trying to do everything."
~ Darren Hardy

As a leadership coach, I work with a lot of people with dreams, often huge dreams. I, myself, also have a huge dream that I am looking to accomplish, and when you have a dream that you can see so clearly, you want to see it happen right now.

It can be difficult to feel happy when you feel like there are so many things you need to accomplish all the time, and there isn't enough time, not enough people or resources or money. If this is you, I ask you to stop.

There is a great Russian proverb that says, "When you chase two rabbits, you catch none."

Follow this advice, and only focus on one step at a time. When you succeed at that step, enjoy it! Realize that you've actually accomplished something! Sometimes when you step back from looking at everything you have to do, and look at what you've already accomplished, you can be amazed at how far you've come.

Your dream may be huge, and you may have a long road ahead of you, but the journey is beautiful. Don't forget to smell the flowers and see the wildlife throughout your journey.

Cody Wooten is a leadership coach, speaker and teacher who helps people unlock their legendary leadership, create dream teams and increase productivity. Find out more at www.MeetOurAuthors.com.

October 27
A Child's Love of Story
Carol A. Peña

"Why was Solomon recognized as the wisest man in the world? Because he knew more stories than anyone else." ~ Alan Kay

When I was young, Mom had a way of finding a little quiet time in a noisy household with storytelling. Her favorites were old folklore and childhood stories of life on the farm. My earliest memory takes me back to a stormy evening at home. She would pop a big bowl of popcorn, then sit all seven of her children in a circle. It was something she learned from her father as a child.

"Let me tell you about La Llorona," she began. A sudden flash of lightning illuminated the room, and a clap of thunder shook the house. As she told of the weeping woman searching for her lost children, we heard a mournful cry come from outside. Mom's scary stories somehow always managed to be perfectly timed to an exposed fence pipe that would howl like an old banshee when the wind was strong and swirling.

I am profoundly grateful to have an amazing mom with a child's love of a good story. Today, we celebrate her and wholeheartedly affirm storytelling does indeed quiet the noise in a busy world.

Carol A. Peña is a native Texan with a passion for creative writing, genealogy and adventures with Buster the Wonder-Yorkie. More at www.MeetOurAuthors.com.

October 28

Joy in the Morning

Kimberly Schramm

"Every breath we take, every step we make, can be filled with peace, joy and serenity." ~ Thich Nhat Hanh

Four white paws click me awake. With Heidi, my miniature poodle, why have an alarm clock? Opening one eye, I look at her. She is sitting upright with that look I know means that she is really ready to go.

My feet hit the floor. She scampers toward the back door, racing and dancing, glancing back to make sure I understand the urgency of the mission. In passing, I hit the brew button on the coffee maker as we head outside.

We greet the morning. At 6 a.m., the air is still warm from the 108-degree day before. The overnight low was 84, so we are enjoying the coolest temperatures of this July day.

Heidi performs her morning ritual. I drink in the sky's unique shade of morning, somewhere between blue and gray as the sun makes its way over the horizon. The air is filled with the sounds of birds, celebrating the dawn of a new day.

A sound signals the end of the coffee maker's brew cycle. I open the door and Heidi dances in. Dumping a scoop of kibble in her bowl, I grab my coffee.

In the quiet of our life, I find everyday joy.

Kimberly Schramm is a business storyteller and marketing strategist. Learn more about how she puts the power of words to work for businesses at www.MeetOurAuthors.com.

October 29

Nurture Happiness with Positive Habits

Tracy Glass

"Happiness is a habit—cultivate it." ~ Elbert Hubbard

Little things in life really can make a difference in creating a sense of joyful well-being. That is why I have found it helpful to sprinkle "happiness habits" throughout my daily routine—small measures I apply throughout my waking hours to promote self-care. Each habit is easy to do and yet contributes greatly to my feeling of contentment. Enjoying a light breakfast upon waking. Making the bed so that it looks pretty and more inviting. Kick-starting my productivity with a delightfully hot cup of coffee. Carving out time to read part of a good book or a favorite magazine. Ending each afternoon with physical activity—an exercise class, a power walk or a set of stretches to erase stress.

None of these happiness habits are elaborate or require immense effort. However, each one helps me remember to take care of myself, since I spend a majority of my time on activities that are focused on helping others. Regular self-care helps me function at a fuller, better capacity.

Tracy Glass is a B2B freelance copywriter serving corporate marketing professionals. She specializes in developing strategic collateral materials and content. Discover more about her at www.MeetOurAuthors.com.

October 30
Finding Joy & Happiness Today
Joyce Blue

"I don't think of all the misery, but of the beauty that still remains."
~ Anne Frank

You have the power to create joy and happiness in your life every day no matter the circumstances you face. When I first heard this message many years ago, I thought the person saying it was crazy. I was in the midst of a roller-coaster marriage and had just found out my husband had been cheating on me. In your darkest hour is when you learn your greatest lessons. Since that time, I've met and worked with so many people that have displayed great joy in horrific situations. How, you may ask? True happiness and joy come from within ourselves.

We really are responsible for our own joy and happiness. The daily practice of gratitude is a great place to start. Each day write three things you are grateful for before you even get out of bed. Some days it might just be the fact you have clothes to wear, air to breathe and water to drink. Being kind to others, smiling, opening doors and saying hello to people you don't know are all great places to start your journey to true joy and cost nothing to implement. Daily joy can be yours!

Joyce Blue is an empowerment coach who shows people how to set aside self-esteem and other struggles to live and lead lives they love. Discover more about her at www.MeetOurAuthors.com.

October 31

Lovely Leo

Katie De Souza

"Whatever the mind of man can conceive and believe, it can achieve." ~ Napoleon Hill

Weighing in at 8lb 10, you were a big baby for me, a small 5-foot-2 frame.

Your little, chubby cheeks were red and blotchy from eczema, yet you were a happy baby who loved to play with his older sister. You loved to play with your legos and would always have identical pieces of the same size and colour held one in each hand.

When you were 4, we took you to the Roman Baths. We gave you and your sister 1p to throw into the wishing well. Gabby threw hers in and made her wish. You put your coin in your pocket. We asked you why, and you said, "It's money. Why are people throwing money away? This is my money. I want to keep it."

I came home to find you with £10. You were 11 and told me you had helped our neighbour unload bags of ice—she gave you the money. Ever the entrepreneur.

Always enjoy life. I am so proud of the young, confident, caring man you have become. Always remember you are loved more than you know and always will be no matter where you are. You are always in our hearts.

Katie De Souza is an author and entrepreneur who inspires couples to achieve their dreams and live a happy and fulfilling life together. Learn more about Katie at www.MeetOurAuthors.com.

November

November 1

My Voice...Set Free!

Judy Morton

"I'm finally sharing my voice, and I inspire others to share theirs!"
~ Judy Morton

What if you found yourself with so much to say, so much to share and a deep-rooted fear that nobody wants to hear your voice. This was me, just a short time ago.

I had a false belief that being a teacher gave the impression I think I know something that you don't know. That it meant somehow, something is missing in you.

This mistaken belief stopped me from being creative. You see, I was hiding behind other people, helping them to share their voice, instead of my own. I thought that was how I could be most helpful.

But I'm not hiding anymore; I want to be someone who inspires. I want to share my voice with the world and share my authentic self: what makes me happy—and what breaks my heart wide open. Most of all, how when I shifted from fear to love and came to a place of deep gratitude for every person and situation in my life, I pulled myself out of a deep, deep depression.

I am never going back again; I am my authentic self!

Judy Morton is a single mom of three and a social media strategist. She loves to light other people up with enthusiasm and joy. Find out more at www.MeetOurAuthors.com.

November 2
Can You Feel It?
Linda Berry

"Our souls speak a language that is beyond human understanding. A connection so rare the universe won't let us part." ~ Nikki Rowe

We're in the soul zone right now. Take advantage of it!

October 31, November 1 and November 2 are the one time of year that the veil is so thin we can touch the other side—and feel it. These three days have been celebrated a multitude of ways over the last couple thousand years by different religions and cultures. Most recently known as Halloween, All Saints Day and All Souls Day, they help the world honor life, death and the unknown in rituals, festivals and esoteric practices.

I'm spiritually grateful for these three days. They offer the most opportune time to get in touch with my soul. There are different aspects of your soul. It's your connection to the creative energy, the god force, the universe—the spark of life. Here in the earthly school for souls, we can pass our tests by using this precious energy.

Cooperate with this energy. Connect to its frequency as it resonates and connects us all. Hear its soft flutters of communication from the other side that help you bond with yourself, your life and others around you. Feel the energy, the energy of the loving force—the soul's only reality on Earth.

Linda Berry is an angel whisperer and the owner, consultant, coach, and reader for the Spiritual Discovery Center. She's also an international astrologer, podcast host, and spiritual and metaphysical book author. Learn more about Linda at www.MeetOurAuthors.com.

November 3

Walking with Memphis

Gregory Paul Hoffmaster

"Until one has loved an animal a part of one's soul remains unawakened." ~ Anatole France

Oh Memphis, where to begin? You were such an amazing and unforgettable being in my life. You were the epitome of a best friend.

You were my friend, my sibling, my parent, and my child all wrapped in one perfect body. I loved all our silly adventures and how you always made me laugh. I loved turning you into the confident, spoiled princess who captured the heart of every person you met. You had my heart from the first moment you fell asleep on my lap and then later woke me up by chewing on my hair. You gave me some of the best years of my life, and I will never forget you. I always try to keep a blue rose nearby in memory of you.

I miss you every day and hope I get to see you again. You were the only thing that continually shined during my darkest hours. You never let my light fully extinguish, and I can never thank you enough for everything you have given me.

You gave me love. You taught me to love. It's as simple as that. I'll forever cherish the memory of waking up to your beaming smile and wagging tail.

Gregory Paul Hoffmaster is one of the lead designers for The Community Book Project and has written in many of the previous editions. He is currently writing a book about social anxiety and other mood disorders. More at www.MeetOurAuthors.com.

November 4

Gratitude for Lilly

Dawn Eileen

"An animal's eyes have the power to speak a great language."
~ Martin Buber

In every moment of life, there is always a lesson of gratitude. Search for a reason to be grateful in every minute of every day. She was a big part of my recovery.

We got her as a family pet, but she turned into so much more. Within a year of getting her, I suffered great losses. Lilly was always by my side. On bad days, she would climb up on my shoulder and put her head against my neck like a huge hug. Through the years, she learned how to detect diabetic highs and lows of my honey. We later realized she also knew when others were sick. She would let me know there was something wrong by patting them and looking at me a certain way saying, "Hey, they are not right."

In her final days, she would try to console me even when she was in pain and having a hard time walking and getting around. I am blessed to have had her for all those years. I believe that people and things are put in our life for a reason. I am grateful for the 14 years I had Miss Lilly.

Dawn Eileen is an inspirational writer, artist, traveler, deep thinker and lover of life who believes in celebrating moments. Check out more about her at www.MeetOurAuthors.com.

November 5

Palm Trees

Donna Burgher

"Attitude is a little thing that makes a big difference." ~ Winston Churchill

Yay, I did it! I moved from gray, cold Michigan to sunny, warm Florida.

I decided I would apply what I teach and manifest my way out of what seemed to be endless snowy, windy and unpleasant days. I choose to focus my attention on the beach poster that I had taped to my office wall. I loved to look at the blue sky and palm trees. I would imagine walking on the hot sand and then the relief my feet would feel as I entered the cool ocean.

The day we arrived I was so excited. I felt like I just moved to paradise. There were palm trees everywhere.

With friends later that day, I enthusiastically said, "Every day can feel like I am on vacation!"

They looked at me like I had two heads. They stated firmly, as if they were the boss of me, "You have to get a job—you are not on vacation."

Almost four years later, I joyfully set up my office outside. I lay out a big beach towel, work under a multicolored umbrella, and sit on my beach chair.

Every day I see palm trees, and I still feel like I am on vacation.

Donna Burgher is the founder and creator of Live a High Vibe Life™. She shows others how to create and manifest a high vibe, abundant life. Find out more at www.MeetOurAuthors.com.

November 6
Try Gratitude, Just for Today
Susan Anderson

"Wear gratitude like a cloak, and it will feed every corner of your life." ~ Rumi

Today, I celebrate another year of being alive; it is my birthday. It is also the 15th anniversary of my daily gratitude practice. Taking different forms over the years, gratitude has become a touchstone for my life. It began as homework for a grief group—the idea being that it is hard to be grateful and sad simultaneously. Remembering that life could still offer even small joys encourages future hope. I now begin and end each day by acknowledging what I am grateful for.

Every day in November, I write a different gratitude on my Facebook page and encourage others to share a gratitude with me. Picking November was natural, with both my birthday and Thanksgiving later in the month. This tradition helps me go into the holiday season with an attitude of gratitude. I find I am more focused on people and memorable experiences and my faith rather than the frantic rush of doing and having and giving more.

Why don't you put on the cloak of gratitude today as the poet Rumi suggests? You could begin slowly with a list on your refrigerator or a few lines in your journal and see where it leads.

Susan Anderson is a lifelong writer and learner. Susan is a business writer, ghostwriter, poet, photographer, and artist. Find out how to connect with Susan at www.MeetOurAuthors.com.

November 7

Eleanor P.
Donna Kozik

Today is my late mother's birthday and I do wish she was still around so I could pepper her with questions. Eleanor was a "city girl" who overnight became the wife of a dairy farmer who was busy from morning to night. She did tell me the story of their first date where they went to the movies, and Dad fell asleep halfway through.

"Were you mad?" I asked. She laughed and said, "No, I knew he had probably been haying all day." I think it was a good early lesson for me to be more easy-going in life.

The farm was a ton of work for Mom and Dad, but we had our fun, too. It was 200 acres of field and woods, so it was natural to build a cabin a mile or so from the house. We'd go up on weekends for weenie roasts and to see the lightning bugs come out at dusk. We had a huge garden there where Dad grew something exotic every year, from yellow watermelon to popcorn.

I think Mom was slightly bemused by the life she lept into when she married Dad. And I am grateful she made the leap!

Donna Kozik is a USA Today and Wall Street Journal best-selling author, along with being the lead editor of *The Community Book Project: Celebrating 365 Days of Gratitude*. Find out more about her at www.MeetOurAuthors.com.

November 8

The Smell of Alfalfa

Lori R. Winslow

"Sometimes you will never know the value of a moment until it becomes a memory." ~ Dr. Seuss

The smell of alfalfa lets me know I'm almost to my happy place, the Colorado River, or just "the river." A drive that lasts four and a half hours, but the last 20 minutes we are engulfed in the smell of alfalfa.

We would get off the main highway and always stop at the Shell Gas Station to refuel and, if we were lucky, get an ice cream. Once we pulled away from the Shell station we left buildings and lights behind and entered farm country. Being raised in the city, it was always so amazing to have the scent of alfalfa overtake the car almost the same way the darkness consumed the landscape.

Alfalfa is an acquired smell. As a kid, I didn't like that smell at all. We would cover our noses and complain for the whole 20 minutes down the last bit of road to camp. As my sisters and I grew older, the smell became the sign that we were almost there. Alfalfa blooming in the summer is not a lovely scent, but it is the scent of my happy place. Now that I live so far away, I rarely get to visit the river, but if I smell alfalfa, I'm already there in my mind.

Lori Winslow helps online business owners develop systems to get and keep their business organized. Learn more at www.MeetOurAuthors.com.

November 9
Finding Joy Through Gratitude
Teresa Miller

"Gratitude is one of the most medicinal emotions we can feel. It elevates our moods and fills us with joy." ~ Sara Avant Stover

I've always considered myself an optimist, so it came as a surprise when I hit my mid-50s and found my optimism waning. I wanted to understand why, so I got to work figuring it out.

After much meditation and soul searching, I came to the realization that what I'd always called optimism was about not living in the present. Instead, I had spent most of my life looking forward to what the future held, to the someday when dreams would come true.

Now, looking back, I felt that my life had not been well spent and that I was running out of time to do better.

The optimist in me refused to wallow in grief over the years I didn't have left. I had to learn to live and love my life in the now. How did I do it?

I started a daily gratitude journal, where every morning I listed 10 things that I am grateful for in my life. Each day had to be a new ten things. And I went to bed each night saying to the universe a heartfelt "Thank you!"

It's amazing how gratitude has healed my negativity and given me true optimism and joy—every day.

Teresa Miller is a publishing and mindset coach for authors and entrepreneurs. She is devoted to inspiring people to discover their own creative joy. Discover more about Teresa at www.MeetOurAuthors.com.

November 10

My First True Love
Marilyn McHenry Fedge

"Fashions fade; style is eternal." ~ Yves Saint Laurent

I love cashmere. I LOVE cashmere!

A black cashmere turtleneck sweater is a classic. Warm and beautiful, it also hides a crepey neck in later years. Yah! Versatile and glorious, wear it with jeans for that smart, casual and polished look. Wear it with black velvet city pants and loads of gold chains, gold hoops or your favorite black skirt, and you are good to go.

I am grateful for many things in my life—my health, family, spring, blueberry pie and cashmere. I saved up for my first cashmere sweater when I was in high school, nearly 50 years ago. It was the beginning of the end for me. A wonderful, black cashmere turtleneck is definitely better than a first kiss.

There is no denying it. Everyone has an obsession for something, be it shoes, jewelry, the beach or lingerie. Whatever it is, it's your thing. Just go for it. If a fire broke out in my home, I would save the obvious—important documents, pictures and, of course, my beloved cashmere sweater.

I am angling for a cashmere robe this Christmas. Forget about it!

For 30 years, Marilyn McHenry Fedge, renowned owner and buyer of McHenry's, built confidence through teaching personal style to hundreds of women. More at www.MeetOurAuthors.com.

November 11
Niece & Nephew Campout
Gloria Howard-Smith

"History will judge us by the difference we make in the everyday lives of children." ~ Nelson Mandela

My greatest joy and my life mission is simple: make children happy. Before I had children of my own, I had many nieces and nephews. We would all attend Friday night church service at my father's church. Before, during, or after service they would ask, "Can I spend the night?" Almost always, my answer was yes. I knew they loved escaping the hum drum of rules and preset bedtimes for the weekend. As my small troop of nieces and nephews would tumble into my small apartment, they would find blankets, fight over the prized sofa or find their spot on the floor. We would eat popcorn and stay up past the usual bedtimes watching movies. Then we had a big breakfast in the morning. I was young, single, unattached, and almost every weekend I had at least four children. A friend asked me, "Are you crazy?" My answer was, "No, I am happy!"

Gloria Howard-Smith is a school counselor, empowerment coach, and forth-coming author of *Glory Girls: 7 Ways to Empower Girls to Live with Confidence.* **Connect with her at www.MeetOurAuthors.com.**

November 12

Gratitude—A Heart's Perspective

Donna Koontz

"That which lies behind you—and that which lies before you—are tiny matters compared to that which lies within you." ~ Ralph Waldo Emerson

BAM!
I'll never forget it.
All I could see was light.
All I could feel was love.
All I could experience was the interconnectedness of life.
The love of all creation within me.
Emanating out from me.
Into the world around me.

Forty-eight luminous hours. Pure bliss inspired by an exploration of my own heart's intelligence accompanied by a profound sense of grace and gratitude.

Since that experience, my heart has become the lens through which I view the world. Soaking in the energetic qualities of gratitude literally charges my soul, revitalizes my body and enhances my capacity to see the light in myself and others, thus keeping my focus on the kindest aspects of humanity.

Imagine 7.6 billion people consciously engaging in life through the lens of their hearts. Humbly and lovingly recognizing the need for positive change. Choosing to express heart qualities innate to us all, such as kindness, compassion and care.

The language of the universe is energy. Our collective intention toward highest good offers a transformational, vibrational impact that serves the whole. The ripples we create radiate out, amplify and return to us. Grateful hearts—ever expanding, all inclusive. Revealing the nature of all that is.

Donna Koontz is a licensed professional specializing in a science-based, heart-intelligent approach to energy management, personal resilience and stress reduction. Find out more about Donna at www.MeetOurAuthors.com.

November 13
Gratitude in Positive Success Journal
Dr. Kanna Krishnan

"It's not happy people who are thankful; it's grateful people who are happy." ~ Arianna Huffington

I still practice writing three most grateful things in my Positive Success Journal today. While writing, I always feel my breath and heart rate become more aligned. My body and nervous system start to relax. I believe, scientifically, certain chemicals are released in the brain as well. These three grateful things, which I call "small successes," are recorded at the end of each day because they help me to limber down, and I feel thankful before going to bed every night. The only condition I impose is that one of three must always refer to an individual and not my own life experience.

I took up this beautiful practice after undergoing a traumatic episode in my life. Journaling helped me to overcome my unhappiness and rekindle what meaningful life really encompasses. I slowly started to find there are so many positive things in life to be thankful for, if only we find ways to recall them somehow—specifically during those low moments! It was not easy writing them at those moments.

However, I am grateful that, rather than reminiscing about the past, I forced myself to look at things Providence has provided for me to positively flourish in this beautiful world!

Dr. Kanna Krishnan is founder of Positive Success Coach and an award-winning entrepreneur focused on positive psychology intervention for individuals and positive workplace culture transformation. Find out how to connect with Dr. Krishnan at www.MeetOurAuthors.com.

November 14
Joy in the Parking Lot
Andy Anderson

"That which we persist in doing becomes easier to do, not that the nature of the thing has changed but that our power to do has increased." ~ Ralph Waldo Emerson

It's 6:35 a.m. My Fitbit's buzzing. It repeats. Twice. Raising my arm up, I blearily push the off button. Blinking. Testing my eyes. One's good enough. Yes. I'm awake. I'm up. I'm ready to go.

Down one flight of stairs. 50 steps. Down two more. Seventy-five more steps. The walk begins.

ITunes is already playing. The same exact playlist as yesterday, the same as 12 months ago. Tough songs to sing along with. Am I able to reach those notes? Complete that phrase with one breath—while I'm walking?

Crossing the street. I get my groove on. These old bones moving again. Singing. Out loud but not "too out loud." How is my voice? Kinda raspy. Not really there yet.

Two thousand three hundred steps. I'm approaching the parking lot of the San Diego Zoo. It's huge. I enter at the northeast end.

I'm ready to sing—at the top of my lungs—without fear of critiques. It's been basic humming for the last few blocks, but now? It's on.

Five thousand. I leave. Convinced I'm on track. It's a good voice day. Other days? Not so much. Sometimes 6,000 or 7,000.

But today, my voice is capable. This. This is an everyday joy. Singing. In a parking lot. Out loud.

Andy Anderson is a local San Diego singer who roams the zoo parking lot. Frequently. You can find his contact info at www.MeetOurAuthors.com.

November 15

The Castleman Boat

Teresa A. Castleman

"Look at that sea, girls—all silver and shadow and vision of things not seen. We couldn't enjoy its loveliness any more if we had millions of dollars and ropes of diamonds." ~ Lucy Maud Montgomery

I'm the shopper of the family with a penchant for shoes. However, when my husband, Brad, buys something, it is usually an investment like a pool table. In 2005, Brad found a reasonably priced 1997 Starcraft aluminum boat.

Fast forward to 2011, when we decided to move 2,300 miles from Indiana to California. The dilemma: to take the boat or not? Since our moving van was a semi, we loaded it up. As Brad says, "It doesn't eat much hay."

Between 2011 and 2020, we used it once or twice a year. We stored it in our garage to keep the "hay costs" down. Who knew that in 2020, our little fishing boat would be the activity that kept us sane!

We both started teleworking 100 percent in March, and other than having conversations with our wonderful cats, our social life dried up. We began taking out the boat on Fridays and weekends, and the sheer joy of lake life and sunshine was rejuvenating and freeing from the daily grind and stress.

We have ordered a bigger motor, and we plan to give the boat a champagne christening when it is mounted. We are truly grateful for our boat!

Teresa is a systems analyst to pay the bills and a health coach to fulfill her soul. However, she is best known as a mother to fabulous cats. Find out more about Teresa at www.MeetOurAuthors.com.

November 16

Joy Is in the Music
Brittany N. Smith

"May your heart always be in a position to seek and choose joy among life's challenges and choices." ~ Nicole Robinson

I remember my mother playing Anita Baker's "You Bring Me Joy" often throughout my childhood. It wasn't until I was much older that I realized my mother suffered with anxiety and depression due to a tumultuous marriage and shattered dreams.

We all need a way to process both triumph and defeat. Music is that one thing that allows me to feel free. The freedom in the journey from pain to joy while moving from verse to chorus is indescribable.

Songs from different genres have the ability to ignite and inspire me. I especially love songs that elevate my mood like Goapele's "Closer," and Elevation Worship's "Fullness," which sparks joy and allows me to visualize days yet to come. Pharrell William's "Happy" and Tasha Cobbs' "Solid Rock" and their playful and upbeat tempos remind me to be grateful of the present.

Acquiring peace and joy is a constant pursuit. If I haven't experienced that joyous calm after one song, I can press repeat or move on to another one.

Something magical happens when I'm dancing and flowing in rhythm to soulful music. I can intentionally exhale negative energy and breathe in only thoughts and feelings that nourish my soul to fuel my life. This is joy.

Brittany N. Smith is a two-time author of *Prayers for Women* devotionals. More at www.MeetOurAuthors.com.

November 17
Celebrate the Progress
Lee Startegies

"It's fine to celebrate success, but it is more important to heed the lessons of failure." ~ Bill Gates

Being a parent is such an awesome privilege. It is easy to get caught up in the busyness of life and miss the small moments. It is in the small moments that parents can find the most joy.

To catch these small moments, be present with your children. Engaging with your kids allows you to see the uniqueness and greatness within them. It also helps you see how they handle setbacks and struggles.

It is in the struggles where you and your child experience and create long-term joy. Finding joy in struggle may sound odd, but it is these moments where the most progress is made.

Think of how exciting it was to see your child crawl and walk their first steps. For them to succeed at these things, they had to struggle. As they get older, the struggles change, and the success can be hidden.

But no matter their age, there is progress to celebrate. To experience everyday joy as a parent, be present, embrace the struggles, and celebrate the progress.

Lee Startegies is an experienced educator and advocate for overlooked youth. He guides families as they transition from frustration and stress to confidence and consistency. Learn more at www.MeetOurAuthors.com.

November 18

How Can I Help?

LuWanda Ford

"Be kind, for everyone you meet is fighting a hard battle."
~ Ian Maclaren

It was December 22, and my husband was moved from intensive care to a regular hospital room.

Things were looking up. Or were they? A nurse broke both his hearing aids trying to disengage the batteries. I could not take them for repair.

When I called the store to see what could be done they didn't have the parts. But they could send them for repair for $135 each. It would take two weeks.

Calling all the stores in the state, I found one an hour away that could fix them. But how to get them there?

A friend asked if there was anything she could do. I thought this was a lot to ask of anyone. But when she heard my story, she only said, "How can I get them from you?"

Early the next morning before leaving, I taped them to the front door. When I brought my husband home from the hospital that evening, the repaired hearing aids were there. They had been fixed and returned.

Even the smallest things can be big things to someone in need. Why do we deny others the chance to help and feel needed themselves?

LuWanda Ford is the founder of the nonprofit Pocket Flag Project and a small business owner focusing on helping people with finances and optimal health. Find out more about her at www.MeetOurAuthors.com.

November 19
Joy on the Dance Floor
Gregory Paul Hoffmaster

"To get the full value of joy you must have someone to divide it with."
~ Mark Twain

Twilight was coming to an end and the wedding reception was beginning. The dance floor was populated with enthusiastic dancers. There were white string lights hung on trees and strung over the dancefloor making the scene enchanting and fairy-like.

I suffer from social anxiety disorder. Simply defined, it's the paralyzing fears and thoughts of being negatively judged by other people and the anxiety that that produces. Currently it's the third largest mental health problem in the world. That being said, dancing is a big no-go for me.

My two-year-old niece, who I helped raise from 4 months old to just over a year old, was a flower girl in the wedding. She's my partner in crime, my monkey, my princess. She skipped over to me, wrapped her little hand around my finger and turned toward the dance floor with me in tow.

Despite having severe social anxiety, I focused only on my niece and her desire to dance with me. I stayed in the present, ignored others around us, and only saw her big blue eyes gazing up at me. Her in her flower girl dress and me in my three-piece navy-blue suit. We danced together, laughing, smiling, not keeping beat, and had a marvelously magical time.

Gregory Hoffmaster is currently working (coached by Donna Kozik) on a book about social anxiety and other mood disorders. Gregory is also a contributing author in *Success Is Yours!* Contact him www.MeetOurAuthors.com.

November 20

The Little Things
Alana Mander

"Learning how to love the little things in life is learning how to be happy." ~ Marcela Reka

Have you ever paid attention to the way a child walks down the street?

My children and I walk the exact same route every morning, yet each day my almost-4-year-old daughter will find something new to marvel at—a flower, a leaf, a snail making its way across the pavement, a bird on a rooftop. All these little things stand out and make her smile. Beauty and curiosity at every turn. How amazing would life be if we, too, could experience that kind of joy every single day?

The truth is we can. Curiosity and joy are innate abilities we are all born with. Somewhere along the road to adulthood our minds become so full of worries and to-do lists, and we spend so much time rushing from one thing to the next, we lose sight of the beautiful moments right in front of us.

So, look up right now and open your eyes. See your surroundings as a child might. Fill your heart with wonder and marvel at the little things. For, as John Kabat-Zinn once said: "The little things? The little moments? They aren't little."

Alana Mander is a writer and mother of two from the United Kingdom who helps people find beauty in the everyday. Find out more about Alana at www.MeetOurAuthors.com.

November 21
The Civil Dusk
Margy Lang

"Nothing can dim the light that shines from within." ~ Maya Angelou

Late fall often reminds me of the beauty of the golden hour, a term to describe the unique gold hue occurring near sunrise and sunset. Golden hour is a favorite time for photographers and filmmakers, offering them an abundance of indirect light that softens the contours of the landscape. In the evening, the meteorological phenomenon is known as "civil dusk."

I relish the evenings when the yellow and rust tones of civil dusk blanket the trees and the pond in my backyard. Even the harsh symmetry of rooftops and buildings are softened in the golden glow. The air seems to be especially still during civil dusk, as if in awe of the solar artistry.

For several years, I've observed more golden hours during the autumn months. Perhaps civil dusk is reflecting the bright hues of fall leaves or the bold color bouncing off the pumpkins sitting patiently in fields waiting to be harvested alongside remains of pale yellow cornstalks. Possibly, civil dusk is a simple invitation for us to step outside, to drink of the glowing light and to pause to give thanks for the sun's artful blend and balance of shimmering gold tones.

Margy Lang assists clients in telling their bold stories to elevate brands, causes and partnerships. Find out how to connect with Margy at www.MeetOurAuthors.com.

November 22

The Return

Lorrie Nixon

"There will come a time when you believe everything is finished; that will be the beginning." ~ Louis L'Amour

It was a Thanksgiving birthday celebration that year, a day full of gratitude and anticipation. What would the next 12 months bring? Sitting quietly, I scrolled through birthday greetings on Facebook. My mind drifted to the past. Our past. A loving relationship had ultimately turned into a long-distance one and eventually faded away. More than 30 years of life's adventures had passed, but a distant longing remained, growing stronger over time.

After many Google searches, I finally found his Facebook page. Checking it from time to time, I was disappointed to see that it had very few updates. That night, I was tempted to write a message but a little hesitant. I started to close the page. Suddenly, as if pushed by an invisible hand, my finger hit "Follow." Startled, and a little nervous, I went to cancel it. Then I thought, "Leave it; he'll never notice."

I awoke to a message asking if he could call me. The years melted away, and he said we should never have parted. For so long, we had both yearned to meet once more. After years apart, we finally found a new beginning. And love grew again. This time, it's a forever love.

Lorrie Nixon is an intercultural communication specialist and a best-selling author. She has trained clients in Italy, Denmark, Greece, Poland and the USA. Contact her at www.MeetOurAuthors.com.

November 23

The Most Amazing Show...
Sally White

"There are only two ways to live your life. One is as though nothing is a miracle. The other is as though everything is a miracle."
~ Albert Einstein

We all have access to the most amazing show on earth, but you won't find it listed in any TV guide. There are no monthly fees. No need of translation nor closed captioning. We'll never see a rerun nor wait six months for a new episode.

We can choose to watch it alone or view it with friends without fear of them getting insulted or upset. It doesn't matter what race, religion, or political beliefs we hold; this show hides no secret agendas.

Often awe-inspiring, this incredible presentation plays once a day with no encore performances. This show gets broadcast across the entire planet. It's celebrated in cultures around the world. It brings people together.

And to view it, we need only step outside.

The sky overhead glowed a bright crimson as far as the eye could see. It looked as if someone had lit a match and set the heavens on fire. Somewhere lost in the red tinted clouds, the sun grinned, another successful performance complete.

Our daily sunset is the most popular form of entertainment, inspiration, and joy in history.

And if cloud cover has marred the day's performance, rest assured, high above, the show must go on.

Sally White is a travel and motivational writer and creator of Adventures of Mom, a family adventure website. Find out more at www.MeetOurAuthors.com.

November 24

When You Open to Life

Kiana Love

"Congratulations! Today is your day.
You're off to great places!
You're off and away!"
~ Dr. Seuss

On my birthday, I'm grateful to be the firstborn U.S. citizen in my family.

I'm grateful my parents met in Toronto in 1967 on a streetcar named Desire. Mom came from the Philippines. Dad worked his way over on a ship from Germany. They were only 21 and 22. I'm grateful my mom didn't leave nursing school with her classmates as usual, or they wouldn't have met.

"May I sit next to you?" my dad said, to which my mom said, "I don't own the seat."

"May I walk you home?" he asked.

She replied, "I don't own the street."

Six months later, they were married, with me on the way. They are still together now. Their story opened me up to believe in possibilities and meet people wherever I go—at the grocery store, on planes, subway stops and even in the bathroom. I've made friends and got clients and great adventures this way.

So I met my husband on New Year's Eve as he bartended, and almost a year later on my birthday, we kissed. We've been together since, going on 13 years. I'm grateful that all is possible when you open to life.

Kiana Love helps women survivors of childhood trauma struggling with upsetting emotions and discomfort in their bodies feel safe and open to life. Discover more about Kiana at www.MeetOurAuthors.com.

November 25
Joy of Conception: Beyond Words
Susan Shatzer

"Even miracles take a little time." ~ Cinderella's Fairy Godmother

Have you ever woken up in the morning and thought, I'm getting older and so is my body? I, too, had this experience five years into my marriage as 30-something rolled around. We wanted to have children, and fertility was required.

To our surprise and amazement, it was Thanksgiving Day when we scored a positive on the home pregnancy test. It was the most joyful day of my life. We sat in astonishment as to the realization that all of our dedication, time, money, and effort had brought us to the most amazing point in our lives. We were going to have a baby.

When asked about names, I would respond, "Nicholas" and pause. It was one of those moments when I just knew it was going to be a boy, and I was right. We named him after Saint Nicholas as he was our early Christmas present. Nicholas James is the ultimate embodiment of joy and the love and dedication that brought him into this world. I am grateful for the joyful opportunity to be his mom.

Susan Shatzer is an eight-time No. 1 international best-selling author, transformation coach and hosts the TV show *Unlocking Your Limitless Life*. Connect with her at www.MeetOurAuthors.com.

November 26

Together Forever

Tammy Atchley

"The most important work you will ever do will be within the walls of your own home." ~ Harold B. Lee

The day had finally arrived—adoption day! It seemed just yesterday we brought a beautiful, 6-day-old little girl into our home. Jazmin is 2 years old now, and none of us could imagine our family without her in it.

Sitting in front of the judge was an experience none of us will forget. Our usually rambunctious, spirited daughter was quiet and just wanted to be held. It seemed like deep down even she knew the significance of this moment. The judge pronounced us a family, and as he smacked the gavel down, it thundered throughout the courtroom.

I couldn't believe she was ours. She is my daughter…forever! A day none of us will ever forget. The day a beautiful little girl became a permanent member of our family. We celebrated all day long.

I held her in my arms that night before bed, and, as I stroked her cheek and hair, the tears began to fall. She whispered, "I love you, Mommy." I thought to myself there was no greater feeling in the world than knowing that my family, including my new daughter, was mine forever.

Tammy Atchley is a parenting coach that helps moms of bullied children. More at www.MeetOurAuthors.com.

November 27
My Lifetime of Inner Joy
Bill McCarthy

"The highest education is that which does not merely give us information but makes our life in harmony with all existence."
~ Rabindranath Tagore

My greatest joy is the realization of this precious gift of life.

Each morning when I rise and meditate, my heart is filled with peace and gratitude for having another day of being alive.

Through meditating for the past 46 years, I have experienced a life of peace, fulfillment and joy. I have become more compassionate and sensitive toward everyone in my life and more conscious and focused on my life's work.

I'm grateful to my teacher, internationally known Ambassador of Peace Prem Rawat, for revealing the source of peace within me and guiding my journey through life.

Before beginning my meditation practice, I was a shy young boy who never wanted to stand out. After experiencing meditation, my life changed dramatically, and I finally had the courage to pursue my dreams. I started the Unity Foundation to promote world peace and cooperation. I produced the nationally broadcast *Positive Spin* television program, the *Peace Day Global Broadcast* streaming live from the United Nations and several major musical events in Los Angeles, San Francisco and New York.

An amazing history for someone who was afraid and insecure growing up. All thanks to meditation, the source of joy in my life.

Bill McCarthy is the founder and president of Unity Foundation. He is a special event, television and internet broadcast producer. Find out more about Bill at www.MeetOurAuthors.com.

November 28

Gratitude: A Prime Manifesting Force

Aryana K. Rollins

"When you are present in this moment, you break the continuity of your story, of past and future. Then, true intelligence arises and also love." ~ Eckhart Tolle

If we aren't grateful for what we currently have, why would the universe give us more? Think about it. It is easy to complain when life isn't going our way, but that attitude will push away any goodness waiting for us. Here is a quick "attitude of gratitude" exercise to prime the pumps of manifesting.

Right now, name 10 things you're grateful for. Such as, I'm grateful for the companionship of my pet, thankful for the food in my cupboards, grateful for the warm, safe space I have to sleep, thankful for the money I already have, grateful for my work, grateful for my best friend.

Go deeper.

I'm grateful for the peacefulness of nature, the flowers, the ocean, the trees. I'm grateful for the air I breathe. I'm grateful for the water flowing from my faucet.

Keep going. Do it fast; don't overthink it. Usually, our attitude will shift well before we get to 10 items.

Now, how do you feel? Do you feel more uplifted and connected with your heart? In just five minutes, this attitude of gratitude exercise can move us out of despair and into appreciation. Practicing it regularly can open up the floodgates of goodness, not only for you but also for the world.

Since 2005, Aryana has taught entrepreneurs on a spiritual path how to clear the blocks in their unconscious mind. Aryana's skill is guiding you to align with your true self so manifesting becomes natural and easy. Discover more about Aryana at www.MeetOurAuthors.com.

November 29

When Cancer Came to Call

Jane Schraceo

"I don't really care whether my glass is half full or half empty. I'm just happy to have a glass." ~ Joe Farrell

Can I be honest? I'm having a little trouble getting into the holiday spirit. There will be an enormous hole at the family table this year and an even bigger hole in our hearts. Some days we just miss Mom more than is bearable. Pancreatic cancer has changed the story of our lives. And it makes gratitude so very hard.

Joe Farrell takes a familiar phrase and adds a twist that gives me pause: "I don't really care whether my glass is half full or half empty. I'm just happy to have a glass."

Pancreatic cancer leaves us with a glass that is so much less than half empty. It can leech happiness from a heart with harrowing intensity. In the midst of the nightmare, practicing gratitude becomes a resolute act of the will.

Breathing sweet air into lungs, embracing the sun's warmth, wrapping arms around a loved one—this is choosing thanks, turning our focus to the blessings that endure despite the pain. Cancer cannot begin to touch the love holding us close.

This year, we are resolving to give thanks for the goodness around us and, yes, for the glass He's given us to hold. Half full or half empty, I choose gratitude.

Jane Schraceo is humbled daiy to come alongside those fighting pancreatic cancer, where she offers hope and encouragement. Learn more about Jane at www.MeetOurAuthors.com.

November 30
Marriage Is the New Wealth
Bryce Thompson

"Love at your highest capacity; it promises the greatest return!"
~ B. Thompson

Intimate, committed relationships require the highest-level communication skill set and emotional currency, more than any other relationship, because of the high stakes involved and the impact on your partner in having your relationship endure.

Emotional intelligence is an essential tool to make possible the maturing of love between two people, and it is key to the development of a soulful relationship. You will discover resources within yourself to embrace and hold up another while honoring yourself. You are able to live with the ebb and flow of your relationship and life. This is the essence of the soul self and the cultivation of a spiritual partnership.

Learn to appreciate and resolve conflict in order to grow and be willing to forgive, appreciate, love and celebrate one another more fully. Show your gratitude for your partner by making it a habit of expressing life- and love-affirming words and deeds in your day-to-day lives. When you are with someone at the highest level of interdependence and intimacy, you can meet the challenges and conflicts couples experience. Your relationship then becomes the emotional and social fulfillment you imagined in the beginning, providing a lifelong investment that keeps on giving.

Bryce Thompson is a licensed psychotherapist and relationship/parenting wellness VIP and group coach. Find out how to connect with Bryce at www.MeetOurAuthors.com.

December

December 1
The Joy of Learning
Frances O. Thomas

"The excitement of learning separates youth from old age. As long as you're learning you're not old." ~ Rosalyn S. Yalow

I remember exactly where I was when I first heard the term "MOOC." Another teacher sitting across the table from me in a meeting told us about a class she was taking. I scribbled down what the acronym stood for: Massive Open Online Courses.

This new learning concept opened up a world of possibilities for me. Unlike my experiences at brick-and-mortar schools, I wasn't tied to a prescribed curriculum of classes I had to take. Instead I could pick and choose whatever caught my eye from a dizzying array of classes offered by some of the top colleges in the world. Best of all? The courses were free.

Since that joyful day, I have studied classical music with Yale, women's leadership with Case Western Reserve University, and even healthy food with Stanford. Without traveling to Europe, I studied Shakespeare with the University of Warwick, entrepreneurship with New Castle University, and community journalism with Cardiff University.

A close friend once called me a perpetual student. Obviously, she had me pegged. My classroom days are far behind me, but isn't it wonderful that technology has provided a perfect way for me to indulge in lifelong learning?

Frances O. Thomas, M.Ed., N. C. C., is the author of *How to Stop #MeToo from Happening to You: Emotional Intelligence for Gen Z Women in the Workplace*. More at www.MeetOurAuthors.com.

December 2

Happiness and Love from Dogs

Shona Battersby

"Whoever said you can't buy happiness forgot little puppies."
~ Gene Hill

One of the dogs we had when I was growing up was an apricot miniature poodle named Teena. She came into our lives as a puppy and brought us so much happiness for several years.

When Dad brought her home, Mum was in hospital. So, what did we do? We put Teena onto a small blanket inside a big brown paper bag from one of our shopping trips and went to the hospital. When we got to Mum's room, we took Teena out of the bag and put her onto the blanket on her bed. I can't believe that we did not get caught as Teena was making a little bit of noise.

There are so many happy memories of our time together. Some of the funniest were around bath time. We would wash her in the laundry sink and as soon as she was wet, she looked so skinny. After her bath we would try and dry her with a towel, but it soon became a game of tug and war with the towel.

I'm grateful our time with Teena was full of love and happiness as she brought so much into our lives.

Shona Battersby does spiritual healing and transformational guidance using Reiki, massage, crystals and other tools. Find out more at www.MeetOurAuthors.com.

December 3

Laughter Gratitude for Life

Teena F. Miller

"C is between B and D...C is the Choice you make between Birth and Death." ~ Jim Kwik

Given the honor of the 2016 California Hero of Hope for the American Cancer Society is, and was, not an honor I signed up for. However, it is a title I am deeply grateful for. Because of this honor, I am invited to share my story around California at various Relay for Life events and Making Strides Against Breast Cancer events.

You see, I needed to overcome my survivor guilt. Why? Because others with my cancer diagnosis were no longer here, and I was. I did it by realizing I was here for a purpose. My purpose is to love as many people as I choose to and irritate the rest! And apparently I am very successful at both! My purpose is to bring hope and a sense of humor wherever I speak before cancer survivors, who I prefer to call "thrivers."

I stand before the audience as an example of living life with hope and humor, and I am filled with gratitude to laughter. I made the choice to laugh between birth and death—to be fully alive!

Teena Miller is a certified laughter yoga teacher and a certified humor professional. More at www.MeetOurAuthors.com.

December 4
Gratitude for My Mom
Lisa Sasso

"A mother is your first friend, your best friend, your forever friend."
~ Unknown

Today is your first birthday in heaven. I am so thankful that God gave me you as my mother. I am eternally grateful to you and that I have many photos of you. Your presence is still here.

From when I was little, I remember you making sacrifices to be able to do things for my brothers and me. You always took me to dance classes as well as soccer and softball practice.

Mom, you were a great cook! Not only did you make us delicious meals every night, but you also made fabulous Sunday dinners that we enjoyed with both sets of grandparents. I always looked forward to that.

You had a smile that would light up a room. Your kind and gentle voice and your loving face drew people to you.

You taught me about love, kindness and gratitude. You also taught me to be a good person, a good mother, wife, daughter, sister, cousin, aunt, godmother and friend. I learned so many lessons from you and for that I am grateful. I just want to say thank you for everything.

I miss you. I love you. Thank you, Mom!

Lisa Sasso is an executive coach and motivational speaker who coaches medical device professionals. She publishes a monthly motivational message for all. Find out more at www.MeetOurAuthors.com.

December 5
Gorgeous Gabby
Katie De Souza

"Today you are You, that is truer than true.
There is no one alive who is Youer than You." ~ Dr Seuss

You were almost born in a toilet. At 3 a.m., my waters broke in bed. Excited and nervous, we went to the hospital. I went to the toilet. Papai came with me. After a while, he shouted, "I can see hair!" The midwife insisted I return immediately to bed. Two minutes later, you, the most perfect little girl, were born. You are the most beautiful girl I know inside and out.

Since 2 years old, you've loved to sing and dance, using hairbrushes as your microphone. Always a free spirit, you would love to crayon over the walls. You loved to give your little brother kisses and cuddles and play with toys for hours. Most times, you would end up snuggled on the sofa together.

As you've grown, you've developed your drawings and art, becoming an excellent illustrator designing artwork for children's books and helping us with our merchandise and marketing.

I'm so proud of the beautiful young lady you have become—strong-minded, determined, friendly and caring. Always living life to the full and going after what you want.

Always remember you are loved more than you know and always will be no matter where you are. You are always in our hearts.

Katie De Souza is an author and entrepreneur who inspires couples to achieve their dreams and live a happy and fulfilling life together. Find out more about Katie at www.MeetOurAuthors.com.

December 6
The Joy of Gelato
Moira Shepard

"Food feeds our souls." ~ Lidia Bastianich

Wickedly burnt caramel?

Or espresso with chocolate bark?

My sister Vicki and I face these decisions daily on vacation in Vancouver, thanks to our discovery of a shop serving world-class gelato. "Look at the map," I say one day. "We meet our Grouse Mountain tour bus two blocks from Bella Gelateria. Want to go there on the way home?"

"Do you have to ask?" Vicki replies.

Another day, Vicki says, "Hey, we catch the train to the dragon boat races near Bella Gelateria. Want to go there before we hop on the train?"

I say, "Is that a rhetorical question?"

So, at some point each day we wait in line for 30 minutes outside the tiny gelateria and talk about our adventures, our lives and the joyful agony of choosing our flavors. Toasted pecan with maple syrup? Salted chocolate?

With our cups of creamy goodness, Vicki and I stroll to a bench on the corner where we can watch ocean liners cruise out of Canada Place dock.

A comfortable silence falls between us as we savor the sweetness of it all.

Who knew sisterhood could taste like caramel?

Moira Shepard helps coaches, healers and writers gain the confidence to share their gifts with the world while making money—and having fun! Find out more about Moira at www.MeetOurAuthors.com.

December 7
The Fun Challenge of Words
Kristi Dement

"The nice thing about doing a crossword puzzle is, you know there is a solution." ~ Stephen Sondheim

I tell myself the only reason my grown daughter beats me at Scrabble is that I taught her everything she knows. The fact is I love words and I love games. So, my everyday joy is playing fun word games.

Ever played the game Taboo? The object of the game is to get another player to say as many words or phrases (like "Ping pong") before the time is up, but the catch is that the clue giver cannot speak any of the taboo words on the card (game, ball, paddle, table, tennis)! I love that challenge.

Oh, don't get me started on my love for Scattergories! After rolling this huge 20-sided letter die to determine the letter all the answers must start with and setting a timer, players have 12 blank lines to answer different categories like "words associated with money" and "things you plug in" during each round of the game.

When I'm by myself, I like to work on crossword puzzles and other puzzles in a variety book. Upon reflection, I suppose I am a "word nerd." If having a love of words and games is a crime, then I am guilty as charged!

Kristi Dement is an experienced hospitality marketing consultant whose informative blog is packed with helpful tips for B&B owners and innkeepers. Connect with her at www.MeetOurAuthors.com.

December 8

Appreciate the Outdoors

Rex Bohachewski

"To me, a lush carpet of pine needles or spongy grass is more welcome than the most luxurious Persian rug." ~ Helen Keller

When I was younger, I moved to different small towns throughout our province. Each town held a new outdoor adventure waiting for me to discover. I hiked mountains, swam in lakes, followed rivers and floated on the ocean, all while making new friends each summer. At times, I missed my school friends, but I knew that I would see them in September, and we would share stories of our summer adventures. Each day, I would head out and explore somewhere new, knowing that I would be back for supper with an appetite and then be ready for slumber, as I was exhausted from the day's activities.

It was not until I was an adult that I realized how fortunate I was that I had the opportunity to explore our province. Only now I realize that most people did not have the childhood that I did. Today, I see people my age travelling throughout the province for a week's vacation and exploring the same towns I did as a kid—only they are doing it as adults. I hope they are in as much awe as I was. I will be forever grateful that I was an outdoor kid.

Rex Bohachewski, author of *How To Get A Loan,* teaches people how to get the credit they want at the interest rate they deserve. Find out how to connect with Rex at www.MeetOurAuthors.com.

December 9

Unanticipated Joy

Lorrie M. Nixon

"Find out where joy resides and give it a voice far beyond singing. For to miss the joy is to miss all." ~ Robert Louis Stevenson

When I consider experiencing joy, my thoughts turn to the usual connections: holidays, family time and vacations. Wonderful occasions and for many of us a sure source of joy. We expect to feel joyful at these times, and often we do. But what if we could capture the positive spirit of joy in our everyday lives? Not with careful planning but instead with actively experiencing our moments as they come to us and pulling out the fine threads of joy.

Every summer, my town hosts concerts in the park on varying weeknights. Different bands, with styles for all musical tastes, relaxing and fun. Sometimes, though, after a long day, I feel too tired to pack up and head out to the park. Too much to do, maybe next week, I tell myself, already disappointed. Then I step outside and feel the warm sunshine on my face, softened by the cool evening breeze. The child in me sees my neighbor's sprinkler dancing in his yard and wants to run across the grass. Too mature, too silly to do that, I think. But my feet don't hear these thoughts and they have their own agenda—joy, once again.

Lorrie Nixon has taught English as a second language/ intercultural communication in the United States, Greece, Italy, Poland and Denmark. She is actively involved in international affairs. Learn more at www.MeetOurAuthors.com.

December 10

Official Lost and Found Day
Beth Munro

"We lose ourselves in the things we love. We find ourselves there too." ~ Kristin Martz

I'm grateful some things are only perceived as lost.

Hearing again, "Where's the...?" led me to plead against male refrigerator blindness.

"Search like a woman!"

Only a wee bottle of ketchup blocked a half-gallon of milk. I've learned our female ancestors had to see beyond poisonous bushes to gather berries while the males hunted animals in open fields.

The next day, hearing again, "Soon, I'll clear my craft supplies from your workbench," he pleaded against temporary clutter blindness.

"Now!"

Why do I stop seeing stuff (and even think it's lost)? I've learned the lizard brain stops seeing immobile things because they're deemed not a threat.

Some things are found where you lost them; others require more effort to be recovered.

While house hunting, longing for my childhood neighborhood, I proclaimed, "All the lost mittens are displayed with care. Community-minded people live here. We should too." We bought a house that needed a new, well, everything, but my husband is grateful my mitten-photo-book-to-be project is not on his workbench.

Still married, we've learned to appreciate what we've found together.

What might you find in a place or relationship different from where you lost it? What would you be grateful to find?

Beth Munro, coach and organizer, helps you clean up your craft room or your life. Seek like a woman with her, and you'll find what you lost. Learn more about Beth at www.MeetOurAuthors.com.

December 11
Gratitude for Healing
Samantha Dorian

"All challenges are a sign of spiritual strength...the readiness of the Soul to move on, to evolve even further." ~ Neale Donald Walsch

The difficulty with healing is the process. Setting a course to heal is the solution. It will take a commitment, dedication to follow through and a strategy to return to the commitment when you falter, which you will.

Every step forward, no matter how itty-bitty it may seem, is a victory. Take nothing for granted. Celebrate what was overwhelming two weeks ago being more manageable today. Be grateful for the challenges as well as the victories because the more grateful you are, the more will be created for you to be grateful for. That's how all of this works. And pay attention to those synchronicities. They're your personal cheerleaders reminding you that you're on the right track.

Your healing will be a foundation of encouragement for others, but don't do it for them; do it for you. You're the key. Give this time and effort to yourself first because you're worth it. You—the magnificent, wondrous, compassionate, valuable, vibrant, spectacular, lovable, compelling, inspirational you. Your evolution allows us all to evolve whether your name or journey is known to us or not.

Thank you for all you are doing and all you are about to do. I salute you.

Samantha Dorian is a psychic and romance writer whose passion for the healing process carries through to the characters She creates. More at www.MeetOurAuthors.com.

December 12

Joyful Magic

Shanley Weston

"You are terrifying and strange and beautiful. Something not everyone knows how to love." ~ Warsan Shire

It's hard to remember that you are magic. It's especially hard when you've lost yourself to the role of mother, father, wife, husband, boss, caretaker. We're so busy changing hats we give up on being joyful and chasing our dreams. I am guilty of this—of giving up my magic and joy to become mother, blogger, entrepreneur.

I reclaimed my magic in an unexpected way—by making a vision board. As I pulled together images that spoke to my soul, I realized the falsity of the business I'd spent the last year building through the eyes of others. I'd allowed myself to be so blinded by what others told me I wanted ("bigger email list!" "higher conversion rates!" "$100K product launches!") that I never noticed these weren't things that took me closer to my dream life. I didn't need any of these to bring me joy. Instead, I tapped back into what I wanted for my business. It was such a relief.

It's OK to forge your own definition of success. You are magic, and if you've forgotten that (like I did), take time for yourself to explore what joy means to you. Keep dreaming. Keep chasing.

Calling herself "the creative disaster," Shanley Weston blogs about running a handmade business, motherhood, and life. Find out more at www.MeetOurAuthors.com.

December 13

From Grumpy to Peaceful

Janet Hollander

"Body follows Mind." ~ Koichi Tohei

I had already tried all my usual ways to get rid of pain in the middle of the night. I had done my yoga stretches, some mindful breathing and moving around a bit, but nothing had worked. I didn't know what to do with inescapable pain. I even tried a different bed, thinking maybe the problem was our aging mattress.

I finally rolled myself into the quilt and remembered that wallowing in negative thoughts would just bring more. So, I started listing in my mind anything I could think of that I was grateful for, starting lamely with the warm blanket, a pillow, a roof … After a few minutes, I must have dropped off to sleep because the next thing I knew, it was morning, and I was making a case to my husband that we needed a new mattress.

My doctor immediately recognized the rash and location of the nerve pain as shingles and put me on medication right away. I have no residual symptoms and got a new mattress out of the deal. But the most valuable take-away was adding gratitude to my tool kit for facing tough times.

Janet Hollander leads workshops, training and classes in the Nia Technique—a wellness and lifestyle movement art—and chair-based fitness focusing on aging with body sustainability and resilience. More www.MeetOurAuthors.com.

December 14

Her Teaching Was Contagious
Bina Kozuch

"How very little can be done under the spirit of fear." ~ Florence Nightingale

Her words were firm when I didn't follow "orders" but soft and directive when it was called for.

"Do not give up!" was her motto.

Where did my mother, Cipora, get the courage to be persistent and never give up when sometimes it became unbearable?

As I reflect on my mother's life, I believe resilience and perseverance were seeded into her soul during the continuous suffering under the German Nazis in Auschwitz-Birkenau, Poland, the infamous death camp. She remained all alone! Her immediate family was gassed and then burned in the crematorium.

Her positive attitude toward life was contagious. I have learned to see the light at the end of the tunnel in times of stress and never give up.

I am grateful for my mother for such a constructive upbringing.

Bina Kozuch is the author of *Triumph After All*. As an educator, she integrates into her lessons the philosophy of courage, tenacity, and the belief in God in the face of desolation. More at www.MeetOurAuthors.com.

December 15
Living in Gratitude
MichelJoy DelRe

"The significant problems we have cannot be solved at the same level of thinking with which we created them." ~ Albert Einstein

At the beginning of the 2020 pandemic, the world of activity came to a stop. Businesses closed. Schools closed. Restaurants and places of entertainment closed. Houses of worship closed. Only essential services remained open as we sheltered in place.

In this quiet, we took a breath, and something remarkable happened. We began to care about those who died. We began to care about one another.

Then, we began noticing changes in the environment. Native Americans reported to NASA that Planet Earth had shifted on her axis. Italians reported that dolphins were swimming in the canals for the first time in 10 years. Californians began to see blue skies in the city of Los Angeles.

At the same time, the U.S. Government upgraded outdated technology. People marched in the streets, protesting racial injustice. Police departments examined their practices. Events shifted to online. Places of worship became creative with technology, reaching more people. And, while most of us were sleeping, NASA planned the launch of its 14th resupply mission, making live coverage in the International Space Station available to the world.

Around the world and in space, we have taken a collective breath, recalibrated and begun to be grateful for one another.

MichelJoy DelRe, international best-selling author in *Ready, Aim, Thrive!,* is a noted entrepreneurial business consultant and leadership coach. Learn more about MichelJoy at www.MeetOurAuthors.com.

December 16

Grandma's Peanut Butter and Jelly

Carol A. Peña

"Grandmothers always have time to talk and make you feel special."
~ Catherine Pulsifer

At Grandma's house, it was okay to be a picky eater. Summer weekends with my grandparents were low-key, from working in the garden to time in the kitchen. Everything tasted better at their house—even a sandwich of peanut butter and jelly.

Grandma would add a heaping tablespoon of peanut butter and a spoonful of apple jelly in a bowl. She would slowly mix the two together until you couldn't tell them apart. Then, she would taste test the blended mixture. A lick of her lips or a smack of her gums was a good sign. If it wasn't quite the right sweetness, she would add a little more jelly and mix again before spreading it onto a slice of bread.

Ah, the anticipation.

That simple PB&J sandwich made with love and a tall glass of cold milk would disappear lickety-split. Now, who was the picky eater?

While sharing at a family reunion, I discovered several relatives with similar stories. We remembered the twinkle in her eyes and a slight nod of her head that seemed to say, "You're going to love it."

Grandma, we still do and always will.

Carol A. Peña is a native Texan with a passion for creative writing, genealogy and adventures with Buster the Wonder-Yorkie. More at www.MeetOurAuthors.com.

December 17

Travels with Missy

Lorrie M. Nixon

"What greater gift than the love of a cat?" ~ Charles Dickens

My sister's cat delivered several kittens, and sis brought them by my house. The orange boy kitties clustered at the foot of my bed. There on my pink satin pillow, though, sat a beautiful tortoiseshell girl. She had decided that she was mine, and I felt drawn to her. But I had just accepted a job far away in Poland. I wanted to take her with me, but was unsure. I realized that I couldn't leave her and soon our adventure began. When we arrived, our apartment wasn't ready. We went to a simple hotel, with Missy snuggled inside my coat.

As we looked out the window at the swirling Silesian fog, I wondered if we would be all right. I heard a knock on the hotel room door. When I opened it, I found an old woman in a babushka scarf, smiling and handing me a plate of cut up fish. "Kot," she said, motioning to Missy. Even in this far away land, Missy was already helping me feel welcome. Over the next eighteen years we had many travels together. With Missy by my side, I always felt right at home-secure, happy, and wonderfully loved.

Lorrie Nixon is an intercultural communication specialist and a best-selling author. She has trained clients in Italy, Denmark, Greece, Poland and the USA. Contact her at www.MeetOurAuthors.com.

December 18
Grateful for Father and Husband
Yvonne Coleman Lowrie

"A family's love is like no other." ~ Unknown

Clarence F. Coleman, who was my father, was born on December 18,1905. My dearest husband, Max Lowrie, was also born on December 18 but several years later in 1927 in Fort Worth, Texas.

During my teenage years, at one of many slumber parties with my closest friends, we discussed the details we envisioned for each of our weddings that would occur when we met the man of our dreams. I remember saying that I dreamed that my wedding would take place on my father's birthday, December 18. I envisioned that my wedding attendants would be wearing red velvet dresses and would also be carrying a red poinsettia attached to a white rabbit fur muff. Additional details of my dream reflected that I would be wearing a luxurious white velvet wedding dress, and I would also be carrying a muff, but mine would have a radiant white poinsettia instead.

On December 18, 1962, my childhood dreams that I had envisioned so many years ago with my teenage friends actually came true in Knoxville, Tennessee, when I married my dearest husband, Max. We celebrated 45 amazing years together in Fort Worth, Texas.

Yvonne spent 65 years as a Girl Scout and volunteer, including the World Foundation for Girl Guides and Girl Scouts, and was a YWCA Y-Teens program participant, including program director, while earning a Masters of Education. Learn more about Yvonne at www.MeetOurAuthors.com.

December 19
How to Plan a Journey
Sally Laird

"Once you start deliberately offering thought, you access the energy that creates worlds." ~ Abraham Hicks

I was nearing the end of my journey when I met Marnie. She was at the start of hers. I loved her the moment I saw her and wanted with all my heart to ease her path. In the end, of course, she eased mine.

I was so busy planning, preparing, worrying. Was I going to miss a sign? Take a wrong turn? Feel stupid? I was missing the moment and the joy of the journey. Marnie was so busy enjoying the moment, she didn't have a plan. She admitted she felt lost. To my delight, we joined forces. She needed a plan; I needed to let go of trying to control everything.

We agreed on a destination and the best route in the available time. Then we enjoyed each day. If anything went wrong, we adapted and kept heading to our chosen destination. Did it go exactly as planned? No! Because we went places we didn't even know existed, and the destination was so much better than we planned.

I found joy, and Marnie found purpose.

Happy birthday, Marnie. Thank you for the adventures. Granny. XX

Sally Laird is the creator and founder of Heart Marketing System, helping holistic practitioners to earn more money doing what they love. Find out more about Sally at www.MeetOurAuthors.com.

December 20
Annie's "Meatballs:" Italian Mother's Love
Janet Spadola

"My mother was my role model before I even knew what that word was." ~ Lisa Leslie

One of the best smells in the world was a pot of my mom's sauce filled with freshly-made meatballs. Everyone loved Annie's. She didn't use a recipe and never had a mother to teach her. She picked it up along the way and loved creating the special dish that others so appreciated. A marvelous combination of pork/beef/veal/fresh parsley/freshly grated parmesan cheese, salt/pepper and, of course, garlic! That was it. If not on the stove, they were in her freezer, tucked into a big, bright yellow Polly-O ricotta container.

When I flew home after her sudden death, I missed her warm smile, and big-breasted hug. After five days of arrangements with family and friends saying goodbye, it was time for me to return to DC. I couldn't think of anything I wanted to bring back with me. But when I looked in the freezer and saw the yellow ricotta container, my eyes filled with bittersweet tears and I knew I had to take her meatballs home.

Ten years and two moves later, that yellow container was still in my freezer. And I smiled inside everytime I saw it.

Janet Spadola, founder of The JAS Group, is a leadership and career transition coach who helps mid and senior level professionals who are stuck at a crossroad in their careers. Find out more at www.MeetOurAuthors.com.

December 21
Return of the Light
Ginny Lang

"There are two ways of spreading light: to be the candle or the mirror that reflects it." ~ Edith Wharton

I'm grateful every year when the days start to get longer. Today is the winter solstice. It's the longest night of the year. Where I live, that means the sun doesn't come up until 9 in the morning and sets by 4:30 in the afternoon. Tomorrow the days start to get longer, but you won't notice it for a few weeks yet. It's a magical, introspective time, deep midwinter, and I feel cozy and sleepy like a hibernating bear. Spring will wake her up again, and us too.

Almost every culture in the world has a festival or holiday that celebrates the days getting longer. Whether you call it Christmas, Hanukkah, Kwanzaa, Yule or Dong Zhi, it celebrates the miracles of light, goodness and community. We break the darkness with twinkling lights in our homes, candles everywhere and sparkling gifts to brighten the days and draw friends close.

I'm grateful for warmth, for company, for celebration and for the spark in darkness that means the light is coming.

Ginny Lang is a veteran management consultant, coach, trainer and facilitator to nonprofit organizations as well as an accomplished speaker and teacher. Discover more about Ginny at www.MeetOurAuthors.com.

December 22

The God Wink

Portia Turner Merriweather

"Kindness is like snow. It beautifies everything it covers." ~ Kahlil Gibran

It was a record-breaking snowstorm. I was home alone. As I watched the snow cover everything in pristine white, I was filled with wonder at its beauty but also with dread at the effort it would take to shovel the porch and walkway. I couldn't even open the front door because the snow was piled so solidly upon it. I went to bed grateful to be warm and cozy, though concerned that I was snowbound.

The next morning after my devotions, I opened the curtains to a great surprise! My porch, walkway and car were free of snow! I sat with my mouth wide open in happy disbelief! Crying, I praised God and thanked Him for the God wink—an act to show me His divine care!

Since my neighbor's walkway was also cleared, I knew her nephew had done it. Later, when I thanked him, he chuckled, "You don't have to thank me. It's really weird! I just started shoveling, and before I knew it, I had done yours and ours, and I wasn't even tired."

God had blessed this young man with stamina to perform an act of kindness for which I will always be grateful.

Portia Merriweather is the author of Nuggets to Nourish Your Soul and Who Made God, Anyway? Find out how to connect with Portia at www.MeetOurAuthors.com.

December 23

Albert
Theresa Scandale

"A true friend is someone who thinks that you are a good egg even though he knows that you are slightly cracked." ~ Bernard Meltzer

Albert,

I admire you for so many things. For the way you carry yourself—for the calm, loving, patient person you are even when you're facing hardships. You always give and are slow to take. No matter what disagreements we have, you're there every time I need you. You answer every call, respond to every text. You never shut me out.

No matter how much or little you have, you're always giving. You've been a consistent and reliable part of my family and my life for so long; I couldn't imagine a life without you. You spend your time comforting me and my broken heart despite how your own heart aches. You are selfless and always on my side. Your loyalty and friendship mean more to me than I can ever say.

I am so proud of the person that you've become and how you've adapted and grown from so many hardships and challenges. You have one of the kindest and purest hearts of anyone I've ever known. You're so deserving of love and happiness. I'm immensely grateful to have you in my life. I know you often feel alone, but you always have a place in our family.

Theresa Scandale is a writer, teacher of English as a foreign language (EFL), aspiring linguist and genealogy enthusiast. She travels with her dog, Topanga, and runs a blog and YouTube channel. Discover more about Theresa at www.MeetOurAuthors.com.

December 24

An Italian Christmas Eve

Angela I. Schutz

"Don't let the past steal your present. This is the message of Christmas: We are never alone." ~ Taylor Caldwell

The water is boiling in the pasta pot, ready for spaghetti, as the brilliant red sauce bubbles on the back burner, soon to marry with the pasta. It's the feast of the seven fishes. There they are waiting to be fried, roasted or boiled into succulent delicacies. The stuffed squid are poaching in a sauce made of garlic and tomatoes, waiting for the addition of peas—a dish we only eat on Christmas Eve.

Lobsters are roasting, and an amazing array of calamari, smelts, cod, scallops and shrimp are coated in flavored crumbs, waiting to be flash-fried to preserve their tenderness. We are debating whether to add shrimp or lobster to the sauce to serve over our spaghetti—a long-standing, yearly debate.

We make baccala soup to honor our heritage—a tomato-based broth with onions, cauliflower, black olives, raisins and salted, dried cod that has been rinsed and soaked for three days before adding it to the soup.

The zeppole dough has been rising all day. See the specks of cinnamon and black pepper throughout. Anchovies are laid out on paper towels, waiting to be encased in the dough before the frying begins.

I am endlessly grateful for the love of family and our time-honored traditions.

Angela Schutz: founder of Driven To Succeed Consulting LLC, published author, professional speaker, adjunct Professor and career coach dedicated to helping others empower their lives. Find out more about Angela at www.MeetOurAuthors.com.

December 25
Love Is Gratitude in Action
Cindy Stock

"Not all of us can do great things.
But we can do small things with great love." ~ Mother Teresa

Every year in November, we Americans celebrate a day devoted to gratitude. Smiling faces gather around tables laden with the familiar fare and enticing aromas of turkey with all the trimmings. But before the forks fly, grace is offered in thanksgiving for blessings received and the bounty before them. And it is good that we do this.

But I also have a personal day of gratitude. Mine is Christmas Day.

Christmas is when God sent the greatest gift of love to the world. His son, Jesus, came to teach us how to love our Creator and how to love one another. He also taught us that since God is love, then love needs to be the most important thing guiding our thoughts and actions in our lives.

I am just an average person. But I try to notice the harried salesperson who could use a kind word, the wheelchair-bound senior struggling to open a door—small things I can do with great love.

And every Christmas morning, before I join my family under the soft, twinkling lights of our Christmas tree, I gaze at our manger and offer a prayer of gratitude for our greatest gift of all.

Cindy Stock is an aspiring research specialist and copywriter. Find out how to connect with Cindy at www.MeetOurAuthors.com.

December 26
Celebrating Life
Alberta Cotner

"Success is not final, failure is not fatal: it is the courage to continue that counts. Never, never, never give up." ~ Winston Churchill

I have experienced several challenges throughout my life. Through sheer determination and will I am a living example that you can overcome anything in life.

When I faced the challenge of losing my son however, I wasn't sure if I would ever recover from that. While I always felt that I was a strong person, this showed me what true strength I held within me.

My son was my best friend and someone that genuinely cared about people. I'm proud that I raised such a wonderful young man and I am thankful he was in my life for at least 24 years. He loved life and lived each and every day to the fullest! I love and miss him dearly. Early in my grief process, I met Ms. Ena Griffin from New York. She had also lost her son at the young age of 19. She has been there for me in so many ways. I appreciate and love her like a sister. I'm very grateful to have her in my life.

Although we grieve for our children, we must remember to be grateful for each and every day we are given. Nothing is granted and life is precious.

Originally from Texas, Alberta Cotner says she has faced her share of challenges throughout her life. "By sharing my stories and experiences, I hope to helpothers navigate similar challenges," she says. Find out more at www.MeetOurAuthors.com.

December 27
Nanny Goat
Angela Boothroyd

"Goats are a special case. Mad as hatters, all of them."
~ Diana Wynne Jones

I don't remember how Mornie the goat came to live with my grandfather and his wife. But the story told to me is that one day, over 40 years ago, granddad went to an auction to buy boat parts and returned home with a fully-grown goat in his car (and no boat parts).

Mornie was everything you'd expect in a goat: intelligent, curious, playful, and a little bit mad. But goats are also said to dislike getting wet, and that definitely wasn't Mornie. My favourite memory of her is her jumping in the car for trips to the coast so she could paddle in the sea.

My little brother and I sometimes walked Mornie on the beach when we visited granddad and his family. Or to be more accurate, she walked us. She happily wore a collar and lead, but goats are very strong and their reputation for being stubborn is well-deserved. Where Mornie wanted to go, we went too. Somehow, we all survived unscathed!

I have a few old photos of the three of us taken one summer holiday and even after all this time they make me smile. She was a great character.

Angela Boothroyd is an English teacher and linguist. She helps non-native English-speaking business owners create business content in English. Find out more at www.MeetOurAuthors.com.

December 28

Be Grateful, Have Faith, and Live Oola

Cynde Canepa

"A hundred years from now, it will not matter what my bank account was, the sort of house I lived in or the kind of car I drove. But the world may be different because I was important in the life of a child."
~ Forest E. Witcraft

In my teens, I was told by an employer, "A hundred years from now, no one will care." Her statement hurt my feelings. I took it as that no one would care about my life 100 years from now.

I pretty much worked myself to death to make my life matter 100 years from now. Working from early morning until I fell asleep at night every day for many years took its toll on my health.

At a conference, I was introduced to the Oola Guys, who shared their formula of how to be balanced and growing in all seven areas of life: fitness, finance, family, field, faith, friends, fun.

Oola has been a lifesaver to me. Practicing the Oola formula, I have pivoted my business to create a virtual academy where I am actively filing it with digital products for business owners, childcare providers and children's activities.

A hundred years from now, my life will have mattered because I was important in the life of a child.

Cynde Canepa is a certified Oola life coach who guides your journey to financial safety while living an Oola life-work balance and growing lifestyle. Find out more about Cynde at www.MeetOurAuthors.com.

December 29
You Make My Life Complete
Georgia R. Day

"If you are not willing to risk the unusual, you will have to settle for the ordinary." ~ Jim Rohn

Irish Wolfhounds are known for their size and giant hearts. I, Patrick Sean, was no exception to this rule. Little did I know, born on Valentine's Day, that my human parents would take me on a lifetime adventure. You see, my parents had retired, sold their home, and began traveling the United States as full-time RV-ers, towing an Airstream travel trailer. I met people from across the world and, of course, was a conversation starter wherever we happened to be.

Then my parents up-scaled my living space, so that I had my very own motor coach and special J-lounge sofa. I could look out, truly see more of the world, and talk to the truckers as they rolled down the highway. My adventures just kept coming! I participated in the Top Dog Fashion Show at the Newport Dunes RV Resort, posed with the Man o 'War statue at the Kentucky Horse Park and visited the Three Dog Bakery annually for my birthday. What I did not expect was international fame, as a British Dog Magazine featured me in a special edition. For nine incredible years, my parents were privileged to be owned by me.

Georgia Day, Career Success and Fulfillment Coach, author and speaker. Find out more about Georgia at www.MeetOurAuthors.com.

December 30
My Best Friend for Life
Marla Hall

"A pet is a forever blessing of mutual love, fun, pampering and devotion." ~ Marla Hall

I'm a dog lover, great playmate, terrible pack leader.

Enter cat love. I begin feeding the feral kitties roaming the apartment building where I live. Each is named, spayed or neutered and given first shots. Tom—correction, Tomasina, Tomi, Poopy and other adoring names—isn't feral. I pick her up and she flops over my arm, half hanging on one side, and the other half dangling head down.

Then, that fateful day. I find her desperately ill and weak. I rush us to the vet. Will she live or die? She pulls through, though never to live outside again. She is FIV positive. Passing across the welcome mat, she checks off litter box, filled food and water dishes, scratching post, toys and best sleeping spots. She moves in.

Tomi is really a dog wearing a tux costume. She loves car rides and diligently monitors bedtime. One day she slips out. I'm hysterical. I tell a friend Tomi's gone. How long—15 minutes. I tote a flashlight, call her name, finally returning home catless and heartbroken.

Under a porch chair appears a familiar face. You're silly, Mommy. I'm home to stay. Best 10 years. We speak daily. She's wise and loving.

Marla Hall believes you never retire, and as CEO of Your Life Inc., you're never unemployed. Let's reinvent your lifestyle and transform those old hours called "work." Find out how to connect with Marla at www.MeetOurAuthors.com.

December 31
The Power of Gratitude
Melody Juge

"Gratitude makes sense of our past, brings peace for today and creates a vision for tomorrow." ~ Melody Beattie

Another year comes to an end! Today, the final day of the year, I'm gently reminiscing, with heartfelt gratitude, on the memorable experiences I've enjoyed throughout this past year. I find that I am most grateful for the shared companionship of those who have touched my heart, especially my sweet four-legged friend Charlie, who continues to be by my side through thick and thin. There is comfort in embracing the joy and peace of mind that this reflection offers as I begin to prepare for a fresh start tomorrow, yet another new beginning.

I toss out the temptation for fixed resolutions and ready myself for the next year to come by using a simple plan: holding a grateful heart. Excitement wells up as I remind myself of the importance of staying in the moment as I embrace a bubbling appreciation for all that is. I'm in awe as I ponder the serendipitous nature of life, looking forward to a new series of miracles that are about to unfold.

As I close out this year, it's now time to surrender to the unknown that will once again begin tomorrow. The sharing of this life journey continues. Happy New Year to all!

Melody Juge is founder of Life Income Management™: Creating Income for Life and creator of RetirementSense™, a proprietary retirement planning process. She is an Investment Advisor registered with fiduciary status. Discover more about Melody at www.MeetOurAuthors.com.

Causes We Support

In the spirit of gratitude, the contributors to *The Community Book Project: Celebrating 365 Days of Gratitude* give a shoutout to these organizations who have helped us and others in the world.

A21

A21's mission is to abolish slavery everywhere forever—to see a world where women are no longer sold for sex, where men are no longer sold for labor, where children are no longer taken from their families and exploited. A world where every single person is free.

www.a21.org

Alannah & Madeline Foundation

The Alannah & Madeline Foundation is one of Australia's most respected children's charities and is dedicated to protecting children from violence and its devastating impact. They care for children who have experienced or witnessed serious violence, reduce the incidence of bullying, cyber bullying and other cyber risks, and advocate for the safety and well-being of children. They believe that every child should have a safe and happy childhood without being subjected to any form of violence.

www.amf.org.au

Alzheimer's Society of Canada

Alzheimer's Society of Canada's mission is to alleviate the personal and social consequences of Alzheimer's and related diseases and to promote the search for causes, treatments and a cure through working with partners to achieve this goal and to ensure Canadians receive personal and responsive services throughout their dementia journey.

www.alzheimer.ca

American Diabetes Association

American Diabetes Association's mission: to prevent and cure diabetes and to improve the lives of all people affected by diabetes. To lead the fight against the deadly consequences of diabetes and fight for those affected by diabetes. To fund research to prevent, cure and manage diabetes.

www.diabetes.org

Annie's Gifts of Love

Annie's Gifts of Love is passionate about helping survivors, especially battered women and their children, rebuild their lives by providing funding to nonprofits that provide direct services.

www.anniesgiftsoflove.org

Associates of Idyllwild Arts Foundation

They act as a nonprofit association for the support of education in the arts, particularly the programs offered by the Idyllwild Arts Academy Boarding Arts High School and Summer Program founded in 1946. They also provide cultural activities for the Community of Idyllwild, California.

www.associatesofiaf.org

The Association for Applied and Therapeutic Humor

The Association for Applied and Therapeutic Humor is a nonprofit organization dedicated to the study and application of humor to effect positive change. All over the world, our members are applying the strategic use of humor in countless ways. AATH is committed to making the world a happier place.

www.aath.org

Association des Humanistes pour le Progrès et le Développement d'Haiti

AHPDH helps underserved children in Haiti receive needed resources by providing healthcare, tuition and school supplies and a sense of community and emotional support. The children are enriched through activities and programs to empower and encourage them and instill hope and faith in their future.

nmonfred60@yahoo.fr

Aussie Helpers

Aussie Helpers is a not-for-profit organization dedicated to supporting Australian farmers, their families and farming communities through times of crisis. The organization is reliant on a dedicated volunteer network to achieve success.

www.aussiehelpers.org.au

Autism Society of North Carolina

The Autism Society of North Carolina supports persons diagnosed with autism through life enrichment, family support and community education. Check out their website for more information.

www.autismsociety-nc.org

Blue Ridge Humane Society

We are dedicated to ensuring the highest quality of life for animals in Henderson County, North Carolina and our neighboring communities through adoption, outreach and education. We embrace the protection, compassionate care and highest quality of life for animals as weassess and treat conditions necessary with animals under our care.

www.blueridgehumane.org

Born Free Foundation

Helping all wildlife to be free, especially against poaching, etc., this organization originally started after the film *Born Free*, starring Virginia McKenna and Elsa, the lion, was shown.

www.bornfree.org.uk

Borneo Orangutan Survival (BOS) Foundation

Borneo Orangutan Survival (BOS) Foundation is a nonprofit organization dedicated to conservation of the Bornean orangutan and its habitat. The foundation is currently caring for almost 650 orangutans with the support of 400 staff, who are experts in primatology, biodiversity, ecology, forest rehabilitation, agroforestry, community empowerment, education and orangutan healthcare.

www.orangutan.or.id

Bread & Roses

Floristry as a tool for social good. Bread & Roses runs floristry training for women from refugee backgrounds. Their programs improve participants' vocational and English skills and give them a chance to build new networks in the UK and enjoy the therapeutic benefits of working with flowers. They provide grants to community organizations that want to offer floristry training to refugee and asylum-seeking women in their communities and run a flower shop to support their work too.

www.wearebreadandroses.com

Butterfly Foundation

Butterfly Foundation is the national charity for all Australians impacted by eating disorders and body image issues and for the families, friends and communities who support them.

www.butterfly.org.au

Caregivers Alberta

Unpaid caregivers support ill, disabled and aging loved ones, saving every health system billions of dollars annually. Caregivers Alberta supports and provides resources to over 1 million caregivers in Alberta and advocates to a much wider audience worldwide.

www.caregiversalberta.ca

City of Lights Dream Center

City of Lights Dream Center is an organization in Alabama that exists to empower the community for a brighter future by eliminating the darkness of poverty and addiction through education, addiction recovery and meal distribution.

www.cityoflightsala.com

Coonhound Companions

Calling all hound dogs, Anna Nirva is your friend! Connected to many rescues throughout the U.S.A. and Canada, Anna helps coordinate adoptions, foster homes, transportation, shelter stays and veterinary care for abandoned hound dogs. See success stories on Facebook, Life with My Rescued Foxhound.

www.coonhoundcompanions.com

Core Dance

Core Dance, a contemporary dance organization, creates, performs and produces compelling original dance that ignites the creative spirit and actively encourages participation and conversation by and with the community. Creating a context for dance that is relevant around the globe, Core Dance uses dance to illuminate, educate and question.

www.coredance.org

Disabled American Veterans

Disabled American Veterans was founded by former U.S. Army Captain Robert S. Marx in 1920 to support America's injured and ill veterans and their families. Since that time, the organization of veterans serving veterans has made the critical transition from military service to civilian life.

www.dav.org

Doors of Change (aka Photocharity)

Doors of Change is a 501(c)(3) organization that has helped over two thousand homeless youth get off the streets into safe housing since 2001. Youth can break the cycle of homelessness and be self-sufficient.

www.doorsofchange.org

Edmonton International Fringe Theatre Festival

The year 2021 is the 40th anniversary of the largest and longest-running fringe festival in North America—second only to the Edinburgh Festival Fringe in Edinburgh, Scotland. It hosts 1200 volunteers and over 250 shows over 10 days.

www.fringefestivals.com/festival/edmonton-international-fringe-theatre-festival

EduCare Foundation

EduCare is one of Los Angeles' largest after-school program providers. Its mission is to inspire and empower young people to become responsible citizens, compassionate leaders and to live their dreams. It specializes in providing social emotional learning and creates live and virtual learning environments in which youth can flourish.

www.educarefoundation.com

Find Picture-Perfect Homes for Dogs

Rita Earl-Blackwell specializes in helping sheltered dogs find homes. Through her "seen equals saved" dog portrait network service, Rita has found homes for hundreds of dogs for over 15 years in Southern California. Contact her for dog adoption, rescue groups and to start your own dog portrait network service.

rita@ritaearl.com

Five Acres Animal Shelter

Five Acres Animal Shelter is the only no-kill animal shelter in St. Charles County, Missouri.

www.fiveacresanimalshelter.org

The Forgiveness Project

The Forgiveness Project collects and shares stories from both victims/survivors and perpetrators of crime and conflict who have rebuilt their lives following hurt and trauma. At the heart of The

Forgiveness Project is an understanding that restorative narratives have the power to transform lives, not only supporting people to deal with issues in their own lives but also building a climate of tolerance, resilience, hope and empathy.

www.theforgivenessproject.com

Friends of Thai Daughters

Friends of Thai Daughters helps prevent child trafficking by empowering vulnerable girls to become valued Daughters, educated women and independent adults.

www.friendsofthaidaughters.org

G.I. Josie

G.I. Josie provides nonclinical programs and support to women veterans (and their children) who endure PTSD and military sexual trauma (MST). The VA doesn't offer nonclinical therapies or programs that help women and children heal together. G.I. Josie provides support for as long as the vet needs to heal.

www.gijosie.org

Graines d'Avenir (Seeds of Future)

Graines d'Avenir (literally "seeds of future") supports Tibetan children in exile to be educated in their culture, provides humanitarian, educational, medical and logistical assistance to Tibetan, secular and religious communities, to disadvantaged non-Tibetan local populations as well as to diverse populations of Buddhist culture.

www.grainesdavenir.com

Gratitude

Gratitude embodies what this book is about. Gratitude feeds hundreds of families and gathers food daily from supermarkets and redistributes it. They are then rewarded with a smile and a thank you! This charity inspires gratitude in everyone everywhere.

www.gratitude.charity

Harvest Project

"Extending a hand up, not a hand out," Harvest Project is a community-based urban relief organization on Vancouver's North Shore. Their mission is to help people who are experiencing challenging life circumstances by providing physical, emotional and spiritual support that empowers each individual to take positive steps in their life.

www.harvestproject.org

Heart For Guatemala

Heart for Guatemala partners with and supports local organizations that provide educational pathways for disadvantaged children and families, enabling them to redefine their narrative of success and opportunity within their communities.

www.heartforguatemala.org

Heartmath Institute

Their cause: Awakening the heart of humanity

HeartMath's research, training and technologies are aimed at guiding all of humanity toward realization of its full potential and relying on the qualities of the heart in its role as caretaker of future generations and our planet.

www.heartmath.org

Heifer International

Heifer International offers practical help for the poor and hungry, from microloans to women farmers in Nepal to training a family to raise chickens for food and profit in Haiti. Their mission to end poverty through agriculture has changed lives and communities worldwide.

www.heifer.org

Helping Families Handle Cancer Foundation

Helping Families Handle Cancer Foundation is an Alberta-based, non-for-profit organization designed to aid families with ill children in order to alleviate some of the financial stress so that families can put their energy both into caring for their children who are battling the life-threatening illness and into everyone's emotional well-being.

www.helpingfamilieshandlecancer.com

Hinds Hospice

The mission of Hinds Hospice is to uphold the dignity and ease the suffering of the terminally ill while supporting their loved ones, and those who are grieving.

www.hindshospice.org

Home-Start Ealing

Home-Start Ealing offers volunteer support to families with at least one child under 5 years facing difficulties in the London Borough of Ealing. They offer confidential, practical and emotional support to help families work through issues they are facing. They strive to build confidence, improve mental health and reduce isolation.

www.instagram.com/homestartealing

Humane Society of Burnett County Inc.

The Humane Society of Burnett County Inc. (HSBC) is a nonprofit whose mission is to provide a safe haven for stray or unwanted animals, to foster the human-animal bond, to promote responsible pet ownership and to end pet overpopulation through spaying/neutering.

www.hsburnettcty.org

Indspire

Indspire, a top-10 Canadian Impact Charity, has supported 42,500

First Nation, Inuit and Métis students with bursaries and scholar-ships. Its vision is that, within a generation, every Indigenous stu-dent will graduate; ninety percent of students it supports graduate. Its mission is to enrich Canada through education and inspiring achievement.

www.indspire.ca

International Students

International Students helps foreign students integrate into society through acculturation and the teaching of English. The students are gifted, talented and want to learn and develop relationships that will help them maximize their gifts and talents such that they create a positive impact and influence that make the world better.

www.internationalstudents.org/national-ministry

Kids Off the Block

Kids Off the Block Inc. (KOB) was founded in 2003 to provide at-risk, low-income youth positive alternatives to gangs, drugs, tru-ancy, violence and the juvenile justice system. Founded by Diane Latiker, who opened her home to youth in her community to help them steer away from daily negative influences.

www.kidsofftheblock.us

Kiva

Kiva is a nonprofit organization through which you can lend money to empower people in need to improve their lives in underserved populations. One hundred percent of funds go to individuals of your choice.

www.kiva.org

Ladies of Virtue

Ladies of Virtue exists to instill purpose, passion and perseverance in girls ages 9 to 18 while preparing them for college, careers and to become change agents in their communities. LOV's vision is to become the premier mentoring and leadership training organization for Black girls in Chicago and beyond.

www.lovchicago.org

Lanark Animal Welfare Society

In 1986, the Lanark Animal Welfare Society officially began an established registered charity. Their mission: "To promote the welfare of animals committed to our care, to provide shelter and care and prevent cruelty and suffering for those animals in need through outreach and education."

www.lanarkanimals.ca

The Leeward Charitable Foundation

Leeward turns donations of surplus clothing, furniture and household items into funds for local charities. They are a unique retailer, valuable recycler and sustainable source of critical funding for important local charities. Since 2009, Leeward has donated over $2.5 million dollars in cash and in-kind donations.

www.leewardfoundation.org

Lhasa Happy Homes

LHH is a dog rescue in Southern California concentrating on lhasa apso, shih tzu, maltese and small breed mixes from kill shelters. Many have critical injuries, require surgery or are senior dogs. LHH rehabilitates them, nurtures them in cozy foster care homes and adopts them to vetted individuals and families.

www.lhasahappyhomes.org

LHCH Charity (Liverpool Heart and Chest Hospital)

The Liverpool Heart and Chest Hospital is one of the largest specialist heart and lung centres in the U.K., with over 115,000 people depending on their services every year. The groundbreaking work carried out there changes lives, and with heart and lung diseases remaining the main causes of death and disability in the U.K., it's never been more needed.

www.lhchcharity.org.uk

Little Flower Penny Dinners

The Little Flower Penny Dinners began over a century ago to provide assistance and care to the needy in Dublin. It was started with donations from parishioners of a penny a week. It continues to offer practical help to Dublin's homeless, providing hot meals, home help care and support.

https://www.littleflowerpennydinners.ie

Make-A-Wish Foundation

A wish is granted every 34 minutes. A wish can be that spark that helps these children believe that anything is possible and gives them the strength to fight harder against their illnesses. This one belief guides us and inspires us to grant wishes that change the lives of the kids we serve.

www.wish.org

Medical Development Group

The premier MedTech community, advancing healthcare by enabling diverse professionals to grow through expert forums, collaboration and knowledge sharing. Members promote their businesses, and members and nonmembers find the products, services and expertise they need. Lisa Sasso was just nominated to the first MDG board emeritus position.

www.mdgboston.org

MEND

MEND (Meet Each Need with Dignity) started in 1971 and offers a range of comprehensive services to lift families and individuals in Los Angeles County out of poverty, from the distribution of food and clothing to medical, dental and vision clinics. MEND is 99% volunteer-driven and almost entirely privately funded.

www.mendpoverty.org

MyLifeLine

MyLifeLine is an online support community where cancer patients can create profiles and then share their experiences and connect to one another.

www.mylifeline.org

New Beginnings for Animals

All-volunteer, 501(c)(3), nonprofit organization based in Mission Viejo, California, dedicated to saving abandoned dogs and cats in overcrowded shelters throughout the state. Many of the animals rescued have a slim chance of getting out alive due to sickness, injury or lack of kennel space. New Beginnings is a lifesaver!

www.greatpets.org

The Ovarian Cancer Circle/Inspired by Robin Babbini

The Ovarian Cancer Circle/Inspired by Robin Babbini is committed to creating a ring of networking, education and support for women of all ages, their extended families and friends affected by ovarian cancer. The Circle is dedicated to funding research that promotes and sustains a national dialogue leading to a cure.

www.theovariancancercircle.org

PACER's National Bullying Prevention Center

Individuals from across the nation and around the world unite with the powerful message that bullying should never be a part of childhood. Uniting our nation to take action at the local level to prevent bullying and promote kindness, acceptance and inclusion in schools, communities and online.

www.pacer.org/bullying

The Pajama Program

The Pajama Program was started by Genevieve Piturro to advocate for underserved children in shelters in New York City. Genevieve started this foundation after seeing the needs of children throughout the Metropolitan area. It is now throughout the United States and Puerto Rico giving pajamas and community to children.

www.pajamaprogram.org

Pancreatic Cancer Action Network

PanCAN's vision is to create a world in which all patients with pancreatic cancer will thrive. Their mission is to take bold action to improve the lives of everyone impacted by pancreatic cancer by advancing scientific research, building community, sharing knowledge and advocating for patients.

www.pancan.org

Pathways to Education

Pathways to Education is a national, charitable organization breaking the cycle of poverty through education. Their award-winning program is creating positive social change by supporting youth in low-income communities to overcome barriers to education, graduate from high school and build the foundation for a successful future.

www.pathwaystoeducation.ca

Pertubuhan Kebajikan Bhagawan Sri Ramakrishna, Malaysia.

The ashram focuses on the education of 26 orphans to help them overcome their learning barriers after identifying their root causes. The organization needs include monthly utilities, groceries, school expenses, tuition fees, petrol expenses, salary of six staffs (as per Welfare Department's requirement) and the entire upkeep of the ashram.

www.sra-melaka.org

Pollinator Partnership

Pollinator Partnership is the largest nonprofit 501(c)(3) organization in the world dedicated exclusively to the protection and promotion of pollinators (bees and butterflies) critical to food and ecosystems through conservation, education and research.

www.pollinator.org

Pregnancy Care Clinic

Pregnancy Care Clinic exists to serve women, men and their unborn children in a judgment-free, loving, supportive atmosphere. Accurate information about the developing life in the mother's womb, ultrasounds, childbirth education, health provider consultations, counseling, parenting classes, maternity and baby items are some of the services provided free of charge.

www.supportpcc.com

Prison Entrepreneurship Program

The Prison Entrepreneurship Program offers released offenders a comprehensive slate of reentry services, including case management, transition housing, assistance in finding employment and connection to social services.

www.pep.org

Rails-to-Trails Conservancy

The mission of the Rails-to-Trails Conservancy is to create a nationwide network of trails from former rail lines, connecting corridors to build healthy places for people to enjoy the outdoors. These trail networks connect people and places, transforming communities.

www.railstotrails.org

Readerfest

Readerfest serves under-represented populations of writers of all age groups by providing arts education, conferences, workshops, exposure and connection to the literary community while focusing on social justice.

www.readerfest.org

Relationships God Style

Relationships God Style connects women of God to the purposes of God through one-on-one and group coaching as well as classes, workshops and seminars.

www.rgscoachingcenter.org

Repair Café Newburyport

Repair cafés aspire to restore unusable items at no cost to the owner or, failing that, to responsibly recycle the raw materials. While a main goal is to kindle people's enthusiasm for a sustainable society, Repair cafés also help people clear out their pile of "someday I could fix this" items!

www.repaircafenbpt.org

Rocky Mountain Down Syndrome Association

RMDSA assures inclusion and enhanced independence of people with Down syndrome. They provide education, resources, support and host events in partnership with individuals, families, professionals and the community.

www.rmdsa.org

Rosie's Ranch

Rosie's Ranch in Parker, Colorado, provides an inclusive therapeutic environment where children, with or without special needs, connect with an equine partner and each other. Under the guidance of qualified staff, these children build self-confidence, literacy and language skills through education and equine-assisted activities.

www.rosiesranch.com

Rotary International

The international service organization Rotary is a global network of 1.2 million people. They focus on two primary goals: bringing clean water to those in need and working to eradicate polio from the planet. Promoting peace and supporting education is also a part of the work done by Rotary.

www.rotary.org

Save the Children

Save the Children believes every child deserves a future. Since their founding over 100 years ago, they've changed the lives of over 1 billion children. In the United States and around the world, they give children a healthy start in life, the opportunity to learn and protection from harm. They do whatever it takes for children—every day and in times of crisis—transforming their lives and the future we all share.

www.savethechildren.org

SEE International

SEE International brings medical volunteers and partners together to care for the people who need it most. They work side by side with local doctors and clinics to improve access to high-quality eye care and surgery in Santa Barbara, California.

www.seeintl.org

Sheldrick Wildlife Trust

As one of Africa's oldest wildlife charities and a leading conservation organization, the Sheldrick Wildlife Trust (SWT) embraces all measures that complement the conservation, preservation and protection of wildlife.

www.sheldrickwildlifetrust.org/faqs

Sisters Empowering the World (S.E.W.)

Dr. Patricia Bailey, who has produced a tremendous impact for more than 40 years in over 145 countries around the world, founded S.E.W, Sisters Empowering the World. S.E.W. equips women to become vessels of honor for their families and transforms them into world changers to impact the nations.

www.sistersempoweringtheworld.com

Sisters of the Incarnate Word and Blessed Sacrament

SIW is a community of women centered in the person of Jesus, faithfully sharing the tradition that has been passed on by Jeanne Chézard de Matel, their foundress. They witness that God's reign is in their midst by walking in the spirit of Jesus.

www.incarnatewordorder.org

Stand Beside Them

Stand Beside Them coaches and inspires America's veterans and their spouses/caregivers to achieve success at home, at work and in the community.

www.standbesidethem.org

Table of Hope MCC

Table of Hope MCC is located in the heart of Kansas. More than just a diverse and all-inclusive church, it is one that inspires hope within their local community via their food pantry, pet food pantry and annual back-to-school project—providing students with backpacks, supplies and more.

www.mccwichita.com

Tails That Teach

Tails That Teach inspires children to be kind to pets through innovative blends of character and humane education. Over 65 thousand compassion-centered books have been donated to animal organizations and schools worldwide. They founded National Rescue Dog Day, observed annually on May 20, bringing awareness to 3.3 million sheltered dogs awaiting homes.

www.tailsthatteach.org

Teen Suicide Prevention Society Inc.

With suicide rates on the rise, the silence around suicide is deadly. The Teen Suicide Prevention Society provides training in confidently starting the conversations that save lives. Their mission at TSPS (internally "teaspoons") is to make suicide, especially teen suicide, a thing of the past.

www.teensuicidepreventionsociety.org

Terebinth Refuge

Terebinth Refuge is a shelter and safe home located in Waite Park, Minnesota, that brings hope, healing services and freedom to sexually exploited and trafficked women.

www.terebinthrefuge.org

Timothy's Gift

Timothy's Gift visits prisons in multiple states, communicating these messages: "You are loved. You have great worth. You are not alone." Professional musicians and other volunteers inspire both inmates and staff. Current visitor restrictions are necessitating a switch to video format that allows these messages to reach even more people.

www.timothysgift.com

TNR Riverside

TNR Riverside's mission is to reduce cat overpopulation through their humane "trap, neuter, return" strategy. Contrary to previous strategies of trap and kill, TNR has cats altered (and often vaccinated) and returns them to their neighborhoods, allowing them to live out the remainder of their lives without contributing to over-population.

www.tnrriverside.org

Unstoppable Foundation

Unstoppable Foundation is a nonprofit humanitarian organization bringing sustainable education to children in impoverished communities. For example, in late 2020 the organization was able to complete two new schoolhouses and one latrine in Nderiat, Kenya, the Sponsor A Village community.

www.unstoppablefoundation.org

VARAS - Volunteers for Ameloriation of Rural Areas

VARAS works tirelessly in the West African country of Ghana to pair volunteers with social programs to further education, women and child empowerment and sustainable enterprise, releasing young, rural Ghanaians from a cycle of poverty and exploitation.

www.varas.org

Veterans LYFE Services

VLS advocates on behalf of veterans at every stage of their lives and helps them navigate through the many resources and services, working closely with collaborative community partners to minimize barriers for the veteran to return them to living a full life after their transition from military service.

https://veteranslyfeservices.org

Whole Life Healing Centers

Their mission is to provide access to comprehensive healing modalities for individuals and families impacted by emotional and physical trauma. Their vision is a world where each person embodies sustainable change, thereby empowering the individual to recog-

nize they are whole and capable of living a life they love.
www.wholelifehealingcenters.org

The Williams Syndrome Foundation

The WSF offers help and support to families, carers and people with Williams Syndrome, a chromosomal disorder presenting as global developmental delays and a profound learning disability.

www.williams-syndrome.org.uk

Wings of Rescue

Wings of Rescue is a 501(c)(3) charity founded in 2012 that flies endangered pets from high-intake and/or high-kill shelters to no-kill shelters from where they have all been adopted into loving homes. So far in 2020, Wings of Rescue has flown 8,524 pets (6,303 dogs, 2,159 cats, 23 rabbits, 38 guinea pigs and one three-legged mouse) a distance of 243,724 miles to safety and delivered 40,290 pounds of emergency humanitarian and pet relief to natural disaster victims.

www.wingsofrescue.org

Women's Resource Center of Greensboro

The mission of the Women's Resource Center of Greensboro is to promote the self-reliance of women by assessing needs, providing services and acting as a gateway to community resources. In seeking solutions for unmet needs, the WRC provides strategic leadership through collaborations and partnerships within the community.

www.womenscentergso.org

World Foundation for Girl Guides and Girl Scouts Inc.

The World Foundation is an independent, not-for-profit organization established in 1971 and granted 501(c)(3) status. The two members are the World Association of Girl Guides and Girls Scouts

Inc. and Girl Scouts of the USA. It is the world's largest voluntary movement for girls and young women.

www.worldfoundationgggs.org

The Writers' Community of Durham Region

The Writers' Community of Durham Region, affectionately called the WCDR, is a network of writers from all genres and all levels of writing, from creative to technical to business and journalistic writing, supporting each other through in-person meetings and a strong online community.

www.wcdr.info

Your Pets Are Safe

Your Pets Are Safe is dedicated to help stop domestic abuse by taking care of the pets of abuse survivors while in shelters (which do not take animals). Pets left behind are usually killed by the abuser. This helps the abused to flee and saves the abused, their children and the pets.

karen@yourpetsaresafe.com

Z-Cares Foundation

Z-Cares stands up to anxiety. Founded in memory of Zachary Nimmo, Z-Cares is dedicated to supporting our youth and shedding the stigma associated with mental health. They work tirelessly every day to develop and deliver programs that will help our youth talk about and cope with their mental health.

www.zcares.org

Get Your Free Gratitude Journal!

Keep a daily record of life's positive moments (big and small) with this printable gratitude journal filled with a year's worth of positive affirmations, insightful prompts, inspiring quotes, and room for reflecting on all the things that make your life a blessing.

- Take 60 seconds to shine a light on what's good!
- Affirmations and inspirational quotes to lift you up.
- Delivered via a colorful PDF printable.

**Pick up your free gratitude journal!
www.TheCommunityBookProject.com**

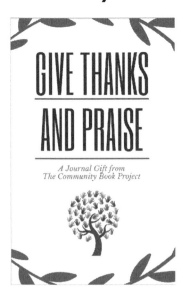

Manufactured by Amazon.ca
Bolton, ON

21848451R00243